Collins
COBUILD
Business
Vocabulary
in Practice

Sue Robbins
Materials Bank by Sarah Horrod

THE UNIVERSITY
OF BIRMINGHAM

HarperCollins Publishers
Westerhill Road
Bishopbriggs
Glasgow
G64 2QT
Great Britain

Second Edition 2004

Latest Reprint 2006

© HarperCollins Publishers 2003, 2004

ISBN-13   978-0-00-719023-2
ISBN-10   0-00-719023-9

Collins®, COBUILD® and Bank of English® are
registered trademarks of HarperCollins Publishers
Limited

www.collins.co.uk

A catalogue record for this book is available from the
British Library

Computer typeset by Wordcraft, Glasgow

Printed in Great Britain by Scotprint

Acknowledgements
We would like to thank those authors and publishers
who kindly gave permission for copyright material to be
used in the Collins Word Web. We would also like to
thank Times Newspapers Ltd for providing valuable data.

CONTENTS

FIRST/SECOND EDITION

Publishing Director
Lorna Knight

Editorial Director   *Managing Editor*
Michela Clari   Maree Airlie

Project Manager
Alison Macaulay

Lexicographers   *Editor*
Bob Grossmith   Maggie Seaton
Jane Bradbury
Liz Potter

We would like to give special thanks to Sian Harris,
BBC Training & Development and Jill Northcott, IALS,
University of Edinburgh for their invaluable advice and
feedback. We would also like to thank The Guardian,
The Times and the New Internationalist
for giving us permission to use their
texts in this publication.

INTRODUCTION

Like all COBUILD texts, **Collins COBUILD Business Vocabulary in Practice** is based on the analysis of real language in use. Over the last few years, we have built up a huge electronic collection of text, both written and spoken, called the *Bank of English®*. At present, the *Bank of English®* stands at over 500 million words, and has been used as the basis of all COBUILD texts. It enables the editors and lexicographers at COBUILD to look at how the language works, and give examples from real texts of how particular words and terms are used.

Collins COBUILD Business Vocabulary in Practice is designed for students at upper-intermediate level and above, and aims to give practice in the use of a wide range of words and expressions that occur when talking about business. In this book, you will find examples of typical business words and phrases, along with relevant practice exercises, so that you can put your knowledge to use straight away. You can use **Collins COBUILD Business Vocabulary in Practice** to consolidate the vocabulary you have already acquired, to help you start using words that you recognize but rarely use, and to build up a wide range of new business words. You may want to use the units in order to systematically develop your knowledge of meaning and usage, or you may want to select units that relate to a particular topic that interests you.

ORGANIZATION OF THE BOOK

The book is divided into 14 topics, each of which contains 5 themed units. The topics and units are listed on the Contents page (iii), and at the beginning of each topic in the text.

Each unit consists of two pages. On the left-hand pages you will find the key vocabulary for the unit, with an explanation in full of the meaning, example sentences using the vocabulary and other useful information. On the right-hand pages, you will find exercises practising all of the vocabulary which is explained on the left-hand pages.

At the back of the book, there are a further 60 pages of practice material in the Materials Bank. The Materials Bank is divided into the same 14 topics as the main text, but it brings together the vocabulary from the 5 units in each topic, and also introduces new vocabulary which is useful for these topics. The exercises in the Materials Bank are particularly useful for work in the classroom, but they can also be used for self-study.

MAIN TEXT

1 Left-hand pages
The left-hand pages provide a wealth of essential information about the most important business vocabulary in English.

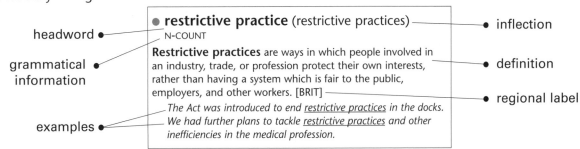

Headwords: These have been carefully chosen to reflect the language needed by students of business and people using English at work. Each unit contains approximately 10 key items of vocabulary. Words which are very closely related (for example 'import' and 'export') are grouped together so that it is easier to compare them.

Grammatical Information: The entries also provide the key grammatical information you need to use the word properly. Noun plurals and verb inflections are given in brackets after the headword, and the part of speech of the word is shown in small capitals. These appear after the headword and inflections if the word only has one part of speech, or before the definitions if the word can be used in different ways. For example, the word 'deregulation' is always an uncountable noun, so it is shown like this:

● **deregulation** N-UNCOUNT

Deregulation is the removal of controls and restrictions in a particular area of business or trade.

Since <u>deregulation</u>, banks are permitted to set their own interest rates.

The bright side of world financial <u>deregulation</u> is that countries such as Mexico have access to private capital on a scale unimaginable even a decade ago.

---

while the word 'yield' can be a verb or a noun, so it is shown like this:

● **yield** (yields, yielding, yielded)

1 VERB

If a tax or investment **yields** an amount of money or profit, this money or profit is obtained from it.

It <u>yielded</u> a profit of at least $36 million.

2 N-COUNT

The **yield** on a tax or investment is the amount of money or profit that it makes.

…the <u>yield</u> on a bank's investments.

The parts of speech used in this book are as follows:

ABBREVIATION
An **abbreviation** is a short form of a word or phrase; EG *HR; WTO*

ADJ
An **adjective** is used to tell you more about a person or thing; EG *generic; online*

ADV
An **adverb** gives more information about when, where, how or in what circumstances something happens; EG *per capita; freelance*

CONVENTION
A **convention** is a word or fixed phrase, often used in conversation; EG *caveat emptor*

N-COUNT
A **count noun** has both singular and plural forms, and normally has a word such as 'a', 'an', 'the' or 'my' in front of it; EG *firm/firms; company/companies*

N-COUNT-COLL
A **countable collective noun** is a count noun which refers to a group of people or things. It behaves like a count noun, but when it is used in the singular form, it can be used with either a singular or a plural noun; EG *staff; works*

N-PLURAL
A **plural noun** is always plural, and is used with plural verbs; EG *communications; economies of scale*

N-PROPER
A **proper noun** refers to one person, place, thing or institution, and begins with a capital letter; EG *Internet; World Trade Organization*

N-SING
A **singular noun** is always singular, and must have a word such as 'a', 'an', 'the' or 'my' in front of it; EG *public sector; telecoms revolution*

N-UNCOUNT
An **uncount noun** has only one form, takes a singular verb and is not used with numbers or with 'a'; EG *globalization; flexitime*

N-VAR
A **variable noun** is a noun which can be used in both count and uncount forms; EG *partnership; acquisition*

PHRASAL VERB
A **phrasal verb** is a combination of a verb and an adverb or a verb and a preposition, which together have a particular meaning; EG *power ahead; turn around*

PHRASE
A **phrase** is a group of words which have a particular meaning when they are used together. This meaning is not always understandable from the separate parts; EG *under licence; go out of business*

VERB
A **verb** is a word which is used to say what someone or something does or what happens to them, or to give information about them; EG *invent; merge*

Definitions: All of the definitions are written in full sentences in simple, natural English. This allows us to show you the typical patterns and grammatical behaviour of a word, as well as the meaning.

Labels: Almost all of the terms in this book are used in all varieties of English. If a term is only used in British English, we have added the label [BRIT] after the definition. If it is mostly used in British English, but is sometimes used in other varieties, we have added the label [mainly BRIT].

Examples: Each headword and definition is followed by examples. All of the examples are taken from the *Bank of English®*, a huge database of real language from a wide variety of sources, including *The Economist, The Times, The New Scientist* and the *Wolverhampton Business English Corpus*. The examples have been carefully chosen to illustrate common patterns and typical uses of the word or phrase, so that you can see how it is really used in English today.

Collocation Boxes: These give you more information about the collocations of a number of terms, showing you words and structures which are commonly used with the headword.

Common Collocations

to <u>file for</u> bankruptcy
to <u>be on the verge of</u> bankruptcy
to <u>be on the brink of</u> bankruptcy
to <u>be facing</u> bankruptcy
to <u>declare</u> bankruptcy

Cross-references: Many terms in the book can be used in several different business contexts. At the bottom of most left-hand pages you will find cross-references to other units in the book where you can find definitions and examples for other useful words related to the topic you are studying. Cross-references look like this:

➲ **just-in-time manufacturing**: Topic 5.1;
sub-contracting: Topic 5.3; **mass production**: Topic
5.5; **order**: Topic 6.3; **supplier partnership**: Topic 12.2

2 Right-hand pages

The right-hand pages contain a variety of exercises to practise all the vocabulary on the corresponding left-hand pages. Exercise types include: fill the gaps exercises; matching exercises; completing diagrams and tables; true/false questions and multiple-choice exercises. You will find answers to all of the exercises in the main text in the answer key at the back of the book. This means that **Collins COBUILD Business Vocabulary in Practice** can be used either in the classroom or for self-study.

MATERIALS BANK

The Materials Bank allows you to practise and extend the vocabulary covered in the main text. The exercises here include reading comprehension (using real texts from authentic sources), discussion activities, suggestions for writing work, crosswords, and word searches. The Materials Bank is divided into 14 topics, and each one brings together the vocabulary practised in each topic of the main text. There is also an answer key for the Materials Bank at the end of the book. Most of these exercises can be used for self-study, and they are all ideal for classroom practice.

INDEX

At the back of the book you will find an index, which contains all the words and phrases that are defined on the left-hand pages in the main text. This will allow you to find the explanation of a particular term quickly and easily.

We believe that **Collins COBUILD Business Vocabulary in Practice** will prove to be an indispensable tool for learners of English. As always, we welcome any comments that users may have about our books, so please contact us if you have any observations, criticisms or questions.

You can contact us on our website at: www.cobuild.collins.co.uk
by email directly to: cobuild@ref.collins.co.uk

or you can write to us at the following address:

Collins COBUILD
Westerhill Road
Bishopbriggs
Glasgow G64 2QT
UK

Topic 1

THE CHANGING WORLD

● **information technology** N-UNCOUNT
  IT N-UNCOUNT

Information technology is the theory and practice of using computers to store and analyse information. The abbreviation **IT** is often used.

> …the <u>information technology</u> industry.
> The UK <u>IT</u> market is growing at a faster rate than in any other country in Europe.

● **business model** (business models) N-COUNT

A **business model** is the structure of a business, including the various relationships between the different parts of the business.

> …the entirely new <u>business models</u> made possible by the Internet.
> …inefficiencies in traditional <u>business models</u>.

● **vertical integration** N-UNCOUNT
  virtual integration N-UNCOUNT

Vertical integration is the merging of two or more companies involved in different aspects of the same business, for example, a brewery might buy a chain of pubs. **Virtual integration** is close cooperation between two or more companies involved in different aspects of the same business, so that they operate almost like a single company. **Virtual integration** is based on the use of IT.

> For the oil business the benefits of <u>vertical integration</u> are that supplies are assured and an immediate customer or outlet is available.
> The biggest attraction of <u>virtual integration</u> is that organizations can integrate care without investing huge amounts of capital or completely altering their structures.
> The most important difference in these new economies is that they favour <u>virtual integration</u> over <u>vertical integration</u>.

● **CAD** N-UNCOUNT
  CAM N-UNCOUNT

CAD is the use of computer software in the design of things such as cars, buildings, and machines. **CAD** is an abbreviation for 'computer aided design'. **CAM** is the use of computer software in the manufacture of products. **CAM** is an abbreviation for 'computer-aided manufacture'.

> A design made with <u>CAD</u> can be transmitted perfectly from one place to another, if they both use the same system.
> The application of <u>CAD/CAM</u> makes traditional procedures more efficient and provides avenues for innovation and new development.
> …<u>CAD/CAM</u> software.

● **microelectronics** N-UNCOUNT

Microelectronics is the branch of electronics that deals with miniature electronic circuits.

> He thinks Daimler should buy its <u>microelectronics</u> from outside suppliers.
> …a <u>microelectronics</u> company.

● **outsource** (outsources, outsourcing, outsourced) VERB
  outsourcing N-UNCOUNT

If a company **outsources** goods or services, it pays workers from outside the company to supply the goods or provide the services. **Outsourcing** is the use of outside companies to supply goods or services.

> Increasingly, corporate clients are seeking to <u>outsource</u> the management of their facilities.
> The difficulties of <u>outsourcing</u> have been compounded by the increasing resistance of trade unions.

● **fast track manufacturing** N-UNCOUNT

Fast track manufacturing is a manufacturing system which aims to speed up manufacturing times, for example by the use of more efficient practices or the pre-manufacture of components.

> Our <u>fast track manufacturing</u> facility can build and ship complete turn-key systems in a matter of weeks.

● **flexible** ADJ

Production methods or working practices that are **flexible** are able to be changed easily so that they suit different conditions and circumstances.

> …<u>flexible</u> production lines that can make whichever versions of its three main products are selling best.
> Thanks to cheaper wages and <u>flexible</u> working practices, BA's operating costs are lower than its American rivals.

Common Collocations

flexible <u>working arrangements</u>
flexible <u>working hours</u>
flexible <u>working patterns</u>
flexible <u>working practices</u>
flexible <u>hours</u>
flexible <u>work schedule</u>

● **multi-skilled workforce** (multi-skilled workforces) N-COUNT

A **multi-skilled workforce** is a workforce that has many different skills, enabling them to do several different types of work within a company.

> The importance of a highly trained, <u>multi-skilled workforce</u> has never been so crucial to the survival of the industry.

➲ **just-in-time manufacturing**: Topic 5.1;
  subcontract: Topic 5.3; **mass production**: Topic 5.5;
  order: Topic 6.3; **supplier partnership**: Topic 12.2

PRACTISE YOUR VOCABULARY

1 Use the terms in the box to complete the paragraph.

> vertical integration   business model   IT   outsourcing   virtual integration

Companies based on a traditional, production-oriented _____ are often rather inefficient, and find it hard to adapt to change. A model where the management of a company owns other companies in the production process and the firm controls a number of successive stages in the supply of a product is an example of _____. Companies which buy in components and only assemble the finished product in-house, however, are using _____. Using other companies to supply goods rather than manufacture them themselves cuts down on costs, but can make it difficult to maintain quality. Many companies use new business models based on the use of _____. Computers can help two different companies work closely and form partnerships. This model is referred to as _____, and uses IT to achieve the benefits of both of the above systems.

2 Look at the information about seven companies. Which one is an example of:

a vertical integration   c CAD   e fast track manufacturing   g CAM
b virtual integration   d outsourcing   f multi-skilled workforce

i Ashdown Components relies heavily on the use of IT in the production process. They work closely with their main customer, who uses their components to assemble cars at their nearby plant.

_____

ii The Dairy Box confectionery company makes chocolates and sweets. 15 years ago it bought cocoa plantations in Africa to produce its own raw materials.

_____

iii Big Eddie's International Trucking and Freight Company used to employ their own mechanics to repair and maintain their vehicles. However, 10 years ago they stopped this and now use a specialist firm to do this work for them.

_____

iv In the past, the company received many complaints from their customers about the length of time they had to wait for their orders to be filled. Following changes to their manufacturing system, this rarely happens now.

_____

v In the Shining Path paint factory the workers are expected to move round the factory, working at different points in the production process as the load of work demands.

_____

vi Hawthorn have invested a great deal of money in updating the production process at their factories, and have introduced sophisticated computer equipment to assist them.

_____

vii The machines at the Apollo sports shoe factory can easily be programmed to make different designs in response to the rapidly-changing demands of fashion.

_____

3 Read the text and say if the sentences below are true or false.

JKM produce microchips that contain the electronic circuits used in spacecraft. Their computer system is networked with the computer system at the Space Agency, and computer specialists from both places work together in the design process. The Space Agency use the finished microchips in their spacecraft. The technicians can work at either site, and can adapt their designs rapidly if they need to.

a JKM operate within the IT industry.   d The relationship between JKM and the Space Agency is an example of
b JKM is a microelectronics company.   virtual integration.
c The microchips are developed using CAD.   e JKM employees use flexible working practices.

● **communications** N-PLURAL

Communications are the systems and processes that are used to communicate or broadcast information, especially by means of telephone wires, underground cables, satellites, or radio waves.

> …a contract for sophisticated <u>communications</u> equipment made by American companies and secretly shipped abroad.
> E-commerce and website design are the next big things in corporate <u>communications</u>.
> One of the main tasks of the five crew members is to put a <u>communications</u> satellite into orbit.

Common Collocations

<u>mobile</u> communications   <u>electronic</u> communications
<u>corporate</u> communications   <u>business</u> communications

● **telecoms revolution** N-SING

If you talk about the **telecoms revolution**, you mean the recent, sudden changes in telecommunications such as the increased use of the Internet and mobile phones.

> For governments and big companies, the <u>telecoms revolution</u> will be unsettling.
> The <u>telecoms revolution</u> has created a new pattern of rural working.

● **disruptive technology** (disruptive technologies) N-COUNT

A **disruptive technology** is a new technology, such as computers and the Internet, which has a rapid and major effect on technologies that existed before.

> …the other great <u>disruptive technologies</u> of the 20th century, such as electricity, the telephone and the car.
> The transistor was a <u>disruptive technology</u> for the vacuum-tube industry in the 1950s.

● **high-tech sector** N-SING

The **high-tech sector** is used to talk about businesses which produce or develop advanced technologies, such as computers and mobile phones.

> Even within the <u>high-tech sector</u> there is some replacement of skilled staff by lower-cost research students.
> With the slump in the <u>high-tech sector</u>, Irish people are once again discovering just how valuable a commodity job security can be.

● **social change** (social changes) N-VAR

Social change is change in human society, such as changes in the way people interact with each other or changes resulting from new technology or new institutions.

> Nationally, the biggest <u>social change</u> over the past 10 or 15 years has been our increasing tolerance of people who are gay, or a different colour.
> Football is under threat from <u>social changes</u>, particularly from computer games, TV, video, stereo etc.

● **consumer behaviour** N-UNCOUNT

Consumer behaviour is the way that groups of consumers typically behave, especially their shopping habits.

> A clearer picture of <u>consumer behaviour</u> is gradually emerging.
> Developments in materials, marketing and styling have all had an effect on <u>consumer behaviour</u>.

● **mobile phone** (mobile phones) N-COUNT
  mobile (mobiles) N-COUNT

A **mobile phone** or **mobile** is a telephone that you can carry with you and use to make or receive calls wherever you are. [BRIT]

> Calls from land lines are generally less expensive than from <u>mobile phones</u>.
> He had already left a message on my <u>mobile</u>.

● **mobile phone operator** (mobile phone operators) N-COUNT

A **mobile phone operator** is a company that runs a mobile phone business.

> Figures this week from the <u>mobile phone operators</u> showed soaring subscriptions over Christmas.

● **pay-as-you-go** ADJ

A **pay-as-you-go** system is a system in which you pay for something, such as a mobile phone call, when you actually use it rather than before or afterwards.

> This is a <u>pay-as-you-go</u> service, each message costing 23.5p (including VAT), billed as a text message on your bill.
> Charges for <u>pay-as-you-go</u> phones tend to be more expensive than those on monthly tariffs.

● **tariff** (tariffs) N-COUNT

The **tariff** for something is a list of prices, especially ones which vary according to the time or day of use. Your mobile phone **tariff** is how much you pay for each call, depending on when you make it and who you make it to.

> The most appropriate choice of system and <u>tariff</u> depends on where and how often a customer uses the phone.

⮑ **Internet**: Topic 1.3; **globalization**: Topic 1.4; **state-of-the-art**: Topic 5.4

PRACTISE YOUR VOCABULARY

1 Complete the sentences with a phrase from the box.

IT has become more accessible   *the falling cost of telephone calls*
different brands of mobile phones   *interconnect with the World-Wide Web*
the increasing willingness of consumers to try products from abroad

a New disruptive technology: patterns of communication have changed since _____ _____ to individuals and to companies.

b The telecoms revolution: the use of technology in business has expanded rapidly due to the number of businesses and customers who are now able to _____.

c The impact of technology: more businesses and customers are able to use Internet technology due to _____.

d Changing consumer behaviour: companies have been able to extend their product range due to _____.

e The rapid growth of the high-tech sector: in a period of enormous technological change, the market has been flooded with _____.

2 The telecoms revolution has introduced many different ways of communicating. Match the products on the left with the extracts from a sales brochure on the right.

Mobile phone   **a** The ultimate tool for organizing your work and your life.

Computer   **b** The whole world of information always available at your desk at the speed of a super highway.

The Internet   **c** Safe and permanent international communications systems delivering a high-quality service.

Satellite communications **d** Always immediately in touch wherever you are.

Cable TV   **e** Choose from 200 channels to receive the entertainment you want when you want it.

3 Use the terms in the box to complete the newspaper headlines.

social changes   pay-as-you-go   tariffs   mobile phone operators   telecoms revolution

a _____ options become popular as phone users say no to hidden charges.

b Half of all households now connected to the Internet thanks to the _____.

c _____ to provide new services in order to attract more customers.

d Mobile phone use brings _____ as interpersonal communication increases.

e Phone users are encouraged to read their contracts as _____ can be higher than expected.

● **Internet** N-PROPER
Net ABBREVIATION
Internet access N-UNCOUNT
surf (surfs, surfing, surfed) VERB

The **Internet** or the **Net** is the computer network which allows computer users to connect with computers all over the world, and which carries e-mail. If you have **Internet access**, you are able to use a computer which allows you to use the Internet. If you **surf** the Internet, you spend time finding and looking at things on the Internet.

> *Opportunities exist, and are being exploited, in selling fast-moving consumer goods over the <u>Internet</u>.*
> *It is well recognised that employees spend at least half an hour a day surfing the <u>Net</u> for private purposes.*
> *Millions of students and schoolchildren already have <u>Internet access</u> provided free by their educational establishments.*
> *No one knows how many people currently <u>surf</u> the Net.*

Common Collocations
to <u>browse</u> the Net
to <u>buy something over</u> the Internet
to <u>sell something over</u> the Internet
to <u>publish something on</u> the Internet
to <u>post something on</u> the Internet

● **World-Wide Web** N-PROPER
WWW ABBREVIATION
Web N-PROPER
website (websites) N-COUNT
site (sites) N-COUNT

The **World-Wide Web** is a computer system which links documents and pictures into a database that is stored in computers in many different parts of the world and that people everywhere can use. The abbreviations **WWW** and the **Web** are often used. A **website** or **site** is a set of information about a particular subject which is available on the Internet.

> *...the rapid growth in the use of the <u>World Wide Web</u>.*
> *...buyers spotted her ads on the <u>Web</u>.*
> *Call 0171-493 2612 or visit <u>www.kaspia.co.uk</u>*
> *Every time you visit a <u>website</u>, you leave a record showing you were there and what pages you viewed.*
> *The <u>site</u> earns its revenue from advertisers.*

Common Collocations
to <u>build</u> a website   to <u>visit</u> a website
an <u>official</u> website   to <u>design</u> a website

● **personal computer** (personal computers)
N-COUNT
PC ABBREVIATION

A **personal computer** is a computer that is used in a business, a school, or at home. The abbreviation **PC** is also used.

> *Apple is lowering prices to attract a larger share of the*

competitive <u>personal computer</u> market.
> *Ultimately, we're going to capture digital images initially and then be able to put them right onto your <u>PC</u>.*

● **Internet Service Provider** (Internet Service Providers) N-COUNT
ISP ABBREVIATION

An **Internet Service Provider** is a company that provides Internet and e-mail services. The abbreviation **ISP** is also used.

> *There's a click-on modem available too, so you can pick up your e-mails from your <u>Internet service provider</u>.*
> *Dixons was the natural company to launch an <u>ISP</u> because it led the market in selling personal computers.*

● **online** ADJ

1 If a company goes **online**, its services become available on the Internet.
> *...the first bank to go <u>online</u>.*

2 If you are **online**, your computer is connected to the Internet.
> *You can chat to other people who are <u>online</u>.*

3 An **online** company or service offers customers the opportunity to order goods or use services via the Internet.
> *Visit Britain's premier <u>online</u> shopping centre, featuring such well-known names as Argos, Interflora, Eurostar and Victoria Wine.*
> *...an opportunity to join the UK's leading <u>online</u> Bank.*

● **dot-com** (dot-coms) N-COUNT

A **dot-com** is a company that does all or most of its business on the Internet.
> *In 1999, <u>dot-coms</u> spent more than $1 billion on TV spots.*

● **e-business** (e-businesses)
e-commerce N-UNCOUNT

1 N-COUNT
An **e-business** is a business which uses the Internet to sell goods or services, especially one which does not also have shops or offices that people can visit or phone.
> *There are plenty of options of what should stay and what should go to keep an <u>e-business</u> afloat.*

2 N-UNCOUNT
E-business or **e-commerce** is the buying, selling, and ordering of goods and services using the Internet.
> *...proven <u>e-business</u> solutions.*
> *...the anticipated explosion of <u>e-commerce</u>.*

● **broadband** N-UNCOUNT

Broadband is a method of sending many electronic messages at the same time, using a telephone line, satellite dish, or undergound cable.
> *The two companies said they planned to develop new <u>broadband</u> services for customers in the UK and Ireland jointly.*
> *As we move into <u>broadband</u>, a wide range of e-commerce services will become available.*

PRACTISE YOUR VOCABULARY

1 **What do these abbreviations stand for?**

ISP   WWW   PC

2 **Complete the paragraph by putting the correct form of the following words or phrases into the gaps.**

websites   going online   Internet   surf the Net   broadband   ISP

Zbig wants to buy some tickets for a concert so he's _____, using his computer at home to

_____ . He's visiting the _____ of several ticket agencies where he hopes to buy the tickets

using his credit card. The company that provides him with Internet services, his _____, has recently

improved its services and can now offer _____ access to the _____ . This will make Zbig's

connection to the Web much faster and easier so he's thinking of getting an upgrade.

3 **Are these statements true or false?**

	True	False
a The World-Wide Web is based in the USA.	☐	☐
b Broadband can only send electronic messages by phone.	☐	☐
c 'Surfing the Net' involves visiting lots of websites.	☐	☐
d Online companies are also known as dot-coms.	☐	☐
e Some companies only trade online and do not have conventional offices or shops.	☐	☐
f 'Going online' means the same as 'surfing the Net'.	☐	☐

4 **Look at this diagram and label it by putting the terms from the box into their correct places to show the process of accessing the Internet. Each letter (a–d) represents one of the terms.**

Internet Service Provider   World-Wide Web   website   personal computer

a _____

a _____

b _____

a _____

a _____

d _____

d _____

c _____

d _____

d _____

● **globalization** N-UNCOUNT

Globalization is used to talk about the way in which big companies do business all over the world.

> Trends toward the _globalization_ of industry have dramatically affected food production in California.
> Some 30% say that _globalization_ will be a vital means of lowering their costs or upgrading their technology.

Common Collocations
anti-globalization   economic globalization

● **market** (markets) N-COUNT

The **market** for a particular type of thing is the number of people who want to buy it, or the area of the world in which it is sold.

> The foreign _market_ was increasingly crucial.
> ...the Russian _market_ for personal computers.

● **global market** (global markets) N-COUNT
global marketplace N-SING
worldwide market (worldwide markets)
N-COUNT

People sometimes use expressions such as a **global market**, a **global marketplace**, and a **worldwide market** to talk about a market for something that exists throughout the world.

> Surely in a _global market_ no country can afford to spend much more than its competitors on welfare if it is to keep down its costs and keep its citizens in jobs.
> Increasingly, the nation's high-tech industries are depending on immigrants, engineers, scientists, and entrepreneurs to remain competitive in the _global marketplace_.
> On-line services, such as the Internet, gave advertisers access to a _worldwide market_ of up to 25 million users.

● **global enterprise** (global enterprises) N-COUNT
global business (global businesses) N-COUNT

A **global enterprise** or a **global business** is a company or industry which sells its products or services in many different parts of the world.

> ..._global enterprises_ based in the advanced industrial nations.
> 'By piecemeal acquisition in Europe and Asia, BT is building a _global business_,' said Mr Roe.
> Mobile phone sales are booming; telecommunications is one of the most profitable _global businesses_.

● **global economy** N-SING

The **global economy** is the economies of all the countries of the world considered as a whole.

> He explained how staying competitive in the new _global economy_ depended on how much a country invested, not just in high-tech machinery, but in training workers to use it.
> Profits started to slide when the Gulf War threatened to paralyse the _global economy_.

● **multinational** (multinationals)

① ADJ

A **multinational** company has branches or owns companies in many different countries.

> ...a _multinational_ company with operations in several countries and tens of thousands of employees performing a wide range of tasks.

② N-COUNT

A **multinational** is the same as a multinational company.
...._multinationals_ such as Ford and IBM.

Common Collocations
a multinational corporation   a multinational firm
a multinational enterprise   a multinational company

● **deregulation** N-UNCOUNT

Deregulation is the removal of controls and restrictions in a particular area of business or trade.

> Since _deregulation_, banks are permitted to set their own interest rates.
> The bright side of world financial _deregulation_ is that countries such as Mexico have access to private capital on a scale unimaginable even a decade ago.

● **liberalize** (liberalizes, liberalizing, liberalized) VERB
liberalization N-UNCOUNT

When a country or government **liberalizes** its laws, it becomes less strict and allows people or companies more freedom.
Liberalization is the process of making laws less strict, so that people or companies have more freedom.

> Negotiators are working to eliminate most tariffs and trade barriers and to _liberalize_ investment opportunities and trade-in services between the US and Canada.
> The American economy stands to benefit the most from future trade _liberalization_.

Common Collocations
to liberalize trade   to liberalize prices
to liberalize an economy

⊃ **global**: Topic 3.4; **restrictive practice**: Topic 10.3

PRACTISE YOUR VOCABULARY

1 Word Partners

a Match each of the terms on the left with a term on the right that has the same meaning.

an enterprise   a worldwide market
a global market   the marketplace
a multinational   a business
the market   a global enterprise

b Look at the word partners with the word <u>global</u>. Use each one to complete the sentences.

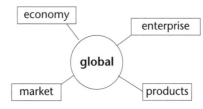

i   Some companies produce _____ that are easily recognized by people all over the world.

ii The _____ has developed with the collapse of Soviet-style communism and the opening up of new countries to trade.

iii Some companies now operate in so many countries that they are described as _____s.

iv Since products are assembled from components made in numerous countries and then sold on to other countries' markets, we can talk of a _____.

2 Use the terms in the box to complete the paragraph.

| *deregulation*   *liberalized*   *globalization*   *global economy*   *multinational* |

The tendency of companies to sell their products into many foreign markets, or _____, has led to the development of a global marketplace. In recent times markets in Eastern Europe have joined the _____. Since the governments of these countries _____ their laws relating to foreign trade many _____ companies have set up operations there to take advantage of the opportunity to enter such a huge new market. The process of _____ has made trade with Eastern Europe easier.

3 Which of these companies can be called a multinational?

a Company A exports its products from Germany, where they are produced, to France and the UK.

b Company B is based in Holland and has production bases in the USA and Mexico.

c Company C is based in Australia, and exports to New Zealand and the Philippines.

d Company D is based in Canada, where it has many production bases, and sells into its home market.

● **flexible working patterns** N-PLURAL

Flexible working patterns are arrangements in which some employees are allowed to vary the hours that they work in order to suit their personal needs.

> *The study found that the growth of <u>flexible working patterns</u> was set to continue.*
> *Seven in ten people who have <u>flexible working patterns</u> outperform their full-time colleagues by a third.*

● **flexitime** N-UNCOUNT

Flexitime is a system that allows employees to vary the time that they start or finish work, provided that an agreed total number of hours are spent at work. [BRIT]

> *The Draft National Plan for Women is committed to promoting family-friendly policies, such as job-sharing and <u>flexitime</u>.*
> *The company is also keen to introduce further <u>flexitime</u> working, with some workers possibly moving onto a four-day week.*

● **teleworking** N-UNCOUNT

Teleworking is working from home using equipment such as telephones, fax machines, and computers to keep in contact.

> *<u>Teleworking</u> has increased substantially, with 39 per cent of businesses saying that their employees worked from home at least some of the time.*
> *<u>Teleworking</u> is becoming a major force as people use the telephone and e-mail to allow them to work from home.*

● **freelance**

1 ADJ

Someone who does **freelance** work or who is, for example, a **freelance** journalist or photographer, is not employed by one organization, but is paid for each piece of work they do by the organization they do it for.

> *Michael Cross is a <u>freelance</u> journalist.*
> *Jill was getting some <u>freelance</u> writing jobs from trade magazines.*

2 ADV

If you work **freelance**, you do freelance work.

> *He is now working <u>freelance</u> from his home in Hampshire.*
> *She had a baby and decided to go <u>freelance</u>.*

> ### Common Collocations
> to <u>go</u> freelance   to <u>work on a</u> freelance <u>basis</u>

● **shift** (shifts) N-COUNT

If a group of factory workers, nurses, or other people work **shifts**, they work for a set period before being replaced by another group, so that there is always a group working. Each of these set periods is called a **shift**. You can also use **shift** to refer to a group of workers who work together on a particular shift.

> *His father worked <u>shifts</u> in a steel mill.*
> *The night <u>shift</u> should have been safely down the mine long ago.*

● **job share** (job shares, job sharing, job shared)

1 VERB

If two people **job share**, they share the same job by working part-time, for example one person in the mornings and the other in the afternoons.

> *They both want to <u>job share</u>.*

2 N-SING

A **job share** is an arrangement in which two people share the same job by both working part-time.

> *One lady who works in a bank <u>job share</u> said 'I can have my career and I can see my kids. It's wonderful.'*

● **career break** (career breaks) N-COUNT

If someone takes a **career break**, they stop working in their particular profession for a period of time, with the intention of returning to it later. A **career break** is usually unpaid.

> *Another major disadvantage for women is that many still take <u>career breaks</u> to bring up children, which cuts down the time they have to save towards a pension.*
> *'I'm considering a <u>career break</u> so I can concentrate on playing rugby,' revealed the Bedford-based police officer.*

● **long-hours culture** N-SING

The **long-hours culture** is the way in which some workers feel that they are expected to work longer hours than they are paid to do.

> *The report concluded: 'Our research confirms that Britain's <u>long-hours culture</u> is seriously undermining the quality of life. We must challenge this culture, for everyone's sake.'*

● **part-time**

1 ADJ

If someone is a **part-time** worker, or has a **part-time** job, they work for only part of each day or week.

> *Many businesses are cutting back by employing lower-paid <u>part-time</u> workers.*

2 ADV

If someone works **part-time**, they work for only part of each day or week.

> *I will continue to work <u>part-time</u> as a consultant after 60.*

● **short-term** ADJ

Short-term is used to describe things that will last for a short time, or things that will have an effect soon rather than in the distant future.

> *The company has 90 staff, almost all on <u>short-term</u> contracts.*

⊃ **work-life balance**: Topic 12.4; **salary**: Topic 14.2; **working conditions**: Topic 14.3; **absenteeism**: Topic 14.5

PRACTISE YOUR VOCABULARY

1 Complete the sentences by putting one of these words or phrases in each space.

teleworking   freelance   flexitime   job sharing   shifts   short-term contract

a John's company demands that he is in the office between 10.00 and 15.00 but he can start earlier than that and finish later than that as long as he works 40 hours per week. He is working _____.

b This is the worst week of the month for Mary because this week she's working nights. Next week is the best, because then she'll be at home when her daughter comes in from school. She's working _____.

c Pat works for a large insurance firm but he only goes to their office one day a week. For the other four he works at home and keeps in touch by e-mail, fax and phone. He's _____.

d Peter is a journalist. He writes for a variety of papers. This week it's the Financial Times, last week it was the Wall Street Journal. He decides how much work he does and when he works and completes his own accounts for tax purposes. He's working _____.

e Heidi is working at a food processing plant in Germany. She's worked there for two months, and her job finishes at the end of this month. She hopes the company will renew her contract for another three months. She's working on a
_____.

f Mary and Jane are both receptionists for a PR firm. Mary works there on Monday and Tuesday, Jane then takes over for the rest of the week. They are _____.

2 Are these statements true or false?

	True	False
a When a worker is on a career break they are unpaid.	☐	☐
b Part-time workers do not have a full-time job.	☐	☐
c Flexitime workers always start their working day at the same time.	☐	☐
d Shift workers always work at night.	☐	☐
e Freelance journalists receive a regular salary from the newspaper company they work for.	☐	☐
f Companies which offer flexible working patterns give their employees more control over their hours of work.	☐	☐
g If a company has a long-hours culture, its workers often stay late at work.	☐	☐

3 Some estimates suggest that up to one third of the workforce could eventually be teleworkers. List the benefits to a company and to the employee of this way of working. Choose from the list below.

| no commuting   smaller premises   flexible working hours   wider choice of potential employees   lower overheads
no restrictions on where you live |
|---|

COMPANY	EMPLOYEE

Topic 2

BUSINESS AND BUSINESSES

● **business** (businesses)

1 N-COUNT

A **business** is an organization which produces and sells goods or which provides a service.

> The company was a family <u>business</u>.
> He was short of cash after the collapse of his <u>business</u>.
> The cost of eating out is likely to rise if Granada succeeds in its £3.4 billion takeover bid for Forte, the international hotel and catering <u>business</u>.

2 N-UNCOUNT

Business is work relating to the production, buying and selling of goods or services. **Business** is also used when talking about how many products or services a company is able to sell. If **business** is good, a lot of products or services are being sold, and if **business** is bad, few of them are being sold. **Business** is also work or some other activity that you do as part of your job and not for pleasure.

> ...young people seeking a career in <u>business</u>.
> Jennifer has an impressive academic and <u>business</u> background.
> They worried that German companies would lose <u>business</u>.
> <u>Business</u> is booming.
> I'm here on <u>business</u>.
> ...<u>business</u> trips.

Common Collocations

a business <u>fails</u>	a business <u>goes bust</u>
a business <u>goes under</u>	the business <u>community</u>
to <u>downsize</u> a business	

● **concern** (concerns) N-COUNT

You can refer to a company or business as a **concern**, usually when you are describing what type of company or business it is.

> If not a large <u>concern</u>, Queensbury Nursery was at least a successful one.
> There used to be a football club at Old Trafford, but now there is a monolithic business <u>concern</u> called Manchester United plc.

● **big business** N-UNCOUNT

Big business is business which involves very large companies and very large sums of money.

> <u>Big business</u> will never let petty nationalism get in the way of a good deal.
> Ministers from 24 nations including Australia meet in Antarctica this week to discuss threats to the region's natural resources, primarily from <u>big business</u> interests.

● **small business** (small businesses) N-COUNT

A **small business** is a business that does not employ many people and earns relatively little money.

> ...information on issues that affect <u>small businesses</u>.
> ...banks interested in attracting <u>small business</u> customers.

● **company** (companies) N-COUNT
  firm (firms) N-COUNT

A **company** or **firm** is a business or organization that makes money by selling goods or services.

> Sheila found some work as a secretary in an insurance <u>company</u>.
> ...the Ford Motor <u>Company</u>.
> The <u>firm</u>'s employees were expecting large bonuses.

● **venture** (ventures) N-COUNT

A business **venture** is a commercial undertaking, such as the launch of a new company, in which there is a risk of loss as well as an opportunity for profit.

> His first business <u>venture</u> was a clothes shop in Rose Street.
> ...people interested in starting a commercial <u>venture</u>.

● **enterprise** (enterprises) N-COUNT

An **enterprise** is a company or business, often a small one.

> There are plenty of small industrial <u>enterprises</u>.
> Pressure from the workers is likely to grow and may eventually force the government to give its oil <u>enterprises</u> freedom to act like private companies.

● **corporation** (corporations) N-COUNT
  corporate ADJ

A **corporation** is a large business or company. **Corporate** means relating to business corporations or to a particular business corporation.

> ...multi-national <u>corporations</u>.
> Lotus Development <u>Corporation</u> co-developed the compact computer with H-P.
> This established a strong <u>corporate</u> image.

● **commerce** N-UNCOUNT

Commerce is the activities and procedures involved in buying and selling things.

> They have made their fortunes from industry and <u>commerce</u>.
> Shifts in agriculture promoted and reflected changes in <u>commerce</u>.

● **commercial** ADJ

1 **Commercial** means involving or relating to the buying and selling of goods.

> Docklands in its heyday was a major centre of industrial and <u>commercial</u> activity.
> Attacks were reported on vehicles and <u>commercial</u> premises.

2 **Commercial** organizations and activities are concerned with making money and profits, rather than, for example, with scientific research or providing a public service.

> Conservationists in Chile are concerned over the effects of <u>commercial</u> exploitation of forests.
> Whether the project will be a <u>commercial</u> success is still uncertain.

➲ **multinational**: Topic 1.4; **turnover**: Topic 6.1

PRACTISE YOUR VOCABULARY

1 Use the terms in the box to complete the sentences.

| big business   commerce   small businesses   corporations   firm |

a A business, company or _____ is an organization that sells goods or services.

b Business is also referred to as _____.

c The term _____ can refer to large business organizations or to any business activity that makes a lot of money.

d Large companies are referred to as _____.

e Small companies are referred to as _____ or small firms.

2 Find five words in the list that are synonyms for a business (list A), and one word that is a synonym for business (list B) and add them to the table.

a company   c enterprise   e commerce
b firm   d business concern   f business venture

List A	List B
a business	business

3 Complete each sentence with the correct form of one of the words from list A or list B.

a Most governments try to create an economic environment that will help _____ and trade.

b Some _____ such as Coca-Cola and Nike are internationally famous.

c Many students study _____ at college.

d In recent years some _____ involved in new technology have become very wealthy.

4 Circle the correct answer to each question. Use the information in the table to help you.

a Seaton Industries has a turnover of around £55m. In other words it is a small firm/corporation

b Robbins Inc. employs around 300,000 people. In other words it is a small/medium/large firm.

c In the UK, firms employing less than 20 staff make up 97% of all businesses. They are small businesses/corporations.

	Number of employees	Turnover
a small business	50 or fewer	£2.8m or below
a medium firm	between 50 and 250	£11.2m or below
a large firm/corporation	usually over 250	usually more than £11.2m

● **industry** (industries)

[1] N-UNCOUNT

Industry is the work and processes involved in collecting raw materials and making them into products in factories.

> *British industry suffers through insufficient investment in research.*
> *...in countries where industry is developing rapidly.*

[2] N-COUNT

A particular **industry** consists of all the people and activities involved in making a particular product or providing a particular service.

> *...the motor vehicle and textile industries.*
> *...the Scottish tourist industry.*

● **sector** (sectors) N-COUNT

A particular **sector** of a country's economy is the part connected with that specified type of industry.

> *...the nation's manufacturing sector.*
> *...the service sector of the Hong Kong economy.*

● **primary sector** (primary sectors) N-COUNT
secondary sector (secondary sectors) N-COUNT
industrial sector (industrial sectors) N-COUNT
tertiary sector (tertiary sectors) N-COUNT
service sector (service sectors) N-COUNT

The **primary sector** is the part of a country's economy that consists of industries which produce raw materials. The **secondary** or **industrial sector** consists of industries which produce things from raw materials, for example manufacturing and construction. The **tertiary** or **service sector** consists of industries which provide a service, such as transport and finance.

> *Developing countries are characterized by very large primary sectors and small industrial and service sectors.*
> *In 1930 a third of all women in the secondary sector worked in the textile industry.*
> *The average Irish woman working in the industrial sector is paid 65% less than her male counterpart.*
> *...economies that are slowly increasing the proportion of their labour force in the tertiary sector.*
> *Industries in the service sector that employ any number of low-paid workers would be especially hit by the implementation of a minimum wage.*

● **private sector** N-SING
public sector N-SING

The **private sector** is the part of a country's economy which consists of industries and commercial companies that are not owned or controlled by the government. The **public sector** is the part of a country's economy which is controlled or supported financially by the government.

> *...small firms in the private sector.*
> *...the gap between the salaries of public and private sector employees.*
> *To keep economic reform on track, 60,000 public-sector jobs must be cut.*

● **corporate sector** (corporate sectors) N-COUNT
financial sector (financial sectors) N-COUNT
personal sector (personal sectors) N-COUNT
household sector (household sectors) N-COUNT

The private sector can be divided into the **corporate sector** (businesses that supply goods and services), the **financial sector** (businesses that provide financial services), the **personal sector** (private individuals) and the **household sector** (private households).

> *...African countries which have an underdeveloped corporate sector.*
> *Many other funds that concentrate on the financial sector have almost doubled over five years.*
> *In the days when the personal sector saved more than it borrowed, falling inflation and high real interest rates meant people had more money.*
> *Wider share ownership is not the way to promote the household sector's investment in new manufacturing industry.*

● **public sector enterprise** (public sector enterprises) N-COUNT

A **public sector enterprise** is a commercial venture that is controlled or supported financially by the government.

> *Investment Corporation of Pakistan (ICP), another public sector enterprise, held 5.86% of the company's stock.*

● **productive sector** (productive sectors) N-COUNT

The **productive sector** is the part of a country's economy consisting of industries and companies which produce goods that can be sold at home or abroad.

> *...goods that are required by the productive sector.*
> *...a rapid diffusion and growth of technologies, such that industry became the dominant productive sector.*

● **goods** N-PLURAL

Goods are things that are made to be sold.

> *Money can be exchanged for goods or services.*
> *...a wide range of consumer goods.*

⊃ **developing**: Topic 4.1; **service industry**: Topic 12.2

PRACTISE YOUR VOCABULARY

1 There are many ways of describing the different parts of the economy. Look at the two diagrams showing the main classifications of economic activity and answer the questions.

STRUCTURE OF THE ECONOMY

| Public Sector |
| Private Sector |

activities undertaken by the state

activities undertaken by private individuals & businesses

| Corporate Sector | Financial Sector | Personal Sector |

businesses supplying goods & services

businesses providing financial services

private individuals & households

STRUCTURE OF INDUSTRY

The Productive Sectors of the Economy

| Primary Sector | Industrial Sector | Service Sector |

- *raw materials*
- *farming*

- *manufacturing*
- *construction*
- *gas & electricity*

- *retailing*
- *banking*
- *tourism*

Put each of the following examples of economic activity in the correct column in the table.

a Machinery hire   e Car production   i Supply of water   m Computer programming   q Gold mining
b Pig farming   f Coal mining   j Ship building   n Financial services   r Producing clothes
c Catering   g Oil drilling   k House building   o Car hire
d Insurance   h Graphic design   l Forestry   p Food processing

the primary sector	the industrial sector	the service sector

2 Developed countries have small primary sectors and large industrial and service sectors, whereas developing countries depend mainly on the primary sector. Look at this table and answer the questions that follow it.

Country	Primary Sector as % of total economy	Industrial Sector as % of total economy	Service Sector as % of total economy
A	10%	35%	55%
B	65%	20%	15%
C	30%	50%	20%

Which country do you think is likely to be described as:

a an underdeveloped economy   b a developing economy   c a developed economy

3 Complete the sentences with an appropriate term from the box.

| *goods*   *public sector enterprises*   *industries*   *public*   *private*   *financial*   *productive*   *service* |

a The manufacturing sector consists of a variety of manufacturing _____.
b Companies that are owned by shareholders or private individuals are in the _____ sector.
c A nationalized industry, run by the state, is in the _____ sector, and the companies in this sector are examples of _____.
d Any company that produces _____ or products is in the _____ sector.
e Banks are located within the _____ sector of the economy, or in the _____ sector of industry.

● **start-up** (start-ups)

☐1 ADJ

A **start-up** company is a small business that has recently been started by someone.

Thousands of <u>start-up</u> firms have entered the computer market.

☐2 N-COUNT

A **start-up** is a small business that has recently been started by someone.

For now the only bright spots in the labor market are small businesses and high-tech <u>start-ups</u>.

> **Common Collocations**
>
> a <u>business</u> start-up   an <u>Internet</u> start-up
> start-up <u>costs</u>   start-up <u>capital</u>
> start-up <u>company</u>

● **business plan** (business plans) N-COUNT

A **business plan** is a detailed plan for setting up or developing a business, especially one that is written in order to borrow money.

She learned how to write a <u>business plan</u> for the catering business she wanted to launch.

● **lender** (lenders) N-COUNT
bank manager (bank managers) N-COUNT
business angel (business angels) N-COUNT
venture capitalist (venture capitalists) N-COUNT
backer (backers) N-COUNT

A **lender** is a person or an institution that lends money to people. A **bank manager** is someone who is in charge of a bank, or a particular branch of a bank, and who is involved in making decisions about whether or not to lend money to businesses and individuals. A **business angel** is a person who gives financial support to a commercial venture and receives a share of any profits from it, but who does not expect to be involved in its management. A **venture capitalist** is someone who makes money by investing in high risk projects. A **backer** is someone who helps or supports a project, organization, or person, often by giving or lending money.

…the six leading mortgage <u>lenders</u>.
These files give details of your credit history and may have influenced your <u>bank manager's</u> decision not to give you a loan.
The number of companies financed by <u>business angels</u> increased by 51 year-on-year.
AME has been given $45m worth of taxpayers' funds to stimulate the growth of multimedia companies by acting as a <u>venture capitalist</u>.
I was looking for a <u>backer</u> to assist me in the attempted buy-out.

● **stakeholder** (stakeholders) N-COUNT

Stakeholders are people who have an interest in a company's or organization's affairs.

The <u>stakeholders</u> in the workers' compensation system – employers, workers and their representatives, and the legal profession – have strong opinions.

You have to involve and seek the agreement of all the <u>stakeholders</u> and interested parties.

● **overheads** N-PLURAL
running costs N-PLURAL

The **overheads** or **running costs** of a business are its regular and essential expenses, such as salaries, rent, and bills.

We are having to cut our costs to reduce <u>overheads</u>.
The aim is to cut <u>running costs</u> by £90 million per year.

> **Common Collocations**
>
> to <u>cut</u> overheads   to <u>reduce</u> overheads
> to have <u>high</u> overheads   to have <u>low</u> overheads
> <u>annual</u> running costs   <u>day-to-day</u> running costs
> to <u>cover</u> running costs

● **cash flow** N-UNCOUNT
break-even figure N-SING
profit forecast (profit forecasts) N-COUNT

The **cash flow** of a firm or business is the movement of money into and out of it. A **break-even figure** is the amount of money a company needs to make over a particular period of time in order not to make a loss. Any more money it makes after this will be profit. A **profit forecast** is a statement or set of figures which aims to predict how much money a company will make over a particular period of time.

A French-based pharmaceuticals company ran into <u>cash-flow</u> problems and faced liquidation.
This should put the operation well on course for a <u>break-even figure</u> by the end of the year.
Woolworths exceeded the <u>profit forecast</u> last year when it lifted profit 17 per cent to $200 million.

> **Common Collocations**
>
> <u>operating</u> cash flow   <u>negative</u> cash flow
> <u>positive</u> cash flow   to <u>reach</u> break-even <u>point</u>

● **budget** (budgets) N-COUNT

The **budget** for something is the amount of money that a person, organization, or country has available to spend on it. The **budget** of an organization or country is its financial situation, considered as the difference between the money it receives and the money it spends.

Some companies have a <u>budget</u> for external training.
The hospital needs to balance the <u>budget</u> each year.

> **Common Collocations**
>
> a budget <u>deficit</u>   budget <u>cuts</u>
> the budget <u>for</u> something   a <u>balanced</u> budget

➲ **return**: Topic 7.5; **expenditure**: Topic 8.2; **market research**: Topic 9.1; **supplier**: Topic 12.2; **income**: Topic 14.2

PRACTISE YOUR VOCABULARY

1 Which people on the following list are backers? Write them in the box below. Which people on the list are stakeholders?

a lenders   **c** employees   **e** customers   **g** business angels   **i** the community

b shareholders   **d** bank managers   **f** suppliers   **h** venture capitalists

BACKERS

2 Look at these titles of business books. Choose one of the terms from the box to fill the gap in each title.

overheads   break-even   backers   cash flow   business plan   budget

a   GETTING _____ FOR YOUR PROJECT.
HOW TO FIND INITIAL CAPITAL

d   CONTROLLING _____ .
KEEPING A HEALTHY BANK ACCOUNT

b   HOW TO DRAW UP A _____ .
DOCUMENTS THAT SHOW YOU MEAN BUSINESS

e   REDUCE YOUR _____ NOW!
CUT COSTS TO BOOST PROFITS

c   BRINGING THE _____ POINT FORWARD.
HOW TO START MAKING A PROFIT FASTER

f   BALANCING YOUR _____ .
HOW TO SPEND WISELY

3 Which book do you think would have a chapter called:

   a Checking income and expenditure

   b The profit forecast

   c When sales income and costs are balanced

   d Allocating money and resources

   e Financing a business start-up

   f Keeping control of your running costs

● **sole trader** (sole traders) N-COUNT
sole proprietor (sole proprietors) N-COUNT

A **sole trader** is a person who owns their own business and does not have a partner or any shareholders. The **sole proprietor** of a business is the owner of the business, when it is owned by only one person.

>　*Finance for a <u>sole trader</u> usually comes from the individual's own savings or from family and friends.*
>　*...a firm of solicitors of which he was the <u>sole proprietor</u>.*

● **partnership** (partnerships) N-VAR

Partnership or a **partnership** is a relationship in which two or more people, businesses, or industries work together as partners.

>　*...the <u>partnership</u> between Germany's banks and its businesses.*
>　*Alex and Mikhail were in <u>partnership</u> then: Mikhail handled the creative side; Alex was the financier.*

● **limited company** (limited companies) N-COUNT
limited liability company (limited liability companies) N-COUNT
Ltd ABBREVIATION

A **limited company** or **limited liability company** is a company whose owners are legally responsible for only a part of any money that it may owe if it goes bankrupt. The word **Limited** or the abbreviation '**Ltd**' is used in the name of a company to show that it is a limited company. [mainly BRIT]

>　*They had plans to turn the club into a <u>limited company</u>.*
>　*There are advantages in being a <u>limited liability company</u>.*
>　*He is the founder of International Sports Management <u>Limited</u>.*

● **plc** (plcs) N-COUNT

In Britain a **plc** is a company whose shares can be bought by the public. **Plc** is usually used after the name of a company and is an abbreviation for 'public limited company'.

>　*...British Telecommunications <u>plc</u>.*
>　*This licence would not allow him to trade as a <u>plc</u>.*

● **franchise** (franchises, franchising, franchised)

① N-COUNT
A **franchise** is an authority that is sold to someone by an organization, allowing them to sell its goods or services or to take part in an activity which the organization controls.

>　*...the <u>franchise</u> to build and operate the tunnel.*
>　*Talk to other <u>franchise</u> holders and ask them what they think of the parent company.*

② VERB
If a company **franchises** its business, it sells franchises to other companies, allowing them to sell its goods or services.

>　*She has recently <u>franchised</u> her business.*
>　*It takes hundreds of thousands of dollars to get into the <u>franchised</u> pizza business.*

● **franchisee** (franchisees) N-COUNT
franchiser (franchisers) N-COUNT
franchising N-UNCOUNT

A **franchisee** is a person or group of people who buy a particular franchise. A **franchiser** is an organization which sells franchises. **Franchising** is the act of selling franchises in a business.

>　*Gianfranco Ferre, the Italian fashion house, has seen its main British <u>franchisee</u> go bust.*
>　*...Dunkin' Donuts, a <u>franchiser</u> of doughnut shops.*
>　*One of the most important aspects of <u>franchising</u> is the reduced risk of business failure it offers to franchisees.*

● **holding company** (holding companies) N-COUNT

A **holding company** is a company that has enough shares in one or more other companies to be able to control the other companies.

>　*...a Montreal-based <u>holding company</u> with interests in telecommunications, gas and natural resources.*

● **subsidiary** (subsidiaries) N-COUNT
parent company (parent companies) N-COUNT
wholly-owned subsidiary (wholly-owned subsidiaries) N-COUNT

A **subsidiary** is a company which is part of a larger and more important company, known as the **parent company**. A **wholly-owned subsidiary** is a company whose shares are all owned by another company.

>　*...British Asia Airways, a <u>subsidiary</u> of British Airways.*
>　*Each unit including the <u>parent company</u> has its own, local management.*
>　*The Locomotive Construction Company Ltd is a <u>wholly-owned subsidiary</u> of the Trust.*

● **sister company** (sister companies) N-COUNT

Sister companies are two or more companies which are owned by the same parent organization.

>　*...Midland Bank's <u>sister company</u>, the Hang Seng Bank.*

● **associated company** (associated companies) N-COUNT

An **associated company** is a company in which between 20% and 50% of the shares are owned by another company or group.

>　*A large shareholding should provide considerable influence (but not control) over the <u>associated company</u>.*

● **group** (groups) N-COUNT

A **group** is a number of separate commercial or industrial firms which all have the same owner.

>　*The <u>group</u> made a pre-tax profit of £1.05 million.*

➲ **multinational**: Topic 1.4

PRACTISE YOUR VOCABULARY

1 Which terms refer to organizations that control another company, and which refer to companies whose shares are held by another company?

a a holding company **b** an associated company **c** a parent company **d** a subsidiary (company)

2 Look at the four diagrams showing corporate relationships and complete each sentence with one of the terms below.

| sister companies   group   associated companies   holding company |

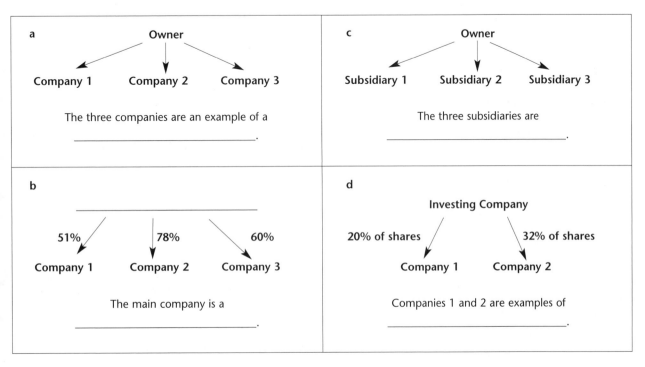

a

Owner

Company 1   Company 2   Company 3

The three companies are an example of a

_____.

c

Owner

Subsidiary 1   Subsidiary 2   Subsidiary 3

The three subsidiaries are

_____.

b

_____

51%   78%   60%

Company 1   Company 2   Company 3

The main company is a

_____.

d

Investing Company

20% of shares   32% of shares

Company 1   Company 2

Companies 1 and 2 are examples of

_____.

3 Use each term in the box to complete the paragraph.

| franchisees   franchise   franchise agreement   franchising   franchiser |

A company that wants to expand rapidly may choose _____ as a method. Ultramoda, an Italian clothing company, is an example of a _____ operation. Ultramoda is the _____ and sells the right to sell goods using its name to _____. These other businesses, which sign a _____ with Ultramoda, are usually small businesses, whereas the franchiser is a large international company.

4 Read the information about the four companies below and say which matches each of the terms in the box.

| a sole trader/sole proprietor   a partnership   a limited company   a plc |

a Mike Cobb set up an art gallery last year. He owns the gallery and manages it by himself.
b Craftplay is a medium-sized firm whose shares are available on the stock market.
c Ovenclean went bankrupt last year, but its shareholders were not made responsible for all the money it owed.
d Brothers Gianfranco and Giancarlo Belen recently set up an import-export company. They run the business together.

● **strategy** (strategies) N-COUNT

A **strategy** is a plan or set of plans intended to achieve something, especially over a long period.

> *What should our marketing strategy have achieved?*
> *Community involvement is now integral to company strategy.*

● **grow** (grows, growing, grew, grown) VERB

If someone **grows** a business, they take actions that will cause it to increase in wealth, size, or importance.

> *To grow the business, he needs to develop management expertise and innovation across his team.*
> *A lot of smaller enterprises have problems raising capital to grow their business.*

● **expansion strategy** (expansion strategies) N-COUNT

An **expansion strategy** is a set of planned policies and actions intended to make a company bigger or more successful.

> *This confidence has enabled NWV to pursue an aggressive expansion strategy. Last year the firm tripled its business on the Continent.*

● **acquisition** (acquisitions) N-VAR

If a company or business person makes an **acquisition**, they buy another company or part of a company.

> *…the acquisition of a profitable paper recycling company.*
> *The high street bank beat six other bidders to make the acquisition.*

● **takeover** (takeovers) N-COUNT

A **takeover** is the act of gaining control of a company by buying more of its shares than anyone else.

> *…the proposed £3.4 billion takeover of Midland Bank by the Hong Kong and Shanghai.*
> *Now the French group is ready to launch a takeover bid for the whole company.*

> ### Common Collocations
>
> a <u>hostile</u> takeover   a <u>proposed</u> takeover
> a takeover <u>offer</u>   a takeover <u>battle</u>
> a takeover <u>bid</u>

● **joint venture** (joint ventures) N-COUNT

A **joint venture** is a business or project in which two or more companies or individuals have invested, with the intention of working together.

> *Financial News Network announced today that it will be sold to a joint venture created by Dow Jones and Westinghouse Broadcasting.*
> *Chiroscience recently signed a joint-venture agreement with Medeva, giving Medeva the rights to license some of its discoveries.*

● **consortium** (consortia *or* consortiums) N-COUNT

A **consortium** is a group of people or firms who have agreed to co-operate with each other.

> *The consortium includes some of the biggest building contractors in Britain.*
> *These teams will be asked to form consortia to take over the new health authorities being set up from next April.*
> *Four consortiums are bidding for two contracts to modernise track, signalling, stations and trains.*

● **join forces** (joins forces, joining forces, joined forces) PHRASE

If you **join forces** with someone, you work together in order to achieve a common aim.

> *Both groups joined forces to persuade voters to approve a tax break for the industry.*
> *William joined forces with businessman Nicholas Court to launch the new vehicle.*

● **merge** (merges, merging, merged) VERB
merger (mergers) N-COUNT

If one company **merges** with another, or **is merged** with another, they combine to form a single company. You can also say that two companies **merge**, or **are merged**. A **merger** is the joining together of two separate companies or organizations so that they become one.

> *The C&G has said it will pay the bonus only to widows and widowers when it merges with Lloyds in August.*
> *He sees sense in merging the two agencies while both are new.*
> *…a merger between two of Britain's biggest trades unions.*
> *…the proposed merger of two Japanese banks.*

● **global reach** N-UNCOUNT

When people talk about the **global reach** of a company or industry, they mean its ability to have customers in many different parts of the world.

> *The company does not yet have the global reach of its bigger competitors.*
> *It would have to grow by acquisitions or joint ventures to achieve global reach.*

● **local partner** (local partners) N-COUNT

A company's **local partners** are companies based in foreign countries with whom they form a partnership in order to help them to start doing business in that country.

> *On-line banking services were already popular in the USA and Microsoft would seek local partners to develop the service in Australia.*

⮕ **vertical integration**: Topic 1.1; **franchise**: Topic 2.4; **ailing**: Topic 7.4

PRACTISE YOUR VOCABULARY

1 Look at the terms in the box and find two terms that refer to:

a two or more companies working together

b an increase in the size of the business

c gaining control of another company

d coming together formally or informally

acquisition   expansion   join forces   consortium   grow the business   merge   joint venture   takeover

2 Are the following statements true or false?

	True	False
a In a consortium, the companies concerned continue to exist independently of each other.	☐	☐
b Only one company invests in a joint venture.	☐	☐
c A merger is intended to be temporary.	☐	☐
d In a takeover, one of the companies may not like the idea of union.	☐	☐
e During an acquisition, one company may be taken over by another.	☐	☐
f Local partners are businesses which are based in a company's local area.	☐	☐
g If a company joins forces with another company, one company takes control of the other.	☐	☐

3 Use the terms in the box to complete the paragraph.

local partner   global reach   business strategy   expansion strategy

A common _____ designed to increase market share is selling into new markets. It can be

quite difficult to break into an overseas market, and finding a _____ can be very helpful. Their

knowledge of local conditions makes it easier for the company to establish itself. If a company pursues such an

_____ aggressively they will eventually have an international presence or

_____.

4 Match the business strategies with the situations below.

takeover   joint venture   local partner

a Cool-Cola is a British company. They would like to launch their product in Japan, and would like a Japanese company to help them to do this. They need a _____.

b Supersavers is an ailing supermarket chain. BigFood plans to buy enough shares to take control of the company. It is planning a _____.

c Max and Sarah have put their money together to develop a new computer game for the British market. This is a _____.

Topic 3

GLOBAL TRADING

● free trade N-UNCOUNT

Free trade is a system which allows certain countries to buy and sell goods from each other without any financial restrictions such as taxes.

The proposed <u>free trade</u> agreement between the US and Mexico came under fire today from environmentalists.
The two presidents want to replace the suspicions of the past with a new commercial relationship based on <u>free trade</u>.

● export (exports) N-COUNT
import (imports) N-COUNT
visible export/import (visible exports/imports)
N-COUNT
invisible export/import (invisible exports/ imports) N-COUNT

Exports are goods which are sold to another country and sent there. **Imports** are products or raw materials bought from another country for use in your own country. Trade in goods such as food, raw materials, and manufactured goods is known as **visible exports** and **visible imports**. Trade in services such as banking, insurance, and tourism is known as **invisible exports** and **invisible imports**.

According to the September estimates, <u>exports</u> rose by 18%.
British video games have always been big in the US, but this year's <u>imports</u> have done particularly well.
In the UK <u>visible imports</u> have traditionally been greater than <u>visible exports</u>.
Tourism is Britain's single biggest <u>invisible export</u>.

> ### Common Collocations
> <u>a ban on</u> imports   imports/exports <u>increase</u>
> imports/exports <u>decrease</u>

● balance of payments (balances of payments)
N-COUNT

A country's **balance of payments** is the difference, over a period of time, between the payments it makes to other countries for imports and the payments it receives from other countries for exports.

Britain's <u>balance of payments</u> deficit has improved slightly.

● trade deficit (trade deficits) N-COUNT
trade surplus (trade surpluses) N-COUNT

If a country has a **trade deficit**, the value of the goods it imports is greater than the value of the goods it exports. If a country has a **trade surplus**, it exports more than it imports.

America's <u>trade deficit</u> grew sharply in February, widening to $13.9 billion from a revised $11.4 billion in January.
The country's <u>trade surplus</u> widened to 16.5 billion dollars.

● exchange rate (exchange rates) N-COUNT

The **exchange rate** of a country's unit of currency is the amount of another country's currency that you get in exchange for it.

The continuing strong performance by Scotland's exporters, despite the relatively high <u>exchange rate</u>, is very good news.

● protectionism N-UNCOUNT

Protectionism is the policy some countries have of helping their own industries by putting a large tax on imported goods or by restricting imports in some other way.

The aim of the current round of talks is to promote free trade and to avert the threat of increasing <u>protectionism</u>.

● tariff (tariffs) N-COUNT

A **tariff** is a tax that a government collects on goods coming into a country.

Each exporting country has an incentive to subsidize exports even when the importing country levies an import <u>tariff</u>.

● customs duty (customs duties) N-VAR

Customs duties are taxes that people pay for importing and exporting goods.

Foreign investors can now import and export goods without paying <u>customs duties</u>.
<u>Customs duty</u> on cotton is being removed to ensure cheaper availability of raw material.

● quota (quotas) N-COUNT

A **quota** of something is an official limit on the minimum or maximum number of them that is allowed.

At present, farmers are given a set <u>quota</u> of sheep to produce in return for a subsidy under the common agricultural policy.
Sometimes it's cod we're throwing back into the water because we can't exceed our <u>quota</u>, other times it's plaice or haddock.

● domestic market (domestic markets) N-COUNT

A **domestic market** is the market which exists within a particular country.

More of us are holidaying at home too – Mr Davern said the <u>domestic market</u> was worth 24 per cent of tourism earnings.

● open market N-SING

Goods that are bought and sold on the **open market** are advertised and sold to anyone who wants to buy them.

The Central Bank is authorized to sell government bonds on the <u>open market</u>.

● World Trade Organization N-PROPER
WTO ABBREVIATION

The **World Trade Organization** is an international organization that encourages and regulates trade between its member states. The abbreviation **WTO** is also used.

… institutions such as the World Bank and the <u>World Trade Organization</u>.
In 1998 the <u>WTO</u> agreed with the US that Europe was going against <u>WTO</u> rules of free trade.

➲ **USP:** Topic 9.4

PRACTISE YOUR VOCABULARY

1 **Use the terms in the box to complete the paragraph.**

free trade   protectionism   tariffs   customs duties   quotas   imports   exports   exchange rates

The WTO was set up in 1995 to encourage free trade in the global marketplace. It is therefore designed to resist
_____. No new barriers to trade can be set up, and governments cannot set new _____ or
_____ or increase ones that already exist as these are really taxes that prevent _____.
Similarly the WTO opposes the use of _____ since these limit the amount of _____
coming into a country. This may protect a country's industry in the short term, but if its trading partners reply with similar
measures, then _____ will suffer. The WTO governs trade in many products and raw materials, but the
world of finance is largely outside of its scope, therefore it has no control over _____.

2 **Circle the terms below which encourage the movement of goods across borders.**

favourable exchange rates   customs duties   WTO   tariffs   import quotas   protectionism   free trade agreements

3 **Match each headword on the left with a set of examples on the right.**

a imports
b free trade
c domestic market
d exports
e open market
f exchange rates
g protectionism

i taxes, tariffs, quotas on imported goods
ii wheat, oil, tobacco being brought into the country
iii no taxes, restrictions or quotas on imports
iv rice, chocolate, wool being sent abroad
v customers in the same country
vi products available to anyone willing to buy
vii £1.00 = $2.50

4 **Look at the list of a country's imports. Which are visible and which are invisible?**

bananas   oil   cars   insurance   tourism   processed food   rice

Visible	Invisible

5 **Look at these figures describing the trade between three states and decide whether the statements which follow are true or false.**

ALAND		BELAND	
exports to Beland	£100M	exports to Aland	£75M
imports from Beland	£75M	imports from Aland	£100M
exports to Celand	£150M	exports to Celand	£55M
imports from Celand	£50M	imports from Celand	£75M

	True	False
a Beland has got a trade deficit with Aland.	☐	☐
b Celand has got a positive balance of payments with Aland.	☐	☐
c Celand has got a trade surplus with Beland.	☐	☐
d Aland has got the best balance of payments figures.	☐	☐
e Beland has got the worst balance of payments figures.	☐	☐

● **flight of capital** N-UNCOUNT

Flight of capital is when people lose confidence in a particular country's economy, and so start to remove their money from that country. This often has the effect of making that country's economic situation worse.

> The interest-rate rise should slow the _flight of capital_.
> TI has seen its shares suffer because of a _flight of capital_ to telecom and Internet-related businesses.

● **infrastructure** (infrastructures) N-VAR

The **infrastructure** of a country, society, or organization consists of the basic facilities such as transport, communications, power supplies and buildings, which enable it to function.

> The _infrastructure_, from hotels to transport, is old and decrepit.
> ...improvements in the country's _infrastructure_.

Common Collocations

an infrastructure project
infrastructure investment
infrastructure spending
infrastructure development

● **deregulate** (deregulates, deregulating, deregulated) VERB
deregulation N-UNCOUNT

To **deregulate** something means to remove controls and regulations from it. **Deregulation** is the removal of controls and restrictions in a particular area of trade.

> Once wholesale prices are _deregulated_, consumer prices will also rise.
> _Deregulation_ of the power market is not necessarily the best option, because free market principles seldom work when there is no free market.

● **dump** (dumps, dumping, dumped) VERB

If one country **dumps** goods in another country, the first country exports a very large quantity of cheap goods to the second country.

> The Commerce Department has ruled that the Japanese companies have been _dumping_ minivans at unfairly low prices in the US.
> The US will _dump_ 22,000 tonnes of subsidised milk powder, butterfat and cheese onto Australia's traditional markets in Asia.

● **subsidy** (subsidies) N-UNCOUNT

A **subsidy** is money that is paid by a government or other authority in order to help an industry or business, or to pay for a public service.

> European farmers are planning a massive demonstration against farm _subsidy_ cuts.
> They've also slashed state _subsidies_ to utilities and transportation.

● **recession** (recessions) N-VAR

A **recession** is a period when the economy of a country is doing badly, for example because industry is producing less and more people are becoming unemployed.

> The _recession_ caused sales to drop off.
> We should concentrate on sharply reducing interest rates to pull the economy out of _recession_.

Common Collocations

a deep recession	to sink into a recession
a severe recession	to come out of a recession
a global recession	to emerge from a recession
recession-proof	recession-hit

● **inward investment** N-UNCOUNT

Inward investment is the investment of money in a country by companies from outside that country.

> The UK is the main location in Europe for _inward investment_ and the third largest recipient of _inward investment_ in the world.

● **law** (laws)

⊡ N-SING
The **law** is a system of rules that a society or government develops in order to deal with crime, business agreements, and social relationships. You can also use the law to refer to the people who work in this system.

> It is against the _law_ to discriminate on the basis of sex, age, marital status, or race.
> Trading-standards officers suspect that many firms are breaking the _law_ by not advertising the full cost of last-minute holidays.

⊡ N-COUNT
A **law** is one of the rules in a system of law which deals with a particular type of agreement, relationship, or crime.

> French lorry drivers say they will be put out of business by the new _law_ which cuts the working week from 39 to 35 hours.

Common Collocations

to change a law	to become law
to pass a law	to break the law
law-abiding	by law
law enforcement	against the law

● **regulation** (regulations) N-COUNT

Regulations are rules made by a government or other authority in order to control the way something is done or the way people behave.

> The European Union has proposed new _regulations_ to control the hours worked by its employees.
> Under pressure from the American government, Fiat and other manufacturers obeyed the new safety _regulations_.

⊃ **boom:** Topic 7.1

PRACTISE YOUR VOCABULARY

1 Match the statements on the left with a sentence on the right that has the same meaning.

a There has been a flight of capital.
b Businesses cannot succeed without the backup of a good infrastructure.
c The government is going to deregulate the industry.
d The company has been dumping its products.
e The government is increasing its subsidies to agriculture.
f There is a recession.
g Inward investment is increasing.
h The government has introduced new car safety regulations.

i Profits are falling and unemployment is rising.
ii It will put more money into the sector to protect it from foreign competition.
iii It is going to remove rules that limit the way management can operate.
iv Large amounts of money have been moved out of the country in a short space of time.
v Manufacturers are obliged to obey national rules relating to the design of their product.
vi Foreign business is putting more capital into its operations in our country.
vii It has been selling abroad at below the cost of production in order to ruin its competitors.
viii They need to use the transport system and they need an educated and healthy workforce.

2 Your company wants to start manufacturing in country X. Which of the following points would make you feel confident (plus points) about investing, and which ones would worry you (minus points)?

	plus points	minus points
a There has been a recent flight of capital from the country.		
b The transport infrastructure is well-maintained.		
c Many industries have been deregulated.		
d Many European countries dump their products there.		
e Government subsidies are available for foreign investors.		
f The country is in recession.		
g There are many regulations concerning workers' wages.		
h The country attracts inward investment from the Japanese.		

3 Which of the following statements are true and which are false?

	True	False
a If an industry dumps its products abroad it can cause problems for the same industry in the receiving country.	☐	☐
b Most governments like to try to prevent any increase in inward investment.	☐	☐
c Some governments give subsidies to sectors of the economy which are threatened by overseas competition.	☐	☐
d Deregulation can increase the range of options for management.	☐	☐
e A flight of capital is a sign that a government's economic policies are popular with business.	☐	☐
f During a recession people buy more and sales figures go up.	☐	☐
g If a government announces that it will be increasing investment in its country's transport infrastructure, most businesses will be pleased.	☐	☐
h All governments like to take credit for economic booms.	☐	☐

● **compete** (competes, competing, competed) VERB
competitor (competitors) N-COUNT

When one firm or country **competes** with another, it tries to get people to buy its own goods in preference to those of the other firm or country. You can also say that two firms or countries **compete**. A company's **competitors** are companies who are trying to sell similar goods or services to the same people.

> *The stores will inevitably end up <u>competing</u> with each other in their push for increased market shares.*
> *Banks and building societies are <u>competing</u> fiercely for business.*
> *The American economy, and its ability to <u>compete</u> abroad, was slowing down according to the report.*
> *The bank isn't performing as well as some of its <u>competitors</u>.*

Common Collocations

to compete <u>successfully</u>	a <u>major</u> competitor
to compete <u>fiercely</u>	to <u>lose ground</u> to a
to compete <u>effectively</u>	competitor
to <u>see off</u> a competitor	a <u>direct</u> competitor
a <u>close</u> competitor	

● **competitive edge** N-COUNT

If a company has a **competitive edge**, it has advantages such as new skills or new technology which make it more likely to attract business than its competitors.

> *The Japanese government also works with its industries to help them develop a <u>competitive edge</u>.*
> *Quality of service is becoming an increasingly important consideration in maintaining a <u>competitive edge</u> in all markets.*

● **competitive advantage** (competitive advantages) N-COUNT

A **competitive advantage** is something that makes one particular company or economy more likely to succeed than others.

> *By keeping wage rises down, Germany and France have made their goods cheaper to buy. That gives them a huge <u>competitive advantage</u> over us.*
> *…a general shift towards using IT systems to gain <u>competitive advantage</u>, rather than merely automating existing processes within the business.*

● **key player** (key players) N-COUNT

If someone or something is a **key player** in a particular organization, event, or situation, they are one of the most important people or things involved in it.

> *The former deputy chairman was a <u>key player</u> in a number of the deals that pushed the bank to the top of the list.*
> *The Federal Government regards BHP's move as a vindication of its concerted effort to confirm Australia as a <u>key player</u> in the financial affairs of Vietnam.*

● **monopoly** (monopolies) N-VAR

1 If a company, person, or state has a **monopoly** on something such as an industry, they have complete control over it, so that it is impossible for others to become involved in it.

> *…Russian moves to end a state <u>monopoly</u> on land ownership.*

2 A **monopoly** is a company which is the only one providing a particular product or service.

> *…a state-owned <u>monopoly</u>.*

Common Collocations

a <u>near</u> monopoly	to <u>break</u> a monopoly
a <u>virtual</u> monopoly	to <u>end</u> a monopoly

● **market leader** (market leaders) N-COUNT

A **market leader** is a company that sells more of a particular product or service than most of its competitors do.

> *We are becoming one of the <u>market leaders</u> in the fashion industry.*
> *It means that the <u>market leader</u> has a very strong grip on the market, so if you want to be profitable you have got to be number one, or maybe number two.*

● **best-seller** (best-sellers) N-COUNT

A **best-seller** is a product which is very popular and of which a great number has been sold.

> *When it goes on sale in June it confronts tough opposition such as the VW Golf, Vauxhall Astra and the UK <u>best-seller</u>, the Ford Focus.*
> *Her books have topped <u>best-seller</u> lists throughout the world.*

● **rival** (rivals) N-COUNT

Your **rival** is a person, business, or organization that you are competing against in the same area or for the same things.

> *BTP, one of Britain's few remaining chemical companies, has been bought by a Swiss <u>rival</u>.*
> *Two problems facing the tourism ministry were how to boost winter tourism, ensure a constant water supply, and see off new <u>rivals</u> such as Croatia and Egypt.*

⊃ **public sector enterprise**: Topic 2.2; **economies of scale**: Topic 8.2; **brand name**: Topic 9.4; **market**: Topic 12.1; **market share**: Topic 12.1

PRACTISE YOUR VOCABULARY

1 Complete the paragraph with the correct term from the box.

| competitive edge   compete   monopolies   competitive advantage   competitors   key players |

_____ are organizations selling products or services in the same market, and they can also be the products

or services themselves. Competitors _____ with each other. Commentators talk about the things that give

one company or product its _____ or_____ over others. Competitors in

a market are players, and the most important ones are _____. Companies without competitors are

_____.

2 Match the beginning of each sentence on the left with the end of the sentence on the right.

i In the global market place companies try   **a** help increase market share.
ii Having a competitive advantage over their rivals can   **b** to gain a competitive edge.
iii Companies can gain an edge   **c** become a market leader.
iv A successful brand can help a company   **d** by having a major brand or best-seller.

3 Look at the pie chart showing the market share of four car manufacturers and answer the questions.

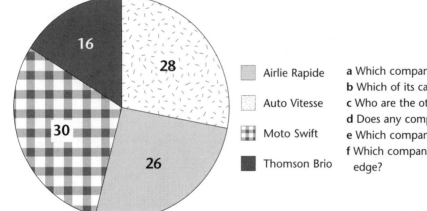

Airlie Rapide

Auto Vitesse

Moto Swift

Thomson Brio

a Which company is the market leader in this sector?
b Which of its cars is a best-seller?
c Who are the other key players in the market?
d Does any company have a monopoly in this market?
e Which company has seen off its rivals most successfully?
f Which company needs to develop a stronger competitive edge?

4 Read the definitions and decide if they are true or false.

	True	False
a A well-established brand name can give a company a competitive edge.	☐	☐
b If a company's profits are good, they don't need to worry about their competitors.	☐	☐
c A company only needs to sell a few of a high-priced product for it to be a best-seller.	☐	☐
d Market leaders often have a competitive advantage.	☐	☐
e Many public sector enterprises have a monopoly in the market.	☐	☐

● **global** ADJ
global brand (global brands) N-UNCOUNT

You can use **global** to describe something that happens in all parts of the world or affects all parts of the world. A **global brand** is a brand which is sold and recognized throughout the world.

> ...a proposed international agreement liberalising _global_ trade.
> We are already familiar with _global brands_ such as Coca-Cola, McDonald's and Microsoft.

● **align** (aligns, aligning, aligned) VERB

If a company **aligns** its products with a particular market, it tries to present them in a way that suggests they are suitable for that market or similar to other products within that market.

> To better _align_ its huge array of products with today's consumer tastes, KGF is now making a concerted effort to become a leader in the low-fat to no-fat foods arena.
> ...a branding strategy to more directly _align_ the group with the globally recognised brand of its French parent, AXA.

● **core values** N-PLURAL

A group or organiazation's **core values** are the things they believe in and consider to be most important.

> With all that change going on, one of my most important jobs is keeping the company focused on our _core values_.
> The _core values_ of this firm are respect for the individual, treating the individual with dignity, and teamwork.

● **standardize** (standardizes, standardizing, standardized) VERB
standardized ADJ

To **standardize** things means to change them so that they all have the same features. **Standardized** products are products which have been changed so that they all have the same features.

> There is a drive both to _standardize_ components and to reduce the number of models on offer.
> If people do not prefer differentiated products to _standardized_ products, why would a business expend resources seeking to destandardize its particular product?

● **product differentiation** N-UNCOUNT

Product differentiation refers to the way that a particular product is presented to the public in order to distinguish it from other, similar products.

> Consumers today enjoy unrivalled choice. But sometimes it is possible to think that what marketing people call '_product differentiation_' has gone too far.
> They cannot seize a significant part of the market unless they achieve _product differentiation_.

● **product line** (product lines) N-COUNT
product mix (product mixes) N-COUNT
product portfolio (product portfolios) N-COUNT
product range (product ranges) N-COUNT

A **product line** is a group of related products produced by one manufacturer, for example products that are intended to be used for similar purposes or to be sold in similar types of shops. A company's **product mix** is the range of products that it produces. A **product range** or **product portfolio** is all the products sold by a particular company.

> A well-known UK supermarket launches more than 1,000 new _product lines_ each year.
> The _product mix_ is 25% toys and games, 25% gifts, 25% design items, 15% electronic items, and 10% fitness-oriented merchandise.
> Unilever's _product range_ spans food, teas, detergents, deodorants, soaps and hair-care.
> We intend to position Kambrook as a value brand within our current _product portfolio_.

● **target market** (target markets) N-COUNT

A **target market** is a market in which a company is trying to sell its products or services.

> We decided that we needed to change our _target market_ from the over-45s to the 35–45s.

⮑ **globalization**: Topic 1.4; **multinational**: Topic 1.4; **corporation**: Topic 2.1; **life cycle**: Topic 9.2

PRACTISE YOUR VOCABULARY

1 Use the terms in the box to complete the paragraph.

product range   product portfolio   global brands   brands   product mix   aligned   brand   product differentiation

The combination of products that a business sells is known as the _____. The American multinational McCann and Muir, for example, have pharmaceuticals, fragrances, consumer products, cleaning products and beauty care products in their _____. Their cleaning products include a _____ of soap powders including _____ such as Brash, Saturn and Brill. A _____ is a product which customers see as different from other similar ones available. McCann and Muir knows that different products satisfy different needs, and that's why _____ is important. Their customers may choose Brill because it's advertised as offering high quality at an affordable price, or Brash because it combines detergent and conditioner for convenience, for example. Many of their _____ are sold around the world, others are _____ to meet the needs of specific markets.

2 Look at the five word pairs and use each one to complete the sentences.

```
           ┌─── range
           │
           ├─── portfolio
 ( product )│
           ├─── line
           │
           ├─── mix
           │
           └─ differentiation
```

a A well-organized business usually tries to manage the _____ by introducing new products into their portfolio as old ones reach the end of their life cycle.

b The product mix includes _____s, or groups of products that are closely related to one another.

c Giving products separate identities, or _____, gives consumers as much choice as possible.

d The particular mix of products that a company is marketing is known as the _____ or _____.

3 Match the two parts of these extracts.

a Boeing is now expanding its product line with its first all-new aircraft for 12 years.	**i** products that weren't included in its product portfolio as little as two years ago.
b Mitre's product range includes	**ii** Nike can change its product mix almost overnight.
c British Aerospace said that more than half of its sales now come from	**iii** that will damage its core values.
d By rearranging what each supplier can do on its network	**iv** It consists of more than 1,000 companies in around 140 different countries of the world.
e Asea Brown Boveri, the world's leading supplier of power and railway equipment, is an example of a global business.	**v** At present the company makes four models, including the $150m 747.
f When managing a brand it is important not to make changes	**vi** soccer and rugby balls and sports footwear.

● marketing mix N-UNCOUNT

A company's **marketing mix** is the combination of marketing activites it uses in order to promote a particular product or service. A typical marketing mix is a combination of product, place, promotion and price.

> The product is the most important element of the _marketing mix_, since it holds together promotion, distribution and pricing policies.

> The key focus of the _marketing mix_ will be on price.

● market conditions N-PLURAL

The **market conditions** are the state of a particular market at a particular time, for example whether there is a lot of demand for a product or little demand for it.

> In current _market conditions_, fundraising for biotechnology companies is difficult.

> The dot-com boom marked one of the most significant periods of change in recent times and highlighted the need for business schools to be responsive to _market conditions_.

● direct marketing N-UNCOUNT

Direct marketing is a method of marketing which involves companies sending advertising material directly to people who they think may be interested in their products.

> The _direct marketing_ industry has become adept at packaging special offers.

> _Direct marketing_ on the Internet needs to be conducted with particular care.

● marketing strategy N-VAR

A **marketing strategy** is a general plan or set of plans intended to organize the sale of a product, for example, deciding on its price, and how it should be advertised, especially over a long period.

> But the customer database must be updated, not only with a full shopping history, but keeping an eye on their lifestyles is vital to our _marketing strategy_. For example, if a customer is no longer single and has started a family, we need to know. It will affect how he or she chooses to holiday.

● launch strategy (launch strategies) N-UNCOUNT

A **launch strategy** is a general plan or set of plans intended to organize the launch of a product, for example, deciding on how it should be advertised, especially over a long period.

> Could you design a cocktail that would help make the brand more appealing to 18-24 year-olds? Or devise a _launch strategy_ for a new chain of student pubs?

> These developments are long term and involve high risks. Established new product development, test and _launch strategies_ will need to be re-examined.

● customize (customizes, customizing, customized) VERB

If you **customize** a product, you change its appearance or features to suit your tastes or needs.

> To accommodate the preferences of homeowners, most manufacturers will _customize_ their products, even the standard models.

> The company makes portable electronic typewriters and personal wordprocessors and markets office supplies, including file folders and _customized_ printed products.

● country-specific ADJ

Something that is **country-specific** relates to a particular country.

> These programs are to be _country-specific_.

> ...losses due to _country-specific_ economic, political, and social events.

● customer profile (customer profiles) N-COUNT

A **customer profile** is a description of the typical sort of customer who is regarded as likely to buy a particular product.

> In stores, between 60% and 70% of all men's underwear purchases are made by women for their men, but on the web, the _customer profile_ is 90% male.

> Each day of the week has its own particular _customer profile_. Mondays and Tuesdays bring in the older, retired customers, while Thursday is mainly dominated by housewives.

➲ **target market**: Topic 3.4; **standardize**: Topic 3.4; **product differentiation**: Topic 3.4; **merchandising**: Topic 6.4

PRACTISE YOUR VOCABULARY

1 Your company is preparing to launch a new product in several different markets. In each pair underline the marketing strategy which shows that you plan to differentiate the product.

a one product at the same price in all countries   one product with a different price for each market

b standardized product for all markets   products customized to each market

c direct marketing campaign   customized marketing campaign

d country-specific advertisements   standardized advert made for all markets

2 Henry Ford once said that his customers could buy one of his cars in any colour they liked as long as they liked black. Did his company sell standardized or customized products?

3 A company which produces a magazine about motorbikes plans to use direct marketing to improve sales. Which of the following activities would they use? Tick all the possible options.

a Send advertising material to selected social/economic groups.

b Put leaflets through the doors of everyone in their local area.

c Target certain age groups.

d Advertise on national television.

e Subscribe to databases about people's leisure activities.

f Send advertising material to local motorbike retail outlets.

4 Match the two parts of the extracts.

a Some businesses are moving away from undifferentiated marketing strategies   **i** is professional males, aged 30–35.

b Market conditions in the oil industry   **ii** as they attempt to target customer needs.

c The typical customer profile for our products   **iii** can be quite variable.

5 Write product, place, promotion or price in each gap to show the elements of the marketing mix.

a _____ making sure that it satisfies customer needs

b _____ making it affordable to the target market

c _____ making sure it's available and convenient for the customer to find it

d _____ making sure that the customer knows about it

6 Look at the four lists of examples of each of the '4 Ps' in the table below and give each list one of the headings from Exercise 5. Then write two more examples of each element in the final column.

element of the marketing mix	examples	more examples
a	coffee, cars, beer, clothes	
b	leaflets, TV advertisements, direct mail	
c	£300, $40	
d	high street stores, specialist retail outlets	

Topic 4

SUSTAINABLE DEVELOPMENT

● ethical consumer (ethical consumers) N-COUNT

Consumers who choose not to buy products from certain companies for moral reasons, for example because a company harms the environment or uses child labour, are sometimes called **ethical consumers**.

A passionate supporter of animal welfare, she too refuses to purchase anything that could possibly be connected with cruelty.
Both are examples of a burgeoning group – ethical consumers.

● business ethics N-PLURAL

Business ethics are the moral beliefs and rules about right and wrong that are involved in business.

Business ethics are coming to the forefront of the agenda.
Companies are seeing that their activities have important social and ethical implications.

● social responsibility N-UNCOUNT

Social responsibility is the duty that some people feel companies have to behave in a correct and proper way, for example towards their workers and the local community.

All businesses have a wider social responsibility and are answerable to more than just their shareholders.

● co-operative (co-operatives) N-COUNT

A **co-operative** is a business or organization run by the people who work for it, or owned by the people who use it. These people share its benefits and profits.

The restaurant is run as a co-operative.
Oxfam aids small farming co-operatives to improve their yields significantly.

Common Collocations

a housing co-operative	a workers' co-operative
a co-operative society	a co-operative movement

● sweatshop (sweatshops) N-COUNT

If you describe a small factory as a **sweatshop**, you mean that many people work there in poor conditions for low pay.

…the dingy, hidden world of garment sweatshops.
…a product that was made with child labor or in a sweatshop.

● child labour N-UNCOUNT

Child labour is the use of children as workers in industry.

Past attempts to ban child labour in various industries have not worked.
… a boycott of goods made with child labour.

● developed ADJ
First World N-PROPER

If you talk about **developed** countries or the **developed** world, you mean the countries or the parts of the world that are wealthy and have many industries. The most prosperous and industrialized parts of the world are sometimes referred to as the **First World**.

Life expectancy in the developed world has doubled.
Although South Africa has many of the attributes of the first world – some good infrastructure, millions of rich people, and a few world-class companies, hospitals and universities – it is still not part of that world.
…wealthy First World countries.

● developing ADJ
Third World N-PROPER

If you talk about **developing** countries or the **developing** world, you mean the countries or the parts of the world that are poor and have few industries. Together the countries of Africa, Asia, and South America are sometimes referred to as the **Third World**, especially those parts that are poor, do not have much power, and are not considered to be highly developed.

In the developing world cigarette consumption is increasing.
The only developing country with large foreign reserves is Taiwan.
As the cities of the Third World expand, there is little hope that their governments' public health systems can cope.
…a campaign to cancel Third World debt.

● GDP (GDPs) N-VAR

In economics, a country's **GDP** is the total value of goods and services produced within a country in a year, not including its income from investments in other countries. **GDP** is an abbreviation for 'gross domestic product'.

He said that in time the UK would match the European average spend on health which is 8 per cent of GDP.

● per capita

1 ADJ

The **per capita** amount of something is the total amount of it in a country or area divided by the number of people in that country or area. **Per capita** means 'per person'.

They have the world's largest per capita income.
Per capita GDP in the richer economies is 74 times that of the poorest.

2 ADV

If something occurs at a certain rate **per capita**, it occurs at a rate calculated by dividing the total number of times it occurs in a particular country or area by the number of people in that country or area. **Per capita** means 'per person'.

Ethiopia has almost the lowest oil consumption per capita in the world.
This year Americans will eat about 40% more fresh apples per capita than the Japanese.

Common Collocations

per capita spending	per capita consumption
to do something on a per capita basis	

➲ **GNP**: Topic 4.5

PRACTISE YOUR VOCABULARY

1 Match two pairs of words that have the same meaning.

a First World   **b** developing countries   **c** Third World   **d** developed countries

2 Look at the list of countries and answer the questions that follow.

a Bangladesh   **c** France   **e** Nepal   **g** Ethiopia
b New Zealand   **d** Singapore   **f** Sudan   **h** Japan

  i Which of these countries are examples of developed countries/developing countries?
 ii Which ones are more likely to have high levels of gross domestic product (GDP)?
iii Which ones are more likely to operate sweatshops?
iv Which ones are likely to have the lowest per capita income?

3 Which of the following do ethical businesses or ethical consumers prioritize?

a values   **c** wealth   **e** morality   **g** personal happiness
b profit   **d** beliefs   **f** greed   **h** social responsibility

4 Which of these four people can be described as ethical consumers?

    Keith: 'I don't buy products that I know have been made by child workers.'

    Steve: 'I choose investment companies that don't do business with firms that have
                connections with dictatorships.'

    Eric: 'We buy the cheapest coffee beans for our café.'

    Brian: 'I invest my money in firms that are likely to make the biggest profits.'

5 Are these statements true or false?

	True	False
a GDP measures the total value of a country's manufacturing industry.	☐	☐
b Sweatshops are retail outlets selling sports clothing.	☐	☐
c Sweatshops do not exist only in Third World countries.	☐	☐
d Child labour exists only in Third World countries.	☐	☐
e Ethical consumers buy goods produced in Third World countries.	☐	☐
f Ethics are usually the main guiding principle in business.	☐	☐

6 Look at the list of courses of action for a retail business operating in a competitive environment. Which courses of action do you think might be priorities for a co-operative retail society, and which for an ordinary retail company? Complete the table.

a providing a service to the local community by
   keeping poorly-performing branches open
b involving staff in all decision-making

c internal democratic organization
d education of workers and customers
e beating the competition

co-operative retail society	ordinary retail company

● **corporate responsibility** (corporate responsibilities) N-VAR

Corporate responsibility is the sense of responsibility that a company considers it has towards things such as the local community and the environment.

> *The European Commission last week published a Green Paper on <u>corporate responsibility</u> designed to create a framework to combine profit generation with social accountability.*
> *While the company is keen to develop its operations in Xinjiang, for example through greater emphasis on training and communication, it is mindful of its <u>corporate responsibilities</u> in the area.*

● **trading relationship** (trading relationships) N-COUNT

If two countries or businesses have a **trading relationship** with each other, they trade with each other on a regular basis.

> *Mr Palaszczuk did not believe New Zealand's actions would affect the close <u>trading relationship</u> between the two countries, he said.*
> *Euro-zone companies will find it relatively easier, says Oxford's Mr Taylor, to develop <u>trading relationships</u> with each other than with British ones.*

● **sustainable** ADJ

You use **sustainable** to describe the use of natural resources when this use is kept at a steady level that is not likely to damage the environment. You also use **sustainable** to describe a business that is able to continue at a steady level without the need to invest more money in it or to develop new markets.

> *…the management, conservation and <u>sustainable</u> development of forests.*
> *Try to buy wood that you know has come from a <u>sustainable</u> source.*
> *The strategy behind the programme is about aggregating a range of services into the one centre to create a commercially <u>sustainable</u> business.*
> *Further, operating without a domestic source of supply in a major market like the USA was not and is not a <u>sustainable</u> business model.*

Common Collocations

<u>ecologically</u> sustainable   <u>environmentally</u> sustainable
sustainable <u>development</u>   sustainable <u>growth</u>
sustainable <u>agriculture</u>

● **ethical policy** (ethical policies) N-COUNT

A company's **ethical policy** is the policy it adopts on ethical issues such as the use of child labour and matters relating to the environment.

> *…a clearly stated <u>ethical policy</u> that covers human rights, the arms trade, fair trade, the environment and animal welfare.*
> *The Co-op Bank's <u>ethical policy</u> stretches to who it does business with. It will not, for example, accept money from fox hunts.*

● **social cost** (social costs) N-COUNT
social benefit (social benefits) N-COUNT

The **social costs** of a policy or scheme are the undesirable effects it is likely to have on society, such as an increase in crime, unemployment, or pollution. The **social benefits** of a policy or scheme are the desirable effects it is likely to have on society, such as a reduction in crime, unemployment, or pollution.

> *'Is it worth the human and <u>social cost</u> of closing down a railway line because it is not competitive?' the spokesman said.*
> *Yet there are heavy <u>social costs</u> to neglecting the countryside, including crowded, car-clogged cities and high urban unemployment.*
> *Sheltered accommodation can produce an additional <u>social benefit</u> by re-housing older people from general and council housing, thus freeing accommodation for homeless people.*
> *…the <u>social benefits</u> of transport investment.*

● **non-profit-making** ADJ

A **non-profit-making** organization or charity is not run with the intention of making a profit. [mainly BRIT].

> *…the Film Theatre Foundation, a <u>non-profit-making</u> company which raises money for the arts.*

● **environmental impact** (environmental impacts) N-VAR

The **environmental impact** of a scheme or product is the environmental effect the scheme or product is likely to have, for example an increase in pollution or a loss of natural habitats.

> *…a scientific adviser whose role was to assess the project's <u>environmental impact</u>.*
> *That there would be some <u>environmental impact</u> in the form of traffic congestion was undeniable.*

● **social audit** (social audits) N-COUNT

If a company carries out a **social audit**, it analyses the social costs and social benefits of its operations in order to measure their success.

> *Some argue that banks should be forced to offer services to poor people and carry out a <u>social audit</u> before closing a branch.*
> *Camelot, the much criticised lottery operator, is putting itself through a <u>social audit</u> to try to come to terms with its critics.*

● **exploitative** ADJ

If you describe something as **exploitative**, you disapprove of it because it treats people unfairly by using their work or ideas for its own advantage, and giving them very little in return.

> *The expansion of Western capitalism incorporated the Third World into an <u>exploitative</u> world system.*
> *No-one knows how far sustainable and non-<u>exploitative</u> practices could go towards providing food, water, shelter and work for the world's people.*

➲ **stakeholder**: Topic 2.3; **regulation**: Topic 3.2; **Third World**: Topic 4.1; **shareholder**: Topic 7.2; **supplier**: Topic 12.2

PRACTISE YOUR VOCABULARY

1 **Which of these factors might act to increase corporate responsibility and which might act as barriers to it?**

a a rise in costs associated with a more responsible approach   **d** social auditing

b shareholder pressure to increase profits   **e** pressure from society

c business secrecy

2 **Use the terms in the box to complete the paragraph.**

> *social audit*   *social costs*   *trading relationship*   *corporate responsibility*   *social benefits*   *ethical policy*

Companies which accept _____ are prepared to accept responsibility for their actions and are able to justify them. They will consider the _____ or the _____ that their actions might have on groups and individuals both inside and outside the organization. Many businesses try to assess the impact of their activities on stakeholders, or anyone who has an interest in the company. They try to maintain a good _____ with their suppliers, for example, and make sure that they are paid on time. This process is known as a _____, and most companies who carry out this kind of auditing also have an _____, or written statement of their non-financial objectives.

3 **Read this extract from a press release and answer the questions below.**

> 'The Green group EcoBusiness has produced a 3-point plan for corporate responsibility:
>
>   1 Non-exploitative trading relationships
>
>   2 Sustainable business practices
>
>   3 Environmental impact assessment
>
> Read on for more details...'

Which point do you think the following extracts refer to:

a   **... such as reducing their use of non-renewable resources and shifting towards non-polluting energy such as solar power.**

b   **... to calculate the effect of, for example, new waste disposal systems on local habitats.**

c   **... this may include guaranteeing a set price for commodities for up to 10 years regardless of the market price.**

4 **Read the text and answer the questions.**

> Oxfam is a non-profit-making organization whose primary objective is to alleviate poverty throughout the world. Most of its funds are used to provide long-term development aid to Third World countries.

a Do you think Oxfam are likely to encourage sustainable development?

b Do you think Oxfam are likely to encourage First World companies to develop trading relationships with companies in the developing world?

c Do you think Oxfam are likely to support companies which have a negative environmental impact in the developing world?

d Do you think Oxfam are likely to encourage companies to conduct a social audit of their business?

● availability of labour N-UNCOUNT

If you talk about the **availability of labour** for a particular task, you mean whether or not there are enough workers available to do that task.

Obviously, the benefits of producing in this country are low labour costs and rentals as well as the <u>availability of labour</u>.

…the eminently sound principle that land should be parceled out according to the <u>availability of labor</u> to cultivate it.

● raw materials N-PLURAL

Raw materials are materials that are in their natural state, before they are processed or used in manufacturing.

…the ships bringing the <u>raw materials</u> for the ever-expanding textile industry.

Back in 1900, the UK imported <u>raw materials</u> such as raw cotton, wool and silk, and converted them into basic manufactured products for export.

Villages became associated with different trades, depending on the availability of <u>raw materials</u> in the area.

● labour costs N-PLURAL

A company's **labour costs** are the money it spends on wages and social security benefits for its employees.

In Sri Lanka, the <u>labour costs</u> are about a tenth of those in the UK.

We know, too, that America's companies are watching their profits shrivel in the face of a slowing economy, rising <u>labour costs</u> and soaring energy prices.

Common Collocations

<u>low</u> labour costs	<u>high</u> labour costs
<u>rising</u> labour costs	to <u>hold down</u> labour costs
to <u>drive down</u> labour costs	to <u>keep down</u> labour costs

● green ADJ

Green issues and political movements relate to or are concerned with the protection of the environment.

The company offers advice on a host of <u>green</u> issues – from council waste strategies to nuclear-waste disposal, to recycling and climate change.

The power of the <u>Green</u> movement in Germany has made that country a leader in the drive to recycle more waste materials.

● infrastructure (infrastructures) N-VAR

The **infrastructure** of a country, society, or organization consists of the basic facilities such as transport, communications, power supplies, and buildings, which enable it to function.

The <u>infrastructure</u>, from hotels to transport, is old and decrepit.

Roads, bridges and other <u>infrastructure</u> have been washed away in the incessant rains.

Common Collocations

<u>transport</u> infrastructure
<u>telecommunications</u> infrastructure
<u>information</u> infrastructure
an infrastructure <u>project</u>
infrastructure <u>investment</u>

● political stability N-UNCOUNT

If there is **political stability** in a country, there is a stable government or political system.

Even though <u>political stability</u> is a major factor in attracting investment, politicians never get any credit.

…fears over the <u>political stability</u> of Russia.

● income distribution N-UNCOUNT

The **income distribution** in a particular country or area is the way in which the amount of money being earned varies between different groups of people.

In Britain too, research by the Institute of Fiscal Studies confirms a similar change in <u>income distribution</u>, in which the rich have become richer, while the poor have become poorer.

…a report on <u>income distribution</u> in OECD countries.

● inflation N-UNCOUNT

Inflation is a general increase in the prices of goods and services in a country.

…rising unemployment and high <u>inflation</u>.

…an <u>inflation</u> rate of only 2.2%.

● factors of production N-PLURAL

An industry's **factors of production** are the things that it needs in order to produce a particular product, such as land, workers, and capital.

The natural rates of output and employment depend on the supply of <u>factors of production</u> and technology.

Sustainable Development – Business Environment

PRACTISE YOUR VOCABULARY

1 A UK-based cosmetics company, BodyBeautiful, is thinking of setting up a manufacturing base in Indonesia. They have drawn up a questionnaire to learn more about the business environment. Use the terms in the box to complete the questionnaire.

infrastructure   inflation   taxation   labour   political stability   raw materials *labour costs   income distribution   green issues*

a Raw Materials

    i Are the _____ readily available?
    What is the cost?
    ii How good is the _____ for transportation?

b The Economy

    Is the economy healthy?
    i How high are levels of _____?
    ii Does the region benefit from _____?
    iii What is the rate of _____?
    iv How even or uneven is _____?
    v Are there any _____ we need to consider?

c Labour

    i Is the supply of _____ good?
    Are workers skilled or unskilled?
    ii How high are _____?

2 Look at the six newspaper headlines. For each one say:

    i Which of the three categories above does the news item relate to?
    ii Will production costs be affected positively (lower costs) or negatively (higher costs)?

    a | Interest rates to fall by 1% | **b** | Oil to run out by 2025 |

    c | Government imposes minimum wage of €25 per hour |

    d | New law requiring students to stay at school to the age of 19 |

    e | Coup d'état imminent, says UN official |

3 Read the paragraph and answer the questions.

> Many factors in a business's immediate environment affect the way it operates. The business is influenced by the availability of labour and raw materials, for example, and by the state of the political environment, including the rate of inflation. A plentiful supply of skilled labour improves productivity and the quality of the finished product, and political stability enables a company to operate more effectively and encourages investment in the country's infrastructure. Labour costs and government taxes make an enormous difference to a company's running costs and customer demand is very much affected by the state of the economy.

    a The article begins by listing three factors in the business environment that affect the way a business operates. What are these factors of production?
    b What type of political environment suits the needs of business and the wider needs of the community?
    c In what area does investment increase if the political situation is stable?
    d Which two costs are mentioned in the text?
    e Do you think businesses prefer these costs to be low or not?

● developing ADJ

If you talk about **developing** countries or the **developing** world, you mean the countries or the parts of the world that are poor and have few industries.

> In the *developing* world cigarette consumption is increasing.
> The only *developing* country with large foreign reserves is Taiwan.

● world market N-SING
world market prices N-PLURAL

The **world market** for a product is all the people throughout the world who wish to buy that product. **World market prices** are the prices paid for something internationally, ignoring any tariffs or subsidies imposed by particular countries.

> The lucrative *world market* for video game consoles is now dominated by three rival Japanese products.
> The three biggest US fruit companies – Dole, Chiquita Brands and Del Monte – control about 66 per cent of the *world market*.
> ...steep rises in fuel prices on the *world market*.
> Beginning in 1981, *world market prices* for farm products and industrial raw materials collapsed.
> Moreover, said the Bank, the farmers would benefit greatly if the nuts were exported at *world market prices*.

● commodity (commodities) N-COUNT

A **commodity** is something that is sold for money.

> The government increased prices on several basic *commodities*.
> ...12 months of increasing *commodity* prices.

● fair trade N-UNCOUNT
fairly-traded ADJ

Fair trade is the practice of buying goods directly from producers in developing countries at a fair price. **Fairly-traded** products are bought from producers in developing countries at a fair price.

> More than five per cent of all roast and ground coffee sold in Britain is now *fair trade*.
> Andy Good, from the Edinburgh-based *fair trade* company Equal Exchange, agrees that we should not underestimate the current impact of the *fair trade* movement.
> Oxfam's food and handicrafts have always been *fairly-traded*.

● Fairtrade mark N-SING

In Britain, the **Fairtrade mark** is a sign that is placed on the packaging of products to show that the product has been bought at a fair price, usually from producers in developing countries.

> The cocoa beans are grown organically in Belize by Maya Indians. It carries the *Fairtrade Mark*, and it tastes delicious.
> If you see the *Fairtrade mark* on a product you will know that a reasonable price has been paid to the people producing it and that the supplier is not exploiting them.

● free trade N-UNCOUNT

Free trade is international trade that is free of government restrictions, for example in the form of import quotas or export subsidies.

> Both want cuts in tariffs on industrial goods, and more *free trade* in agriculture and services.
> ...barriers to *free trade.*

Common Collocations

a free trade *agreement*   a free trade *area*
a free trade *zone*

● cash crop (cash crops) N-COUNT

A **cash crop** is a crop that is grown in order to be sold.

> Cranberries have become a major *cash crop*.
> The weather has also affected around twelve-thousand acres of banana plantations – Costa Rica's principal *cash crop*.

● producer (producers) N-COUNT
grower (growers) N-COUNT

A **producer** of a food or material is a company or country that grows or manufactures a large amount of it. A **grower** is a person who grows large quantities of a particular plant or crop in order to sell them.

> The estate is generally a *producer* of high quality wines.
> ...Saudi Arabia, the world's leading oil *producer*.
> England's apple *growers* are fighting an uphill battle against foreign competition.
> ...a former coca *grower* in Bolivia's Chapare valley.

⊃ **sweatshop**: Topic 4.1; **corporate responsibility**: Topic 4.2; **exploitative**: Topic 4.2

PRACTISE YOUR VOCABULARY

1 Use the terms in the box to complete the paragraph.

> fair trade (2)   world market prices   fairly-traded products   commodities
> producers and growers   developing   Fairtrade mark   cash crops

The trading company Traidfair describes itself as a social enterprise. It attempts to bring justice to international trade by promoting _____ with_____ countries. The company sells a range of _____ from the Third World into First World markets.

Social responsibility is their main priority, and the setting up and maintaining of non-exploitative trading relationships with their Third-World suppliers, i.e. the _____. Their suppliers produce_____ and Traidfair pay _____ for the crop or the _____ they purchase, which then carry the _____.

Traidfair's customers are loyal to them even though their prices are often higher than those of other similar products. More and more people are coming to view _____ and social responsibility as more important than the pursuit of profit.

2 Which of the following are characteristics of the free trade system and which of the Fairtrade system?

   a Producers are often divided by competition.
   b Producers in developing countries have more power.
   c The consumer wants a cheap product.
   d The consumer's main aim is not financial.
   e Companies are motivated by profit.
   f The company's main objective is social responsibility.

free trade system	Fairtrade system

3 Which of these two Third-world farmers is producing a cash crop?

Paulo and Pedro are both farmers working with about 5 hectares of land. Pedro grows maize, potatoes and fruit, keeps 2 pigs, some chickens, 3 goats and a cow. His family eat most of what they produce but sometimes have a little left over which they sell for cash. Paulo grows coffee on his land. He and his family tend the plants and pick the beans which are sold to buyers from America in the local market.

● **eco-tourism** N-UNCOUNT
 eco-tourist (eco-tourists) N-COUNT

Eco-tourism is the business of providing holidays and related services which are not harmful to the environment of the area visited. An **eco-tourist** is a tourist who buys holidays and related services which are not harmful to the environment of the area visited.

> *Having been a part of it for a week, I now truly believe that eco-tourism is the only hope for the islands' survival.*
> *Mexico's government has been trying to promote eco-tourism in the area, believing that this will save the butterflies' trees from the attentions of woodcutters.*
> *…an environmentally sensitive project to cater for eco-tourists.*
> *Perhaps the most popular eco-tourist destination is the Brazilian rainforest.*

● **tourism** N-UNCOUNT
 tourist (tourists) N-COUNT

Tourism is the business of providing services for people on holiday, for example hotels, restaurants, and trips. A **tourist** is a person who is visiting a place for pleasure and interest, especially when they are on holiday.

> *Tourism is vital for the Spanish economy.*
> *Albania desperately needs more tourists to help it escape poverty.*
> *Blackpool is the top tourist attraction in England.*

● **global tourism** N-UNCOUNT

Global tourism is tourism considered as a global industry.

> *Yet global tourism is booming; numbers have more than doubled to nearly 600 million a year in the last 20 years.*
> *By the mid-1980s, the global tourism business employed more people than the oil industry.*

● **tourism sector** (tourism sectors) N-COUNT

A country's **tourism sector** is that part of its economy that earns money through tourism.

> *This is one of the new steps proposed to generate more income from the tourism sector.*
> *…a booming tourism sector.*

● **mass tourism** N-UNCOUNT

Mass tourism is tourism which involves very large numbers of people.

> *When mass tourism began to overtake elite travel following World War II, most travel occurred within and between North America and Western Europe.*
> *…the harm caused by mass tourism.*

● **tour operator** (tour operators) N-COUNT

A **tour operator** is a company that provides holidays in which your travel and accommodation are booked for you.

> *Baby-sitting can be arranged through the tour operator.*
> *…Britain's largest tour operator.*

● **ethical tourism** N-UNCOUNT

Ethical tourism is tourism that is based on ethical principles, such as a desire not to harm the environment of the place visited and to support its local economy.

> *The campaign is a fun, upbeat way of getting more out of your holiday while also getting a fairer deal for local people. Our campaign sets out to demonstrate the strength of consumer demand for ethical tourism.*

● **capital inflow** (capital inflows) N-VAR

In economics, **capital inflow** is the amount of capital coming into a country, for example in the form of foreign investment.

> *As Mr Stals points out, over half the capital inflow in the 12 months to June was in the form of short-term investment, which can be easily withdrawn.*
> *…a large drop in the capital inflow into America.*

● **added value** N-UNCOUNT

In marketing, **added value** is something which makes a product more appealing to customers.

> *It opens up a new market to us and also benefits Tesco as it is able to offer customers added value.*
> *To maintain our market share and provide added value to consumers, we need to upgrade the standard of product design.*

● **socio-cultural** ADJ

Socio-cultural circumstances or developments involve a combination of social and cultural factors.

> *You'll discover the political, economic and socio-cultural effects they had on a wider society.*

● **contract rate** (contract rates) N-COUNT

The **contract rate** for a service is a reduced price that is available, for example because you agree to use the service on a regular basis.

> *If a hotel that is known to have a State of Texas Contract Rate does not honor the rate, ask to speak to the hotel manager.*

● **GNP** (GNPs) N-VAR

In economics, a country's **GNP** is the total value of all the goods produced and services provided by that country in one year. **GNP** is an abbreviation for 'gross national product'.

> *By 1973 the government deficit equalled thirty percent of GNP.*

● **cultural awareness** N-UNCOUNT

Someone's **cultural awareness** is their understanding of the differences between themselves and people from other countries or other backgrounds, especially differences in attitudes and values.

> *US exporters' weaknesses in cultural awareness.*
> *…programs to promote diversity and cultural awareness within the SEC and the industry.*

➲ **primary sector**: Topic 2.2; **balance of payments**: Topic 3.1; **inward investment**: Topic 3.2; **sustainable**: Topic 4.2; **green**: Topic 4.3

PRACTISE YOUR VOCABULARY

1 Read the text about tourism in developing countries and answer the questions.

> The governments of developing countries have realized that the capital inflow generated by tourism offers many economic and political benefits. The tourist industry, on the other hand, has been criticized for making little contribution to the local economies in developing countries, for failing to employ sufficient local people and for offering low contract rates for accommodation. Sustainable tourism is an emerging concept that aims to deal with the negative environmental and socio-cultural impacts of tourism development, and to offer tourists added value.

a Are the governments of developing countries generally in favour of tourism?

b What aspect of tourism offers benefits?

c Are commentators critical of or in support of the tourist industry?

d What three things has the tourist industry been criticized for in relation to the economy, the workforce and accommodation?

e What does sustainable tourism aim to offer tourists?

2 Put each of the advantages and disadvantages of tourism into the correct place in the table.

a provides seasonal, not continuous employment

b benefits the balance of payments

c creates employment

d has a negative socio-cultural impact

e contributes to gross national product (GNP)

f aids economic development

g involves loss of workers from primary industry

h provides income to be used to help conserve the environment

i contributes to the destruction of the environment

j can increase cultural awareness

advantages of tourism	disadvantages of tourism

3 Use each term in the box to complete the sentences.

> Mass tourism   Tour operators   tourism sector   Global tourism   Tourists

a _____ may not think about the damage they cause to the environment and culture of the countries they visit.

b _____ are now branching out and offering specialist trips to holidaymakers who are concerned about green issues.

c _____ has been a growth industry over the last 20 years due to the fall in the cost of international travel.

d The _____ employs many millions of people worldwide.

e _____ does not appeal to people who prefer to make their own travel and accommodation arrangements.

4 Which of these signs on a hotel noticeboard would appeal to an eco-tourist?

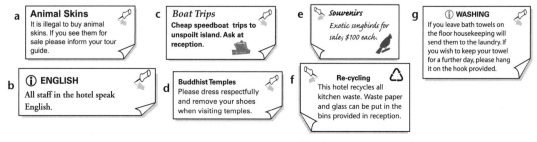

a Animal Skins It is illegal to buy animal skins. If you see them for sale please inform your tour guide.

b ⓘ ENGLISH All staff in the hotel speak English.

c Boat Trips Cheap speedboat trips to unspoilt island. Ask at reception.

d Buddhist Temples Please dress respectfully and remove your shoes when visiting temples.

e Souvenirs Exotic songbirds for sale; $100 each.

f Re-cycling This hotel recycles all kitchen waste. Waste paper and glass can be put in the bins provided in reception.

g ⓘ WASHING If you leave bath towels on the floor housekeeping will send them to the laundry. If you wish to keep your towel for a further day, please hang it on the hook provided.

Topic 5

PRODUCTION

● **production** N-UNCOUNT

Production is the process of manufacturing or growing something in large quantities. **Production** is also the amount of goods manufactured or grown by a company or country.

> *That model won't go into <u>production</u> before late 1990.*
> *We needed to increase the volume of <u>production</u>.*

● **manufacture** (manufactures, manufacturing, manufactured)

☐ VERB

To **manufacture** something means to make it in a factory, usually in large quantities.

> *They <u>manufacture</u> the class of plastics known as thermoplastic materials.*
> *We import foreign <u>manufactured</u> goods.*

② N-UNCOUNT

The **manufacture** of a product is the work involved in making it.

> *…the <u>manufacture</u> of nuclear weapons.*
> *…celebrating 90 years of car <u>manufacture</u>.*

● **manufacturing** N-UNCOUNT
  manufacturer (manufacturers) N-COUNT

Manufacturing is all the processes involved in making a product. A **manufacturer** is a business or company which makes goods in large quantities to sell.

> *…the <u>manufacturing</u> of a luxury type automobile.*
> *…the world's largest doll <u>manufacturer</u>.*

● **manufacturing facility** (manufacturing facilities) N-COUNT

A **manufacturing facility** is a more formal word for a factory.

> *The company has a sales and marketing office in St Albans, as well as a <u>manufacturing facility</u> near Glasgow.*

● **factory** (factories) N-COUNT
  plant (plants) N-COUNT
  works N-COUNT-COLL

A **factory** is a large building where machines are used to make large quantities of goods. A **plant** is a factory or a place where power is produced. A **works** is a place where something is manufactured or where an industrial process is carried out. **Works** is used to refer to one or to more than one of these places.

> *He owned furniture <u>factories</u> in New York State.*
> *The <u>plant</u> provides forty per cent of the country's electricity.*
> *The steel <u>works</u>, one of the landmarks of Stoke-on-Trent, could be seen for miles.*
> *…the <u>works</u> canteen.*

● **output** N-UNCOUNT

Output is used to refer to the amount of something that a person or thing produces.

> *Manual workers need a good breakfast for high-energy <u>output</u>.*
> *Statistics show the largest drop in industrial <u>output</u> for ten years.*

● **capacity** N-UNCOUNT
  full capacity N-UNCOUNT
  spare capacity N-UNCOUNT

The **capacity** of something such as a factory, industry, or region is the quantity of things that it can produce or deliver with the equipment or resources that are available. If a factory or industry is working at **full capacity**, it is using all its available resources. If there is **spare capacity**, it is not using all its available resources.

> *The region is valued for its coal and vast electricity-generating <u>capacity</u>.*
> *Bread factories are working at <u>full capacity</u>.*
> *Building the new model at one of its American factories with <u>spare capacity</u> would have been cheaper.*

● **lean** ADJ
  lean manufacturing N-UNCOUNT
  lean production N-UNCOUNT
  just-in-time (JIT) manufacturing N-UNCOUNT
  just-in-time (JIT) production N-UNCOUNT

If you describe an organization as **lean**, you mean that it has become more efficient and less wasteful by getting rid of staff, or by dropping projects which were unprofitable. **Lean manufacturing** and **lean production** are manufacturing methods which aim to reduce wastage, for example by keeping stocks low and by working more flexibly. **Just-in-time manufacturing** or **just-in-time production** is a manufacturing method which aims to reduce wastage by keeping stocks low and by producing goods only when they are required. The abbreviation **JIT** is also used.

> *The value of the pound will force British companies to be <u>leaner</u> and fitter.*
> *…efficiency-raising techniques such as <u>lean manufacturing</u>.*
> *…Japanese-style <u>lean production</u> techniques.*
> *…Japanese firms which understood customers better and pioneered more efficient <u>just-in-time manufacturing</u>.*
> *If you can achieve <u>just-in-time production</u>, everyone's holdings of stocks can be kept to a minimum, with immense savings in capital.*
> *…examples of genuine <u>JIT</u> operations.*

● **chain of production** N-SING

The **chain of production** is all the stages of production that a product passes through before it is passed to a consumer.

> *The rationale for green detergents was that they would prevent discharges of phosphate into rivers. But there are other environmental costs attached to washing powders, earlier in the <u>chain of production</u>.*

➲ **primary sector**: Topic 2.2; **industrial sector**: Topic 2.2; **service sector**: Topic 2.2; **producer**: Topic 4.4; **product**: Topic 5.2; **produce**: Topic 5.2; **mass production**: Topic 5.5; **stock**: Topic 6.3; **low-cost centre**: Topic 10.4

PRACTISE YOUR VOCABULARY

1 **Use the words in the box to complete the paragraph.**

| factory   production process   lean production   production   just-in-time |

If companies adopt lean manufacturing or _____ techniques they are interested in making the
_____ more efficient. They try to keep all inputs to the process to a minimum. This could mean using the
fewest workers they can, cutting down on the amount of raw materials needed, or using as little _____
space as possible, for example. One of the operations that is central to lean manufacturing is _____
production. This manufacturing method aims to reduce costs by keeping stocks low. Instead of keeping stocks in the
warehouse, the company asks its suppliers to make frequent deliveries so that they can be used straight away.
_____ can then exactly match the amount of goods required, so that the company does not incur costs on
warehousing finished goods.

2 **Which word is the odd one out in each line?**

a manufacturing	factory	production
b plant	manufacturer	factory
c works	manufacturing facility	output
d output	producer	manufacturer
e produce	manufacture	works

3 **Are the sentences true or false?**

	True	False
a The capacity of a factory refers to how many products it can produce in a given time.	☐	☐
b A company operating with spare capacity is not making as much profit as it could.	☐	☐
c A company using lean production techniques is likely to have a large warehouse full of finished products.	☐	☐
d The JIT manufacturing system is a part of the lean production approach.	☐	☐
e Car production is usually carried out at a plant.	☐	☐
f A factory operating at full capacity is operating efficiently.	☐	☐

4 **Fine Field, a company which manufactures garden tools, uses the JIT system of manufacturing. What do you know about the following, therefore?**

a The amount of stock Fine Field hold

b The amount of space available in their factory

c Bulk buying (buying in very large quantities)

d The costs of holding stock in their warehouse

5 **Read the paragraph and answer the questions.**

> ### The Chain of Production
> The primary, industrial (or secondary) and service (or tertiary) sectors are linked together by a chain of
> production. For example, the cocoa-bean growers of Africa form part of the primary sector. They sell their
> product worldwide, and some of their beans are bought by a UK-based company. This company operates in the
> secondary, or industrial sector manufacturing chocolate from the beans. Many restaurants, or companies in the
> tertiary or service sector buy chocolates from the company to give to their customers along with a cup of coffee
> after their meal.

a In which sector (primary, industrial or service) does each of the following operate?

  i The UK-based company

  ii African cocoa-bean growers

  iii Restaurants/companies buying chocolate products for their customers

b What is the 'chain of production'?

● **research and development** N-UNCOUNT
  R&D N-UNCOUNT

Research and development is the part of a company's activity that is concerned with applying the results of scientific research to develop new products and improve existing ones. **Research and development** is also the department within a company that is responsible for this work. The abbreviation **R&D** is often used.

> Companies that spend a lot of money on research and development tend to be the most successful.
> Businesses need to train their workers better, and spend more on R&D.
> ...investment in R&D.

● **laboratory** (laboratories) N-COUNT

A **laboratory** is a building or a room where scientific experiments, analyses, and research are carried out.

> ...a leading research laboratory which tests products on animals.
> ...the Aeronautical Research Laboratory in Melbourne.

● **product** (products) N-COUNT
  goods N-PLURAL
  merchandise N-UNCOUNT
  FMCG (FMCGs) N-COUNT

A **product** is something that is produced and sold in large quantities, often as a result of a manufacturing process. **Goods** are things that are made to be sold. **Merchandise** is a formal word for goods that are bought, sold, or traded. **FMCGs** are inexpensive products that people usually buy on a regular basis, such as supermarket foods or toiletries. **FMCG** is an abbreviation for 'fast-moving consumer goods'.

> Try to get the best product at the lowest price.
> South Korea's imports of consumer products jumped 33% in this year.
> Money can be exchanged for goods or services.
> ...a wide range of consumer goods.
> Several stores have reported running out of merchandise.
> For fast moving customer goods (FMCG) customers shop less frequently, and like to make all their purchases at one go rather than in several different outlets.

● **focus group** (focus groups) N-COUNT

A **focus group** is a specially selected group of people who are intended to represent the general public. **Focus groups** have discussions in which their opinions are recorded as a form of market research.

> In surveys and focus groups, the shoppers said they wanted Tesco to go back to its roots as the "pile it high, sell it cheap" chain.
> ...focus-group studies.

● **reverse engineering** N-UNCOUNT

Reverse engineering is a process in which a product or system is analysed in order to see how it works, so that a similar version of the product or system can be produced more cheaply.

> Xerox set about a process of reverse engineering. It pulled the machines apart and investigated the Japanese factories to find out how they could pull off such feats.
> So, through reverse engineering, Indian companies have been able to make drugs still on patent internationally, and to sell them at a tenth of the international price or less.

● **staff suggestion scheme** (staff suggestion schemes) N-COUNT

A **staff suggestion scheme** is a scheme in which the employees of a company are encouraged to suggest ways of improving the company's performance or its working conditions.

> Individual staff can submit suggestions. This can be encouraged by introducing a staff suggestion scheme which offers good rewards to viable suggestions no matter how apparently trivial the suggestions.

● **product-oriented** ADJ
  product-orientated ADJ
  product-led ADJ

A company that is **product-oriented** or **product-orientated** or **product-led** aims to develop new products and then create a market for them.

> I feel that we need to become a little more product-oriented.
> ...the man behind Fiat's product-orientated return to health.
> The new S-Type represents the first stage of a dramatic product-led expansion of the company over the next four years.

➲ **benchmarking**: Topic 5.3; **patent**: Topic 5.4; **under licence**: Topic 5.4; **department store**: Topic 6.5

PRACTISE YOUR VOCABULARY

1 Use the terms in the box to complete the paragraph.

> research laboratories   reverse engineering   new products   product
> R & D   existing products   goods   product-led

A _____ is something that is produced or manufactured and sold, often in large quantities. Products are

sometimes referred to as _____, although it is very unusual to talk about a good. Many businesses are

_____, which means that they design and make a product, and then try to convince consumers to buy it. In

companies, _____ are developed and _____ are improved through research and

development (_____) carried out in _____. Often a process of _____ is used,

where a product or a system is analysed to see how it works. R & D is potentially risky, although it's worth taking the risk if

it leads to a successful, profitable product.

2 Match each sentence on the left with the sentence which follows it on the right.

a In our company all the employees are encouraged
to contribute ideas for new products.

b We produce a range of consumer goods.

c Our research department often dismantles our
competitors' latest products to see how they are built.

d We develop new products in our laboratories and then
research the market to find out how to sell them.

e We are a large department store that sells luxury goods.

i This reverse engineering can be very enlightening.

ii Some very good ideas have come out of this staff
suggestion scheme.

iii Most of our merchandise is very expensive.

iv We need to sell large quantities of these FMCGs in
order to make a profit.

v We adopt a product-led approach.

3 Match each word on the left with a word on the right to make word pairs associated with product development,
then use each word pair to complete the sentences.

a research

b reverse

c focus

d staff

e research

i groups

ii laboratory

iii suggestion schemes

iv and development

v engineering

a The strength of Rolls is that after spending £2 billion on _____ in the last six years, its range of engines
is wider than ever.

b William Powers is executive director of Ford's _____s.

c Through _____, companies have been able to copy products and sell them more cheaply.

d Some _____ offer rewards for useful suggestions from employees.

e In _____, the shoppers said they wanted Tesco to go back to its roots as 'the pile it high, sell it cheap'
chain.

● **quality control** N-UNCOUNT
quality assurance N-UNCOUNT

In an organization that produces goods or provides services, **quality control** or **quality assurance** is the activity of checking that the goods or services are of an acceptable standard.

> *One of the ways to ensure that finished homes are perfect products is to tighten up <u>quality control</u>.*
> *...<u>quality control</u> checks.*
> *The report also calls for national standards of <u>quality assurance</u> for all x-ray units.*

● **subcontract** (subcontracts, subcontracting, subcontracted)

1 VERB

If one firm **subcontracts** part of its work to another firm, it pays the other firm to do part of the work that it has been employed to do.

> *The company <u>is subcontracting</u> production of most of the parts.*
> *They cut costs by <u>subcontracting</u> work out to other local firms.*

2 N-COUNT

A **subcontract** is a contract between a firm which is being employed to do a job and another firm which agrees to do part of that job.

> *Contracts and <u>subcontracts</u> for the reconstruction of Kuwait have begun to flow in.*
> *European companies expected to win major <u>subcontracts</u> include Thorn EMI.*

● **quality circle** (quality circles) N-COUNT

A **quality circle** is a small group of workers and managers who meet to solve problems and improve the quality of the organization's products or services.

> *Riddick's first move was to form a <u>quality circle</u>.*
> *<u>Quality circles</u> may work well in Japan, but have not been quite as successful in factories in the United States.*

● **benchmarking** N-UNCOUNT

Benchmarking is a process in which a company compares its products and methods with those of the most successful companies in its field, in order to try to improve its own performance.

> *<u>Benchmarking</u> is important. You need to know where you stand compared with your global competitors.*
> *The reviews will include <u>benchmarking</u> against other countries to ensure that UK customers are getting a deal at least as good as those abroad.*

● **TQM** N-UNCOUNT

TQM is a set of management principles aimed at improving performance throughout a company, especially by involving employees in decision-making. **TQM** is an abbreviation for 'total quality management'.

> *One of the main themes of <u>TQM</u> is employee involvement.*
> *Under <u>TQM</u> principles the search for quality is continuous.*

● **monitor** (monitors, monitoring, monitored) VERB
monitoring N-UNCOUNT

If you **monitor** something, you regularly check its development or progress, and sometimes comment on it. **Monitoring** is the process of checking the development or progress of something.

> *Our prices are determined by local markets and we <u>monitor</u> prices on and off the motorway.*
> *Dr Phillips called for greater <u>monitoring</u> of home conversions by local authorities.*

● **routine check** (routine checks) N-COUNT

If someone carries out a **routine check** on a product, place, or piece of equipment, they examine it as part of a regular checking procedure in order to see if there are any problems with it.

> *He carried out <u>routine checks</u> on the integrity of the circuits, and replaced faulty valves in the tape recorders.*
> *The museum said that it came across the asbestos during <u>routine checks</u> on its premises.*

● **inspect** (inspects, inspecting, inspected) VERB
inspection (inspections) N-VAR

When officials **inspect** a place or a group of people, they visit it and check it carefully, for example in order to find out whether regulations are being obeyed. An **inspection** is an instance of inspecting a place or a group of people. **Inspection** is the act of inspecting a place or a group of people.

> *The Public Utilities Commission <u>inspects</u> us once a year.*
> *Each hotel <u>is inspected</u> and, if it fulfils certain criteria, is recommended.*
> *The plant never had a safety <u>inspection</u> in the 11 years it was in operation.*
> *A truly independent system of <u>inspection</u> by specialist teams should be introduced.*

⮑ **outsource**: Topic 1.1; **outsourcing**: Topic 1.1; **focus group**: Topic 5.2; **R & D**: Topic 5.2; **market research**: Topic 9.1; **guarantee**: Topic 11.2; **warranty**: Topic 11.2

PRACTISE YOUR VOCABULARY

1 Choose one of the terms to complete each definition.

total quality management   quality control   benchmarking   subcontract   quality assurance   routine checks

a The collection of management techniques known as _____ aims to improve the company's performance, and is based on the principle that it is cheaper in the long term to do the job right the first time round, rather than making mistakes and fixing them afterwards.

b Companies using TQM believe that quality is the responsibility of every department and every worker. This is very different from the traditional view in which _____ is a process in the chain of production, and is the sole responsibility of a quality controller. He or she may carry out _____ and inspections.

c Many companies consult their customers about their views on quality, and use market research to find out what their customers think. This kind of consultation forms part of the _____ process.

d A distribution company used to employ its own mechanics to repair and maintain their vehicles. Recently, however, they stopped this and now _____ this work to another firm.

e _____ is the practice of comparing business practices between companies.

2 Match each statement on the left with one on the right.

a Our company is starting a quality assurance programme.

b Our R & D department will adopt a benchmarking strategy.

c We will set up quality circles.

d We will take a total quality management approach.

i We will be examining the leading competitor in our field and trying to meet or improve on their standards.

ii We will get members of staff to meet and resolve problems we have with particular products.

iii We will be focusing on quality with a view to increasing our effectiveness, flexibility and competitiveness.

iv We hope to involve all employees in making decisions about quality control.

3 When assessing the quality of a product, which of these factors should be considered?

a physical appearance   **c** reliability   **e** image   **g** suitability
b after-sales service   **d** durability   **f** reputation   **h** price

4 The following are all quality control techniques. Which ones are features of traditional quality control (QC) and which ones are specific to total quality management (TQM)? Tick (✓) the appropriate column.

	QC	TQM
a making everyone in the company take responsibility for quality		
b making quality the responsibility of the quality control department		
c constant monitoring and routine checks of the whole business		
d using a quality controller to check finished work for defects		
e the use of quality circles to generate discussion about the cause of quality problems and their solutions		
f being committed to one's customers and knowing about their needs and expectations		
g assuming customers are happy unless they complain about the quality of goods		

- **invent** (invents, inventing, invented) VERB
  invention (inventions) N-VAR
  inventor (inventors) N-COUNT

If you **invent** something such as a machine or process, you are the first person to think of it or make it. An **invention** is a machine, device, or system that has been invented by someone. **Invention** is the act of inventing something that has never been made or used before. An **inventor** is a person who has invented something, or whose job is to invent things.

> He _invented_ the first electric clock.
> It's been a tricky business marketing his new _invention_.
> …the _invention_ of the telephone.
> …Alexander Graham Bell, the _inventor_ of the telephone.

- **not-invented-here (NIH) syndrome**
  N-UNCOUNT

People sometimes use **not-invented-here syndrome** to refer to the resistance that exists within a company towards accepting ideas or inventions that have been developed by other companies. The abbreviation **NIH** is also used.

> IT developers do tend to suffer from the _not-invented-here syndrome_.
> Mr Bucknor grumbled about the _not-invented-here_ mentality that had kept his predecessors from using off-the-shelf software designed for computers made by rival companies.

- **researcher** (researchers) N-COUNT
  technologist (technologists) N-COUNT

A **researcher** is a person whose work involves studying something in order to discover facts about it. A **technologist** is a specialist in technology, usually within a large company or organization.

> …the country's leading _researcher_ into breast cancer.
> German _technologists_ have derived a process to recycle carpets made from a widely used type of nylon called polyamide-6.

- **innovation** (innovations) N-VAR

An **innovation** is a new thing or a new method of doing something. **Innovation** is the introduction of new ideas, methods, or things.

> They produced the first vegetarian beanburger – an _innovation_ which was rapidly exported to Britain.
> …the technological _innovations_ of the industrial age.
> We must promote originality, inspire creativity and encourage _innovation_.

- **leading edge** N-SING
  leading-edge ADJ

The **leading edge** of a particular area of research or development is the area of it that seems most advanced or sophisticated. **Leading-edge** technology is very advanced or sophisticated technology.

> I think he is at the _leading edge_ of technological development.
> The equipment is truly _leading-edge_ technology.

- **state-of-the-art** ADJ

If you describe something as **state-of-the-art**, you mean that it is the best available because it has been made using the most modern techniques and technology.

> …the production of _state-of-the-art_ military equipment.
> The programme uses _state-of-the-art_ technology.

- **CIM** N-UNCOUNT

CIM is a manufacturing method which uses computers to improve the speed and efficiency of the production process. **CIM** is an abbreviation for 'computer-integrated manufacture'.

> _CIM_ allows manufacturers to make customized products in small batches, at costs close to those of mass-produced goods.

- **patent** (patents, patenting, patented)

1 N-COUNT

A **patent** is an official right to be the only person or company allowed to make or sell a new product for a certain period of time.

> P&G applied for a _patent_ on its cookies.
> He claims that their products infringe the _patent_.

2 VERB

If you **patent** something, you obtain a patent for it.

> He _patented_ the idea that the atom could be split.
> …a _patented_ machine called the VCR II.

Common Collocations

to _file_ a patent _on/for_ something
to _grant_ somebody a patent _on/for_ something
to _have_ a patent _on/for_ something
to _obtain_ a patent _on/for_ something
patent _infringement_

- **under licence** PHRASE

If someone does something **under licence**, they do it by special permission from a government or other authority.

> Japanese pharmaceutical firms began life by learning how to make foreign drugs _under licence_.
> The company also manufactures Marlboro _under licence_ from Philip Morris.

- **intellectual property rights** N-PLURAL

If someone has the **intellectual property rights** to an idea or invention, they are legally allowed to develop the idea or invention, and nobody else can do so without their permission.

> The company said that it has retained the _intellectual property rights_ to its latest light commercial vehicle.
> …new rules to protect _intellectual property rights_.

➲ **R & D**: Topic 5.2; **CAD**: Topic 5.5; **CAM**: Topic 5.5; **mass production**: Topic 5.5

PRACTISE YOUR VOCABULARY

1 Use the terms in the box to complete the paragraph.

patenting	invention	NIH syndrome	innovation	under licence	intellectual property rights	researchers

_____ is the creation of totally new products or production techniques through a process of innovation. _____ is the process of refining and developing an original invention into a usable product or technique, usually carried out by _____. When there is resistance in an organization to ideas or inventions that come from elsewhere, people talk about the not-invented-here, or _____. Inventors protect their inventions by _____ them. Others may be permitted to use ideas for which there is a patent if they pay a royalty. They are then said to use the invention _____. If a person owns the _____ to an invention, they have the right to develop it.

2 Match each sentence on the left with the sentence which follows it on the right.

a Our research department recently developed a new computer programme used to guide the production robots in the factory.

b We recently installed new computers in our factory. We bought the most sophisticated equipment available.

c Our bottling and soft drinks plant is the only one in the region that can legally make Cool Cola.

d Our company's head of R&D was sacked last year after the company was prosecuted for copying a new idea from one of our rivals.

e R&D is very expensive in the pharmaceutical industry, so our legal department gets full protection for our new developments.

f We are a small company that specializes in designing computer programmes for the print business. We employ some of the best technicians in the country.

i Making products under licence like this has been very good for our firm.

ii These patents are essential to modern medicine.

iii We are really at the leading edge of design.

iv The machines use state-of-the-art technology.

v The head of the legal department should have advised him that the company was infringing a patent.

vi After manufacturing the software we kept the intellectual property rights to it.

3 An invention can be created by any of the following:

inventor   researchers   technologists

Use each term to complete the sentences.

a _____ in America have found a new way to make newspaper edible.

b University _____ discovered that the drug could be used for people who had cancer.

c ...Bill White, the _____ of chewing gum.

4 Which of these companies is using CIM?

a Company A used to mass produce moulded plastic sections of toys. They recently introduced computers to improve the production process.

b Company B uses highly sophisticated computers to help its design team to develop new products.

c Company C has a computerized ordering system designed to make ordering easier for their customers.

● **assembly line** (assembly lines) N-COUNT
production line (production lines) N-COUNT

An **assembly line** is an arrangement of workers and machines in a factory, where each worker deals with only one part of a product. The product passes from one worker to another until it is finished. A **production line** is an arrangement of machines in a factory where the products pass from machine to machine until they are finished.

> …a man who works on an <u>assembly line</u>.
> Their first car rolls off the <u>production line</u> on December 16.

● **batch production** N-UNCOUNT
flow production N-UNCOUNT
job production N-UNCOUNT

Batch production, flow production and **job production** are methods of producing goods in a factory. In **batch production**, a large number of goods are produced for several customers. In **flow production,** a very large number of goods are produced in a continuous process on a production line. In **job production**, a small number of goods are produced for one particular customer.

> …<u>batch production</u> of transistors.
> Examples of very capital-intensive production are oil refining, chemical production, electricity generation and any major <u>flow production</u> system.
> He was being interviewed for <u>job production</u> engineering manager.

● **small-scale** ADJ
large-scale ADJ
mass production N-UNCOUNT

A **small-scale** activity or organization is small in size and limited in extent. A **large-scale** activity involves a lot of people or things. **Mass production** is the production of something in large quantities, especially by machine.

> …the <u>small-scale</u> production of farmhouse cheeses in Devon.
> …the first <u>large-scale</u> Internet venture aimed at revolutionising the UK's £62.5 billion construction industry.
> …<u>large-scale</u> job losses.
> …equipment that would allow the <u>mass production</u> of baby food.
> …the introduction of <u>mass production</u> at the turn of the century.

● **automation** N-UNCOUNT
mechanization N-UNCOUNT

Automation and **mechanization** refer to the use of machines to do work that was previously done by people.

> In the last ten years <u>automation</u> has reduced the work force here by half.
> <u>Mechanization</u> happened years ago on the farms of Islay.

● **robot** (robots) N-COUNT
robotics N-UNCOUNT

A **robot** is a machine which is programmed to move and perform certain tasks automatically. **Robotics** is the science of designing and building robots.

> …very light-weight <u>robots</u> that we could send to the moon for planetary exploration.
> Wales has low overheads and you could use <u>robotics</u> to reduce labour costs.

● **CAD** N-UNCOUNT
CAM N-UNCOUNT

CAD is the use of computer software in the design of things such as cars, buildings, and machines. **CAD** is an abbreviation for 'computer-aided design'. **CAM** is the use of computer software in the manufacture of products. **CAM** is an abbreviation for 'computer-aided manufacture'.

> A design made with <u>CAD</u> can be transmitted perfectly from one place to another, if they both use the same system.
> The application of <u>CAD/CAM</u> makes traditional procedures more efficient and provides avenues for innovation and new development.
> …<u>CAD/CAM</u> software.

PRACTISE YOUR VOCABULARY

1 **Use the terms in the box to complete the paragraph.**

> *robotics   production line   automation   assembly line   robots*
> *computer-aided design/computer-aided manufacturing*

Products such as cars are made on a _____ or _____. Many of the tasks previously carried

out by workers have been taken over by _____ – part of the process of_____ . The use of

robots in manufacturing is known as_____. CAD/CAM, or _____, refers to

the use of computers in designing and manufacturing products.

2 **a Match each of the three products to the most suitable production method.**

  a building a bridge   **i** flow (or mass) production

  b growing a crop   **ii** job production

  c producing cans of orange juice   **iii** batch production

b Label each definition with the correct of method of production.

  i A single item (e.g. an aeroplane) is produced from start to finish.   = _____ production

  ii A product is made continuously, often through the use of an assembly line.   = _____ production

  iii One operation, which produces large or small quantities of a product,
     is completed before starting the next.   = _____ production

3 **Which of the following are unlikely to be features of flow production?**

  a high start-up costs   **d** uses highly-skilled labour

  b reduced need for labour   **e** produces small quantities of products

  c produces a simple, uniform product   **f** low level of automation

4 **Read the entry from the *Collins Dictionary of Economics* and answer the questions.**

> **mass production** the manufacture of a product in very large quantities using continuous-flow
> capital-intensive methods of production. Mass production is typically found in industries
> where the product supplied is highly standardised, which enables automated machinery and
> processes to be substituted for labour.

a What method of production is used in the manufacture of mass-produced goods?
b What is the main characteristic of products made on an assembly line? Is each product individual, or are all the products
   identical?
c Are factories using mass production methods staffed by highly-skilled workers, or are they automated and staffed by less
   skilled workers?

Topic 6

SALES

- **sales** N-PLURAL
  sales revenue (sales revenues) N-VAR
  turnover (turnovers) N-VAR

The **sales** of a product are the quantity of it that is sold. **Sales revenue** is money that a company or organization receives from sales of its goods and services. The **turnover** of a company is the value of the goods or services sold during a particular period of time.

> The newspaper has _sales_ of 1.72 million.
> …the huge Christmas _sales_ of computer games.
> …retail _sales_ figures.
> The company spends a tiny 4% of _sales revenues_ on marketing.
> Dairy Vale estimates that _sales revenue_ will rise to $134 million.
> Her annual _turnover_ is around £45,000.
> The company had a _turnover_ of £3.8 million.

- **target** (targets) N-COUNT

A **target** is a result that you are trying to achieve, such as a particular number of products sold or produced within a particular period.

> Stanford's initial _target_ of 4,500 subscribers within three years was exceeded by ten times that amount.
> When the FT began its push into America two years ago it set a _target_ of reaching 100,000 in sales within five years.

Common Collocations

to <u>meet</u> a target	to <u>reach</u> a target
to <u>miss</u> a target	to <u>set</u> a target

- **unit sales** N-PLURAL

The **unit sales** of a product are the numbers of that product that are sold.

> _Unit sales_ this year should climb by more than 9 per cent to more than 900,000 vehicles.
> His research suggests that, in the past 12 months alone, _unit sales_ of T-shirts increased 6% to about 1.7 billion.

- **sales territory** (sales territories) N-COUNT

A salesperson's **sales territory** is the area or areas where he or she tries to sell the company's products.

> He was responsible for a six-state _sales territory_.
> Article 16 of the Regulation states that if the supplier allocates an exclusive _sales territory_ to the dealer the Regulation ceases to be applicable.

- **sales forecast** (sales forecasts) N-COUNT

A company's **sales forecast** is the number of products that it expects to sell during a particular period.

> Baltimore said it would fail to meet _sales forecasts_ of between £21 million and £22 million for the second quarter.
> Mr Gerry gently trimmed his full-year _sales forecast_ from £1.32 billion to £1.28 billion.

- **sales figures** N-PLURAL

Sales figures are the numbers of a product or products that have been sold and the money resulting from these sales.

> This week Marks and Spencer, Britain's biggest clothes retailer, will reveal its Christmas _sales figures_.
> He pointed to disappointing _sales figures_ in Poland.

- **sales force** (sales forces) N-COUNT
  sales team (sales teams) N-COUNT
  sales rep (sales reps) N-COUNT
  salesman (salesmen) N-COUNT
  saleswoman (saleswomen) N-COUNT
  salesperson (salespeople) N-COUNT
  sales executive (sales executives) N-COUNT

A company's **sales force** or **sales team** is all the people that work for that company selling its products. A **sales rep** is a member of the sales team. A **salesman**, a **saleswoman** or a **salesperson** is a person whose job is to sell things, especially directly to shops or other businesses on behalf of a company. A **sales executive** is a senior member of a sales force.

> …the biggest financial _sales force_ in the country.
> …a _sales team_ of twenty.
> I'd been working as a _sales rep_ for a photographic company.
> …an insurance _salesman_.
> …a _saleswoman_ from npower who called at his home.
> When you go to buy cosmetics, the _salesperson_ often suggests that you buy several products from the same line.
> …an advertising _sales executive_.

PRACTISE YOUR VOCABULARY

1 Use the terms in the box to complete the diagram, which shows the relationship between members of the sales team.

salesmen   sales force   sales executives (2)   salespeople   saleswomen

a   the _____

b   senior _____   c   senior _____

d   _____

e   _____   f   _____

2 Use each term in the box to complete the paragraph.

unit sales   sales revenue   sales figures   sales turnover   sales target

It is important for the sales force to know in detail how many products they have sold, and how much money they have made. Many companies produce _____ at the end of each month, which show the _____, or the number of goods sold, and the _____or _____, or the money resulting from these sales. The salespeople then know whether they have met their _____.

3 Circle the correct term to complete each sentence.

a The sales forecast attempts to predict **sales areas/sales targets/sales figures**.
b The sales target is the amount that the company wants **the sales territory/the sales force/the sales figures** to achieve in a fixed amount of time.
c Sales figures give the details of the **unit sales/sales team/sales forecast** the company has achieved.
d Sales turnover is the total amount of money coming into a company as a result of **sales figures/sales forecast/sales**.
e Each salesperson is responsible for sales in a **sales target/sales territory/sales figures**.

4 Put the terms in the box into the correct column in the table.

sales figures   sales team   sales force   sales revenue   sales target   saleswomen   salesmen   sales turnover sales forecast   salespeople   sales executive

people involved in selling	amount of sales

Use an appropriate term (from the above sets) to complete the sentences. In some cases, more than one answer is possible.

i   After only a month, the company reached its annual _____ for Pert-Plus shampoo in Poland.
ii   The company's _____ are a closely guarded commercial secret.
iii   HarperCollins Publishers' _____ have instructions to visit bookshops at least once a week.
iv   Richard Bagnall has joined Rival Bowman as head of the company's _____.
v   Fleming Pooled Pensions has appointed Christopher Grade as _____.
vi   _____ in Queensland regional shopping centres has been stagnant for the past four years.

- **distribution** N-UNCOUNT
  distributor (distributors) N-COUNT

The **distribution** of goods involves supplying or delivering them to a number of people or places. A **distributor** is a company that supplies goods to shops or other businesses.

> Scottish Courage will also take on <u>distribution</u> of all beers, cider and soft drinks to the pubs.
> He admitted there had been <u>distribution</u> problems.
> …Spain's largest <u>distributor</u> of petroleum products.
> Theater owners lease films from film <u>distributors</u>.

- **distribution chain** (distribution chains) N-COUNT
  distribution network (distribution networks) N-COUNT
  channel of distribution (channels of distribution) N-COUNT

A **distribution chain** is all the stages that goods pass through between leaving a factory and arriving at a retailer. A **distribution network** is a set of distribution chains. A company's **channel of distribution** is the method it uses in order to distribute its goods.

> …all the companies in the <u>distribution chain</u> involved in bringing the mussels to Montreal.
> Cadbury has widened its European <u>distribution network</u>.
> They have to develop other <u>channels of distribution</u>, especially direct selling via the telephone and internet.

- **warehouse** (warehouses) N-COUNT
  warehousing N-UNCOUNT

A **warehouse** is a large building where raw materials or manufactured goods are stored until they are exported to other countries or distributed to shops to be sold. **Warehousing** is the act of storing materials or goods in a warehouse.

> Sainsbury will open a big <u>warehouse</u> this summer that will deliver groceries to households throughout London.
> …the <u>warehousing</u> and distribution of consumer goods.

- **end user** (end users) N-COUNT

The **end user** of a product or service is the user that it has been designed for, rather than the person who installs or maintains it.

> You have to be able to describe things in a form that the <u>end user</u> can understand.
> … the final <u>end-user</u> of the finished product.

- **freight** N-UNCOUNT

1

Freight is the movement of goods by lorries, trains, ships or aeroplanes.

> France derives 16% of revenue from air <u>freight</u>.

2

Freight is goods that are transported by lorries, trains, ships or aeroplanes.

> …26 tons of <u>freight</u>.
> 90% of managers wanted to see more <u>freight</u> carried by rail.

- **forwarding** N-UNCOUNT
  freight forwarding N-UNCOUNT
  forwarding agent (forwarding agents) N-COUNT
  freight forwarder (freight forwarders) N-COUNT

Forwarding or **freight forwarding** is the collection, transportation and delivery of goods. A **forwarding agent** or **freight forwarder** is a person or company that is involved in the forwarding of goods.

> …Montreal, the great <u>forwarding</u> centre for wheat and flour.
> Add costs for <u>freight forwarding</u> to Moscow – around $4 a kilo.
> You authorize Federal Express to act as a <u>forwarding agent</u> for you.
> If a <u>freight forwarder</u> requests information from an airline, the airline's computer can immediately reply to the request.

- **wholesaler** (wholesalers) N-COUNT

A **wholsaler** is a person whose business is buying large quantities of goods and selling them in smaller amounts, for example to shops.

> There were a lot more small <u>wholesalers</u> then, and competition was really keen for the business of the independent grocer.
> GEHE is the largest drugs <u>wholesaler</u> in Europe.

- **factory shop** (factory shops) N-COUNT

A **factory shop** is a shop where a factory sells damaged or out-of-date goods to customers at reduced prices.

> Quantities of fabric may be sold direct to customers in the <u>factory shop</u>.
> We took advantage of visiting the <u>factory shop</u> where you can buy very fashionable shoes at cost prices.

- **agent** (agents) N-COUNT

An **agent** is a person who looks after someone else's business affairs or does business on their behalf.

> You are buying direct, rather than through an <u>agent</u>.
> …a written declaration, authorizing another person to act as his <u>agent</u>.

⮑ **retail outlet**: Topic 6.5; **consumer**: Topic 11.2; **customer**: Topic 11.2

PRACTISE YOUR VOCABULARY

1 Use the terms in the box to complete the paragraph.

distribution network   end users   wholesalers   factory shops   distribution   warehouse   distributor   agent

_____ is concerned with getting a product to the customers (or, for technical products, _____). The _____ makes the product available to the customers through various retail outlets. Products may be distributed directly to retailers, or through a _____ to _____ who store the goods in a _____. The wholesalers then forward the products to the retailers or retail outlets. Some businesses use an _____ to bring buyers and sellers together, who works on a commission basis. Some products may be sold directly to the consumer. One British shoe shop, for example, has several _____ where goods are sold direct to the public.

2 Label the diagram using the terms in the box.

manufacturers   factory shop   wholesaler   end users   agent   warehouse

a_____
b_____
c_____
d_____
e_____
f_____

3 Read the text below, then decide whether the statements that follow are true or false.

Fizz, the company most of us recognize as an airline or music company, also owns cinemas. Through the distribution channel of its cinemas it is able to promote its own version of a cola soft drink. By controlling the channel of distribution it is able to be competitive in the cola market.

	True	False
a Fizz owns an airline, a music company, and a chain of cinemas.	☐	☐
b Fizz promotes its own brand of cola through its airline.	☐	☐
c Fizz's cola is competitive because the company controls the channel of distribution.	☐	☐

4 Read this dictionary entry (from the _Collins Dictionary of Economics_) and answer the questions.

Freight forwarder or forwarding agent a firm that specializes in the physical movement of goods in transit, arranging the collection of goods from factories, depots, etc., and delivering them direct to the customer in the case of domestic consignments and to sea-ports, airports, etc., in the case of exported goods. In the latter case, the forwarder also handles the booking arrangements and the documentation required by the customs authorities.

a Find three terms that refer to a firm specializing in the movement of goods.
b Which word is used in the text to mean freight?
c In a domestic context the forwarding agent offers a delivery service to the customer from which two places?
d Where does the freight forwarding company take goods for export?

● order (orders, ordering, ordered)

1 N-COUNT

An **order** is a request for something to be brought, made, or obtained for you in return for money.

> They are going to place an <u>order</u> for 188 trains.

2 VERB

When you **order** something that you are going to pay for, you ask for it to be brought to you, sent to you, or obtained for you.

> A mixture of e-commerce and shops will enable people to <u>order</u> items such as books, CDs, and insurance on the Web, while going to a shop for the things they need to touch, feel or try on. If <u>ordering</u> a T-shirt or sweatshirt, please indicate where you would like the logo to go.

● on order PHRASE

Something that is **on order** at a shop or factory has been asked for but has not yet been supplied.

> The airlines still have 2,500 new aeroplanes <u>on order</u>.

● stock (stocks, stocking, stocked)

1 VERB

If a shop **stocks** particular goods, it keeps a supply of them to sell.

> The shop <u>stocks</u> everything from cigarettes to recycled loo paper.

2 N-UNCOUNT

A shop's **stock** is the total amount of goods which it has available to sell.

> We took the decision to withdraw a quantity of <u>stock</u> from sale.

3 N-VAR

A company's **stock** is the raw materials or components it has ready to be made into finished goods.

> That buyer ordered £27,500 worth of <u>stock</u>.
> The performance of the textiles side might have looked worse had it not been for the fact that <u>stocks</u> have been kept to a minimum.

● stock control N-UNCOUNT

Stock control is the activity of making sure that a company has the right amount of goods available to sell.

> Paul's first priority should be to get a <u>stock control</u> system which would re-order automatically when an item is bought.
> The combination of a widespread transport network and computerised <u>stock-control</u> has become a powerful one.

● buying department (buying departments) N-COUNT

purchasing department (purchasing departments) N-COUNT

The **buying department** or the **purchasing department** of a company is the section that is responsible for buying products sold by the company or materials used by the company.

> Now that consumers have familiarised themselves with all the popular designer labels, naturally cautious <u>buying departments</u> have become more conservative than ever.
> Company policy on raw materials must be flexible enough to enable the <u>purchasing department</u> to exploit price opportunities.

● re-order level (re-order levels) N-COUNT

The **re-order level** of a particular stock is the point at which the existing stock becomes so low that new stock needs to be ordered.

> But the exact nature of the stock-control system and the <u>re-order level</u> will depend upon the rate of usage of the stock, how frequently new stock can be brought in and the lead time.

● work-in-progress N-UNCOUNT

In book-keeping, **work-in-progress** refers to the monetary value of work that has not yet been paid for because it has not yet been completed.

> The idea is to avoid tying up capital in <u>work in progress</u>.
> …five million pounds' worth of finished goods and two million pounds' worth of <u>work-in-progress.</u>

● logistics N-UNCOUNT

Logistics is the management of the flow of materials through an organization, from raw materials to the finished product.

> <u>Logistics</u> is now more important in our industry than technology.

● lead time (lead times) N-COUNT

The **lead time** is the time between the original design or idea for a particular product and its actual production. The **lead time** is also the period of time that it takes for goods to be delivered after someone has ordered them.

> They aim to cut production <u>lead times</u> to under 18 months.
> <u>Lead times</u> on equipment orders can run as long as 3 years.

● vendor rating (vendor ratings) N-COUNT

Vendor ratings are a measure of the relative performances of a group of suppliers, produced by asking a business to evaluate them on factors such as price and flexibility.

> You can search the <u>vendor ratings</u> either by vendor's name or by category.

● component (components) N-COUNT

The **components** of something are the parts that it is made of.

> Enriched uranium is a key <u>component</u> of a nuclear weapon.
> …as <u>component</u> costs come down, PC prices come down.
> They were automotive <u>component</u> suppliers to motor manufacturers.

➲ **raw materials**: Topic 4.3; **just-in-time manufacturing**: Topic 5.1; **wholesaler**: Topic 6.2

PRACTISE YOUR VOCABULARY

1 Use the terms in the box to complete the paragraph.

stocks	lead times	orders	work-in-progress	components

Most manufacturing companies have a warehouse full of _____ waiting to be assembled. These parts are known as stocks. Keeping _____ low reduces the need to finance, store and handle them. In order to do this, manufacturers get their suppliers to make and deliver components just before they are needed. This shortens _____, or the time it takes to make and deliver goods, or to fill customers' _____.
Companies may also have stocks of _____ and finished products.

2 Whitewash, a washing machine manufacturer, has several suppliers of the raw materials and components they need to produce their machines. Read the text answer the questions.

> Businesses purchase raw materials, semi-finished goods and components, which they use to produce products they can sell to consumers and other businesses. The purchasing department of a firm deals with suppliers and maintains adequate stock levels. Managing the materials is an important part of any business. Logistics is the term used to describe the management of materials flow through an organization from materials to finished goods.

a What is the term used to describe the management of materials through a company?

b Who is responsible for maintaining the stock levels Whitewash need to produce the finished washing machines?

c Whitewash buys metal, electric motors and other parts needed to assemble its machines. Which is an example of a raw material, and which is an example of a component?

d Whitewash sell 70% of their finished products through their chain of retail outlets. The other 30% are sold to other businesses. Which of the following businesses do you think are customers of Whitewash: manufacturers of consumer goods, hotels, launderettes, firms of architects?

3 For each of the three suppliers, add their scores together to get a rating out of 100, and find out which supplier has the best vendor rating.

CRITERIA	MAXIMUM SCORE	ACTUAL SCORE		
		Supplier A	Supplier B	Supplier C
Price	25	17	18	18
Delivery	25	18	15	17
Quality	25	20	25	22
Flexibilty	25	25	25	21

4 Are the sentences true or false?

	True	False
a If you have a product on order you are waiting for it to be delivered.	☐	☐
b Re-order levels do not depend on the level of stock.	☐	☐
c The term 'stocks' can cover supplies of raw materials, components, and work-in-progress.	☐	☐
d Customers are usually happier with short lead times than with long lead times.	☐	☐

● **online booking** N-UNCOUNT
online retailing N-UNCOUNT
online shopping N-UNCOUNT

Online booking is the activity of booking services such as rail tickets or holidays via the Internet. **Online retailing** is the business or activity of selling goods or services via the Internet. **Online shopping** is the activity of buying goods and services via the Internet.

> *Travel agency and flight consolidator Flightbookers (www.flightbookers.com) was the first to offer <u>online booking</u>.*
> *Good old-fashioned marketing principles apply as much to <u>online retailing</u> as to conventional retailing.*
> *Flextech owns a string of websites and provides interactive services such as <u>online shopping</u>.*

● **shopping channel** (shopping channels) N-COUNT
home shopping N-UNCOUNT
direct sales channel (direct sales channels) N-COUNT

A **shopping channel** is a television channel that broadcasts programmes showing products that you can contact the channel and buy. **Home shopping** is the activity of buying things from a shopping channel or from an online retailer. A **direct sales channel** is something such as a website where you can buy things directly from a company.

> *...the growing awareness and use of interactive <u>shopping channels</u> on digital television.*
> *...the QVC <u>home shopping</u> channel.*
> *A higher portion of total sales came through <u>direct sales channels</u>, which have lower margins than retail sales.*

● **cold call** (cold calls, cold calling, cold called)

☐ N-COUNT
If someone makes a **cold call**, they telephone or visit someone they have never contacted, without making an appointment, in order to try and sell them something.

> *She had worked as a call centre operator making <u>cold calls</u> for time-share holidays.*

☐ VERB
To **cold call** means to make a cold call.

> *You should refuse to meet anyone who <u>cold calls</u> with an offer of financial advice.*

● **sample** (samples) N-COUNT

A **sample** of a substance or product is a small quantity of it that shows you what it is like.

> *We're giving away 2000 free <u>samples</u>.*
> *You'll receive <u>samples</u> of paint, curtains and upholstery.*

● **loyalty card** (loyalty cards) N-COUNT

A **loyalty card** is a plastic card that some shops give to regular customers. Each time the customer buys something from the

shop, points are electronically stored on their card and can be exchanged later for goods or services.

> *...a <u>loyalty card</u> that rewarded shoppers with money-off vouchers.*
> *...<u>loyalty card</u> schemes.*

● **direct mail** N-UNCOUNT
direct marketing N-UNCOUNT
direct selling N-UNCOUNT

Direct mail or **direct marketing** is a method of marketing which involves companies sending advertising material directly to people who they think may be interested in their products. **Direct selling** involves the use of direct mail or similar sales techniques.

> *...efforts to solicit new customers by <u>direct mail</u>.*
> *...the use of data for <u>direct marketing</u>.*
> *...<u>direct selling</u> via the telephone and internet.*

● **merchandising** N-UNCOUNT

Merchandising is used to refer to the way shops and businesses organize the sale of their products, for example the way they are displayed and the prices that are chosen.

> *The company has lost money every year because of poor store locations, an unfocused <u>merchandising</u> strategy and inventory problems.*

● **point of sale** (points of sale)

☐ N-COUNT
The **point of sale** is the place in a shop where a product is passed from the seller to the customer. The abbreviation **POS** is also used.

> *Demand-chain management captures information on consumer behaviour at the <u>point of sale</u> and feeds it up the supply chain.*
> *...the vast amount of information collected by <u>POS</u>.*

☐ ADJ
Point-of-sale is used to describe things which occur or are located or used at the place where you buy something. The abbreviation **POS** is also used.

> *Introduction of electronic <u>point-of-sale</u> systems is improving efficiency.*
> *...<u>POS</u> terminals.*

● **personal selling** N-UNCOUNT

Personal selling is the selling of a company's goods or services by means of direct contact between the company's sales representatives and potential customers.

> *Avon concentrates on <u>personal selling</u> in the home.*

➲ **intermediary**: Topic 6.5; **mail order**: Topic 6.5; **call centre**: Topic 12.5

PRACTISE YOUR VOCABULARY

1 Read the text answer the questions.

> When sales are made without any intermediaries being involved, this is known as direct selling. Direct selling means consumers can buy products from their own home, and is an increasingly popular method of distribution. It suits both the customers – who can choose how and when to shop, and companies, who do not have to hand over part of their profits to intermediaries. There are various direct selling techniques including the use of direct mail, personal selling, cold calls and catalogues.

a What is direct selling?
b Why do customers like direct selling methods?
c Why do companies like using direct selling?
d Name four direct selling techniques, and say what each one involves.

2 Match each of the sales methods in the box to one of the comments.

> *direct sales channel   personal selling   free samples   online retailing   loyalty cards   cold calls   direct mail*

a 'I really hate it when someone phones me at home and starts trying to sell me something.'

b 'It's OK for buying books and CDs, because seeing them on the screen is all you need.'

c 'Yesterday some people were handing out sachets of shampoo at the railway station. I used it today and it's really good, so I think I'll buy some.'

d 'Every time I buy petrol they give me points on my card which add up so that every six months or so I can choose something nice from their catalogue.'

e 'I hate it because you can't see the things you want like you can online, only what they choose to show you.'

f 'I get so much junk mail through the post – I put most of it straight in the bin.'

g 'I like it because it's good to have everything demonstrated and explained.'

3 For each of the sales methods choose one business that is unlikely to use that method to sell its products.

a **Loyalty cards:**   i petrol stations   ii supermarkets   iii high-fashion boutiques
b **Personal selling:**   i bathroom fitting company   ii industrial cleaners   iii breakfast cereal company
c **Free samples:**   i shoe manufacturers   ii soft drinks company   iii cosmetics company
d **Cold calls:**   i insurance company   ii supermarket   iii gas/electric company

4 Use the terms in the box to complete the paragraph.

> *merchandising   point of sale   in-store demonstrations*

Merchandising is an attempt to influence the customer at the _____. This is anywhere that a consumer buys a product, e.g. supermarket, car showroom, bookshop, petrol station, etc. _____ aims to encourage sales of a product. Instead of a sales assistant persuading them, consumers are persuaded to buy a product based on its physical appeal. Examples of merchandising techniques include point-of-sale displays, _____, the use of smells and lighting, and so on.

5 Which of the following are features of merchandising?

a creating an appropriate ambience   c designing the layout of the stores   e setting the price
b maintaining the stock levels in shops   d displaying the products attractively   f collecting customer data

- **retail outlet** (retail outlets) N-COUNT
retailer (retailers) N-COUNT
retailing N-UNCOUNT

A **retail outlet** is a shop or other place that sells goods direct to the public. A **retailer** is a person or business that sells goods direct to the public. **Retailing** is the activity of selling goods direct to the public, usually in small quantities.

> ...the largest <u>retail outlet</u> in the city.
> Furniture and carpet <u>retailers</u> are among those reporting the sharpest annual decline in sales.
> She spent fourteen years in <u>retailing</u>.
> ...the car <u>retailing</u> industry.

- **retail park** (retail parks) N-COUNT
shopping centre (shopping centres) N-COUNT

A **retail park** is a large specially built area, usually at the edge of a town or city, where there are a lot of large shops and sometimes other facilities such as cinemas and restaurants. A **shopping centre** is a specially built area containing a lot of different shops.

> But finding large sites, which allow ranges to be better displayed, is no easy task, given the small number of shopping centres and <u>retail parks</u> and the increasing number of retailers hunting them down.
> ...large out-of-town <u>retail parks</u>.
> The new <u>shopping centre</u> was constructed at a cost of £1.1 million.

- **department store** (department stores) N-COUNT
supermarket (supermarkets) N-COUNT

A **department store** is a large shop which sells many different kinds of goods. A **supermarket** is a large shop which mainly sells foods and household goods.

> ...Britain's biggest <u>department store</u> after Harrods and Selfridges.
> Most of us do our food shopping in the <u>supermarket</u>.
> How do those prawns find their way from Norway to the <u>supermarket</u> shelf?

Common Collocations

a supermarket <u>chain</u>	a <u>leading</u> supermarket
a <u>local</u> supermarket	a <u>major</u> supermarket

- **bar code** (bar codes) N-COUNT

A **bar code** is an arrangement of numbers and parallel lines that is printed on products to be sold in shops. The **bar code** can be read by computers.

> The moment a <u>bar code</u> is scanned in one of its US stores, a computer is alerted and checks when the item needs replacing.
> ...a <u>bar code</u> scanner.

- **checkout** (checkouts) N-COUNT

In a supermarket, a **checkout** is a counter where you pay for things you are buying.

> ...queuing at the <u>checkout</u> in Sainsbury's.
> Shopping centres are reporting long queues at the <u>checkout</u> and record numbers of bargain hunters.

- **mail order** N-UNCOUNT

Mail order is a system of buying and selling goods. You choose the goods you want from a company by looking at their catalogue, and the company sends them to you by post.

> The toys are available by <u>mail order</u> from Opi Toys.
> Many of them also offer a <u>mail-order</u> service.
> They have two shops in London and a <u>mail order</u> catalogue.

Common Collocations

a mail order <u>catalogue</u>	a mail order <u>service</u>
a mail order <u>company</u>	a mail order <u>business</u>
<u>available by</u> mail order	

- **intermediary** (intermediaries) N-COUNT

An **intermediary** is a person or organization that provides a link between two other people or organizations.

> However, it says it has no plans to be a car dealer. Instead it will act as a non-profit <u>intermediary</u> putting buyers in touch with a participating dealer.
> ...the rule that investment products must be sold through an independent <u>intermediary</u>.
> ...financial <u>intermediary</u> companies.

➲ **franchise**: Topic 2.4; **franchiser**: Topic 2.4; **franchisee**: Topic 2.4; **wholesaler**: Topic 6.2; **agent**: Topic 6.2; **stock**: Topic 6.3; **online shopping**: Topic 6.4; **online retailing**: Topic 6.4; **direct marketing**: Topic 6.4; **after-sales service**: Topic 11.2

PRACTISE YOUR VOCABULARY

1 List each term in the box under the correct heading.

| supermarket   mail order   online retailing   shopping centre   retail park |
| department store   home shopping   franchising |

Retail outlets	Retailing methods

2 How many intermediaries are there in each of the three relationships?

producer → a → wholesaler → retailer → consumer
producer → b → consumer
producer → c → retailer → consumer

a _____   b _____   c _____

3 Use the terms in the box to complete the text.

| computerized checkout system   bar code   checkout |

When you pay for your goods at the supermarket _____ they are passed over a laser, which reads the

_____ on the packaging. The sale of each item is recorded on the _____

and the system automatically subtracts the items from total stock levels. The system can be used to check stock levels and

the store's takings at any time of the day.

4 Read the text answer the questions.

> Direct marketing is the practice of selling directly to consumers without using an intermediary. There are benefits to
> the consumer in <u>not</u> buying directly from the manufacturer, however. Customer service and after-sales services
> offered by retailers are two examples. Retailers may also buy in bulk from the manufacturer to keep the costs of a
> product down.

According to the text, are the following sentences true or false?

	True	False
a Companies that use direct marketing sell to intermediaries.	☐	☐
b Customers who buy from intermediaries can receive better service than those who buy from the manufacturer.	☐	☐
c Customers who buy from the manufacturer always get the product cheaper than other customers.	☐	☐

Topic 7

BUSINESS PERFORMANCE

● **boom-bust cycle** (boom-bust cycles) N-COUNT

A **boom-bust cycle** is a rapid increase in business activity in the economy, followed by a rapid decrease in business activity.

> *We must avoid the damaging <u>boom-bust cycles</u> which characterised the 1980s.*

● **stock-market collapse** (stock-market collapses) N-COUNT

☐ A **stock-market collapse** is a sudden decrease in value among all the shares on a particular country's stock market, for example because of a political crisis.

> *In the early nineties there was a tremendous boom. And then there was the great <u>stock-market collapse</u> and the peso devaluation.*

☐ If a particular company suffers a **stock-market collapse**, its shares suddenly decrease to a very low value.

> *…a share support operation designed to prevent the <u>stock market collapse</u> of Maxwell Communication Corporation.*

● **bond** (bonds) N-COUNT

When a government or company issues a **bond**, it borrows money from investors. The certificate which is issued to investors who lend money is also called a **bond**.

> *Most of it will be financed by government <u>bonds</u>.*
> *…the recent sharp decline in <u>bond</u> prices.*

● **default** (defaults, defaulting, defaulted) VERB

If a company or country **defaults** on its bonds, it is unable to pay back the money it had guaranteed to the buyers of its bonds.

> *Purchasers of bonds need to know whether a corporation is likely to <u>default</u> on its bonds.*

● **booming** ADJ

If a market is **booming**, the amount of things being bought or sold in that market is increasing.

> *Certain British companies gather business intelligence and collect information to help to fight a <u>booming</u> market in counterfeit luxury goods.*
> *For U.S. manufacturers, there's a growing realization that to fuel growth, they must broaden their customer base overseas and take advantage of <u>booming</u> markets in Europe and the Far East.*

● **boom** (booms) N-COUNT
  slump (slumps) N-COUNT

If there is a **boom** in the economy, there is a sudden large increase in economic activity, for example in the amount of things that are being bought and sold. If there is a **slump** in the economy, economic activity falls suddenly and by a large amount.

> *The industry has spent the years since that initial <u>boom</u> 'downsizing' to a more realistic level.*
> *The 1980s continued their stately progress towards the Great Boom and the subsequent <u>slump</u>.*

Common Collocations

a <u>consumer</u> boom	boom <u>time</u>
an <u>economic</u> boom/slump	a slump <u>in sales</u>
a <u>market</u> boom/slump	a slump <u>in profits</u>
boom <u>years</u>	a slump <u>in demand</u>

● **bubble** (bubbles) N-COUNT

A **bubble** is a situation in which a lot of people try to buy shares in a company that is not financially successful, or which is so new that no one knows how successful it will be. As a result, people pay more for the shares than they are worth.
When people realise that the shares are not worth what they paid for them, they often try to sell them at a lower price. When this happens, people say that the **bubble** has burst.

> *Everyone is hoping that these hi-tech companies will turn out to be the Microsofts of the future. Some of them may be, but at the moment they look more like the focus of a speculative <u>bubble</u>. One New York development lawyer says the 1980s lending frenzy created an atmosphere of euphoria. When the development <u>bubble</u> burst, federal regulators started probing the balance sheets of the biggest banks.*

● **bull market** (bull markets) N-COUNT
  bear market (bear markets) N-COUNT

A **bull market** is a situation on the stock market when people are buying a lot of shares because they expect that the shares will increase in value and that they will be able to make a profit by selling them again after a short time. A **bear market** is a situation on the stock market when people are selling a lot of shares because they expect that the shares will decrease in value and that they will be able to make a profit by buying them again after a short time.

> *Interest rates quite often rise in the early stages of a <u>bull market</u>. The bank said that the <u>bear market</u>, which followed last April's crash in Internet, telecoms and technology stocks, had deterred many companies from going public.*

➲ **market**: Topic 1.4; **share**: Topic 7.2; **stock market**: Topic 7.2; **downturn**: Topic 7.3; **go bust**: Topic 7.4; **borrow**: Topic 8.4; **lend**: Topic 8.4; **interest**: Topic 8.4; **peak**: Topic 10.1

PRACTISE YOUR VOCABULARY

1 Put these four words into two pairs – one pair that means prices are rising, and one pair that means prices are falling.

> boom   bust   bear   bull

a prices rising: _____   _____   **b** prices falling: _____   _____

2 Use the terms in the box to complete the paragraph.

> boom-bust   stock-market collapse   boom   slump   booming

An economic _____ is a period of increased demand and production. The period of booming economic growth inevitably peaks, following which there is a _____, or a downturn in the economy. This pattern is known as the business cycle, and an extreme example of this cycle is called the _____ cycle. A _____ market is good for shareholders, but when the economy slumps it can be accompanied by a _____, when the value of shares on the exchange falls significantly.

3 Read these headlines from the business press and answer the questions.

a   **City analysts describe emerging markets as 'bubble' economies**

Are these emerging markets a good long term investment?

b   **We are on the edge of a bear market in technology shares**

Will technology shares be sold or bought in increased numbers?

c   **Economic boom set to run for years**

Will demand in the economy increase or decrease?

d   **New market about to go bust**

Will output increase or decrease?

e   **Bull market set to last all year**

If you buy shares today and sell in a few months' time, will you make money?

4 Use the terms in the box to complete the sentences.

> defaulting   defaulting on its bonds   bond (x 2)

a When a company borrows money from its investors it issues the investor a _____.
b This _____ runs for several years, and the company is obliged to pay back the money at the end of that period. During this period investors earn interest on the amount of money they have lent the company.
c It can happen that a company is unable to pay back the money to an investor, and when this happens the company is _____ on its bonds.
d Investors need to have a clear idea about the likelihood of a company _____.

● **share** (shares) N-COUNT
bonus share (bonus shares) N-COUNT

A company's **shares** are the many equal parts into which its ownership is divided. **Shares** can be bought by people as an investment. **Bonus shares** are shares which are given to shareholders when a company's profits are distributed.

This is why Sir Colin Marshall, British Airways' chairman, has been so keen to buy <u>shares</u> in US-AIR.
The maximum number of <u>bonus shares</u> you can receive is 248.

● **ordinary share** (ordinary shares) N-COUNT
preference share (preference shares) N-COUNT

Ordinary shares are shares in a company that are owned by people who have a right to vote at the company's meetings and to receive part of the company's profits after the holders of preference shares have been paid. **Preference shares** are shares in a company that are owned by people who have the right to receive part of the company's profits before the holders of ordinary shares. They also have the right to have their capital repaid if the company fails and has to close. [BRIT]

He sold 259,349 <u>ordinary shares</u> at yesterday's price of £10.12.
Overnight, the value of <u>preference shares</u> dropped by 20%.

● **shareholder** (shareholders) N-COUNT

A **shareholder** is a person who owns shares in a company.
Each of the four <u>shareholders</u> now has 25%.

● **share price** (share prices) N-COUNT

The **share price** is the price at which a company's shares are bought and sold.
The impact is reflected in the company's <u>share price</u>, which has slumped to £10.13.

● **stock** (stocks) N-COUNT

Stocks are shares in the ownership of a company, or investments on which a fixed amount of interest will be paid.
...the buying and selling of <u>stocks</u> and shares.

● **quoted company** (quoted companies) N-COUNT

A **quoted company** is a company in which you can buy or sell shares on a particular stock exchange.
The figures are based on stakes held in <u>quoted companies</u>.
He has made a significant contribution to the development of smaller <u>quoted companies</u>.

● **invest** (invests, investing, invested) VERB
investment (investments) N-VAR
investor (investors) N-COUNT

If you **invest** in something, or if you **invest** a sum of money, you use your money in a way that you hope will increase its value, for example by paying it into a bank, or buying shares or property. **Investment** is the act of investing money. An

investment is an amount of money that you invest, or the thing that you invest it in. An **investor** is a person or an organization that buys stocks or shares, or pays money into a bank in order to receive a profit.

They intend to <u>invest</u> directly in shares.
When people buy houses, they're <u>investing</u> a lot of money.
...changes concerning the <u>investment</u> of pension contributions.
...an <u>investment</u> of twenty-eight million pounds.
The main <u>investor</u> in the project is a French bank.

● **dividend** (dividends) N-COUNT

A **dividend** is the part of a company's profits which is paid to people who have shares in the company.
The first quarter <u>dividend</u> has been increased by nearly 4%.
In 1998, PP&L Resources reduced the level of its annual <u>dividend</u> to $1.00 per share.

● **yield** (yields, yielding, yielded)

[1] VERB
If a tax or investment **yields** an amount of money or profit, this money or profit is obtained from it.
It <u>yielded</u> a profit of at least $36 million.

[2] N-COUNT
The **yield** on a tax or investment is the amount of money or profit that it makes.
...the <u>yield</u> on a bank's investments.

● **stock exchange** (stock exchanges) N-COUNT
stock market (stock markets) N-COUNT

A **stock exchange** is a place where people buy and sell stocks and shares. The **stock exchange** is also the trading activity that goes on there and the trading organization itself. The **stock market** consists of the general activity of buying stocks and shares, and the people and institutions that organize it.

The shortage of good stock has kept some investors away from the <u>stock exchange</u>.
...the New York <u>Stock Exchange</u>.
<u>Stock markets</u> could suffer if interest rates rise.

Common Collocations

stock markets <u>rise</u>
stock markets <u>crash</u>
the stock market <u>closes up/down</u>
<u>on the</u> stock market

● **go public** (goes public, going public, went public) PHRASE

If a company **goes public**, it starts selling its shares on the stock exchange.
In 1951 AC <u>went public</u>, having achieved an average annual profit of more than £50,000.

⊃ **market**: Topic 1.4; **plc**: Topic 2.4; **return**: Topic 7.5; **creditor**: Topic 8.4

PRACTISE YOUR VOCABULARY

1 Read the sentences and circle the correct <u>underlined</u> term.

a A quoted company is one whose shares are available <u>privately/publicly.</u>

b Shareholders earn <u>interest/a dividend</u> on their shares.

c If a company gives its shareholders bonus shares they <u>do/do not</u> pay for them.

d When a company distributes dividends, holders of <u>ordinary/preference</u> shares get priority.

2 Look at the list of shares and answer the questions.

The three columns tell you:

1 the market price of the shares in UK sterling (100 pence = £1.00)

2 the percentage change in price over a 7-day period (a minus sign indicates a fall in price)

3 the percentage yield, or the dividend investors can expect to receive.

Company	1 Price/pence	2 Change %	3 Yield %
A	204.50	2.3	9.0
B	1339.00	1.4	2.9
C	180.50	-0.9	0.0
D	122.15	1.5	1.6
E	366.25	-1.6	2.6
F	374.83	-1.4	N/A
G	180.00	-3.4	4.4

a Which shares are the most expensive?

b Which shares are the cheapest?

c Which shares have performed best over the last seven days?

d Which shares have performed worst over the last seven days?

e Which shares offer the highest yield?

f Which shares offer the lowest yield?

3 Use the information in the table above to write sentences about the seven companies listed there. One has been done as an example.

a At close of business on the stock market the price for Company D's shares was £1.22. This was an increase of 1.5%. Investors can expect to receive a yield of 1.6%.

b _____

c _____

d _____

e _____

f _____

g _____

4 Use the terms in the box to complete the paragraph.

investment　　stock exchange　　go public　　investors　　invest

Some companies are publicly owned. The shares of public limited companies are tradeable on a _____.

Shareholders, or _____ buy the company's shares and are the owners of the company. Other companies are privately owned, and there is no open market for their shares. This can be a problem when they need to raise finance, and for that reason they may choose to _____, or to make their shares available on the stock exchange.

Shareholders _____ their money in the stock market in the hope that their _____ will pay a good dividend, or, in other words, that they will make a good profit.

● **power ahead** (powers ahead, powering ahead, powered ahead) PHRASAL VERB
steam ahead (steams ahead, steaming ahead, steamed ahead) PHRASAL VERB

If an economy or company **powers ahead** or **steams ahead** it becomes stronger and more successful.

The most widely held view is the market will continue to power ahead – at least in the first half of next year.
It all leaves the way clear for Tesco to power ahead.
The economy is powering ahead, the number of jobless has fallen for eight months in succession in the west, and for three months in a row in the east.
The latest figures show industrial production steaming ahead at an 8.8 per cent annual rate.
Corporate profits, meanwhile, have steamed ahead. Quarter after quarter companies have reported profit rises of 20 per cent or more.

● **sparkling** ADJ

If a company is described as having **sparkling** figures or **sparkling** results, it has performed very well and made a lot of money.

Shareholders in supermarket giant Tesco were laughing all the way to the bank yesterday following another sparkling set of figures.
Top retailer Marks & Spencer has romped in with another set of sparkling results.

● **sink** (sinks, sinking, sank, sunk) VERB

If something **sinks** to a lower level or standard, it falls to that level or standard.

Share prices would have sunk – hurting big and small investors.
Pay increases have sunk to around seven per cent.
The pound had sunk 10 per cent against the schilling.

● **spike** (spikes) N-COUNT

If there is a **spike** in the price, volume, or amount of something, the price, volume, or amount of it suddenly increases.

Although you'd think business would have boomed during the Persian Gulf War, the owners say they saw only a small spike in interest then.
Westpac economist Nigel Stapleton said forecasts of a 1 per cent to 1.5 per cent seasonally adjusted spike in sales for December were 'not unreasonable'.

● **soar** (soars, soaring, soared) VERB

If the amount, value, level, or volume of something **soars**, it increases quickly and by a large amount.

Shares soared on the stock exchange.
…soaring unemployment.
Insurance claims are expected to soar.

● **downturn** (downturns) N-COUNT
upturn (upturns) N-COUNT

If there is a **downturn** in the economy or in a company or industry, it performs worse or becomes less successful. If there is an **upturn** in the economy or in a company or industry, it improves or becomes more successful.

They predicted a severe economic downturn.
It typically takes at least a year for an economic upturn to reduce the number of business failures.

Common Collocations

an economic downturn/upturn
a sharp downturn/upturn
a severe downturn
a sustained upturn
a strong upturn
a slight upturn
a downturn/upturn in business
a downturn/upturn in demand

● **rally** (rallies, rallying, rallied)

① VERB
When something, for example the price of shares, **rallies**, it begins to recover or improve after having been weak.

Markets began to rally worldwide.

② N-COUNT
If there is a **rally** in the price of shares, it begins to improve after having been weak.

After a brief rally the shares returned to 126p.

Common Collocations

a strong rally   a powerful rally

● **recover** (recovers, recovering, recovered) VERB
regain ground (regains ground, regaining ground, regained ground) PHRASE

When something, for example the economy or a currency, **recovers** or **regains ground**, it begins to improve after having been weak.

The Chancellor of the Exchequer told sceptical businessmen at the annual Institute of Directors' conference that the economy would recover in the second half of the year.
After falling back, the dollar then regained ground in London, trading to close at 93.73 against the yen.

PRACTISE YOUR VOCABULARY

1 If you were a shareholder in ABC Co., which of these headlines would you like to read in the morning newspaper?

a | ABC's new management team steam ahead

d | Foreign competition power ahead in ABC's markets

g | ABC issue sparkling interim results

b | ABC's competitors sinking fast

e | Soaring costs of raw materials for ABC

h | ABC's share prices soar

c | Following a recent fall, prices for ABC's products are rallying

f | Economists predict economic downturn

i | ABC's share prices are finally recovering

2 Look at the graph and decide whether the four descriptions below are true or false.

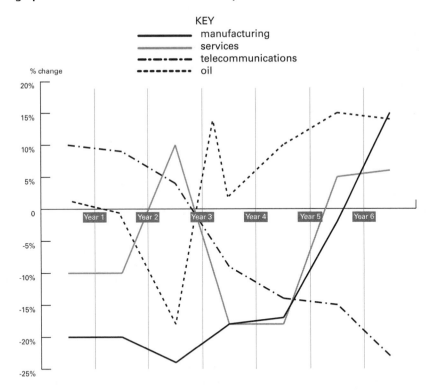

KEY
manufacturing
services
telecommunications
oil

	True	False
a After a steady 3-year period the manufacturing sector has started to power ahead.	☐	☐
b The service sector suffered a serious downturn 3 years ago but stocks have soared recently.	☐	☐
c The telecommunications sector is experiencing an upturn.	☐	☐
d After a period of steady growth in the oil industry there was a sudden spike in oil prices.	☐	☐

3 Correct the sentences above that give false information.

● **decline** (declines, declining, declined)

1 VERB

If something **declines**, it decreases in quantity, importance, or strength.

> The number of staff _has declined_ from 217,000 to 114,000.
> Hourly output by workers _declined_ 1.3% in the first quarter.

2 N-VAR

If there is a **decline** in something, it becomes less in quantity, importance or quality.

> The first signs of economic _decline_ became visible.
> The primary reason for the scheme's failure, Bush argued, was a slumping economy and a _decline_ in the value of real estate.

● **turn around** (turns around, turning around, turned around) PHRASAL VERB

If something such as a business or economy **turns around**, or if someone **turns** it **around**, it becomes successful after being unsuccessful.

> _Turning_ the company _around_ won't be easy.
> In his long career at BP, Horton _turned around_ two divisions.
> If the economy _turned around_, the Prime Minister's authority would quickly increase.

● **bankrupt** ADJ

People or organizations that go **bankrupt** do not have enough money to pay their debts. They can be forced by law to close down their business and sell their assets so that the money raised can be shared amongst the people they owe money to.

> If the firm cannot sell its products, it will go _bankrupt_.
> He was declared _bankrupt_ after failing to pay a £114m loan guarantee.

> ### Common Collocations
> to _go_ bankrupt   to _be declared_ bankrupt

● **bankruptcy** (bankruptcies)

1 N-UNCOUNT

Bankruptcy is the state of being bankrupt.

> Many established firms were facing _bankruptcy_.
> It is the second airline in two months to file for _bankruptcy_.

2 N-COUNT

A **bankruptcy** is an instance of an organization or person going bankrupt.

> The number of corporate _bankruptcies_ climbed in August.

> ### Common Collocations
> to _file for_ bankruptcy
> to _be on the verge of_ bankruptcy
> to _be on the brink of_ bankruptcy
> to _be facing_ bankruptcy
> to _declare_ bankruptcy

● **go out of business** PHRASE

If a company **goes out of business**, it stops trading.

> 50,000 companies _have gone out of business_.
> Many airlines could _go out of business_.

● **liquidation** (liquidations) N-VAR

If a company goes into **liquidation**, it is closed down and all its assets are sold, usually because it is in debt.

> The company went into _liquidation_.
> The number of company _liquidations_ rose 11 per cent.

● **ailing** ADJ

An **ailing** organization is in difficulty and is performing poorly.

> The rise in sales is good news for the _ailing_ American economy.
> …the _ailing_ Asda supermarket chain.

● **fold** (folds, folding, folded) VERB

If a business or organization **folds**, it is unsuccessful and has to close. [mainly BRIT]

> 2,500 small businesses _were folding_ each week.

● **go bust** PHRASE

If a company **goes bust**, it loses so much money that it is forced to close down.

> A Swiss company which _went bust_ last May.

● **troubleshooting** N-UNCOUNT

Troubleshooting is the activity or process of solving major problems or difficulties that occur in a company.

> You realize that the problem must be resolved. A little _troubleshooting_ is needed.

● **management consultant** (management consultants) N-COUNT

A **management consultant** is someone whose job is to advise companies on the most efficient ways to run their business, especially companies that are not performing very well.

> Only after a _management consultant_ visited the office was a solution to the problem found.
> Lybrand, a leading firm of _management consultants_, were asked both to evaluate our analysis and verify our conclusion.

● **insolvent** ADJ
insolvency (insolvencies) N-VAR

A person or organization that is **insolvent** does not have enough money to pay their debts. **Insolvency** is the state of not having enough money to pay your debts.

> Two years later the bank was declared _insolvent_.
> …eight mortgage companies, seven of which are on the brink of _insolvency_.
> The economy has entered a sharp downturn, and unemployment and _insolvencies_ can be expected to increase.

PRACTISE YOUR VOCABULARY

1 Use the terms in the box to complete the paragraph.

> ailing   go out of business   fold   turn around   management consultant
> going bankrupt   troubleshooting

Unsuccessful companies may collapse, _____ or _____. Companies in financial difficulty
are often described as sick or _____. When this is the case, the company may bring in a
_____ to try to help the company, or _____ it _____. This kind of
_____ or problem-solving is often a final attempt to stop the company _____. If this
happens, it will be forced to close down.

2 Match each phrase on the left with one on the right that has a similar meaning.

a The company cannot pay its creditors, and must
close down and use its assets to pay them.

b The company needs someone from the outside to
come and give them advice.

c The new MD was brought in to try and improve the
company's poor trading results.

d Profits are falling.

e The management consultants are looking for ways
to improve the company's performance.

i The company is ailing.

ii They need a management consultant.

iii It is going into liquidation.

iv She turned the company around in less than six months.

v They are doing some troubleshooting.

3 Put these four events into the order in which they might occur:

a The firm goes into decline.   1 _____

b The firm goes bankrupt.   2 _____

c The firm calls in management consultants.   3 _____

d The firm cannot be turned around.   4 _____

4 Which of the following do you think management consultants would be pleased to find, and which would they be
worried about?

	pleased	worried
a a company in danger of insolvency	☐	☐
b a company about to go bust	☐	☐
c management trying to turn things around	☐	☐
d a company threatened with liquidation if its results don't improve	☐	☐
e the company about to fold or go out of business	☐	☐
f troubleshooting strategies to improve the situation	☐	☐

● **profit margin** (profit margins) N-COUNT
gross margin (gross margins) N-COUNT

A **profit margin** is the difference between the selling price of a product and the cost of producing and marketing it. A **gross margin** is the difference between the selling price of a product and the cost of producing it, excluding overheads such as electricity, water, rent etc.

> *The company said profits had also been boosted by sales of vehicles that had better profit margins.*
> *Overall sales rose 11.6 per cent, while gross margins improved 2.7 per cent.*

● **mark-up** (mark-ups) N-COUNT

A **mark-up** is an increase in the price of something, for example the difference between its cost and the price that it is sold for.

> *Restaurants make a decision as to what mark-up they require.*
> *They use dollars to buy Western items such as video recorders and personal computers and then sell them at a huge mark-up.*

● **profit** (profits) N-VAR
profitability N-UNCOUNT
profitable ADJ
profit-making ADJ

A **profit** is an amount of money that you gain when you are paid more for something than it cost you to make, get, or do it. A company's **profitability** is its ability to make a profit. A **profitable** or **profit-making** organization makes a profit.

> *The bank made pre-tax profits of £3.5 million.*
> *You can improve your chances of profit by sensible planning.*
> *Changes were made in operating methods in an effort to increase profitability.*
> *Drug manufacturing is the most profitable business in America.*
> *He wants to set up a profit-making company, owned mostly by the university.*

> **Common Collocations**
>
> interim profits   pre-tax profits   record profits
> an operating profit   annual profits

● **gross** ADJ
net ADJ

① ADJ
Gross means the total amount of something, especially money, before any has been taken away. A **net** amount is one which remains when everything that should be subtracted from it has been subtracted.

> *…a fixed rate account guaranteeing 10.4% gross interest or 7.8% net until October.*
> *…a rise in sales and net profit.*

② ADV
If a sum of money is paid **gross**, it is paid before any money has been subtracted. If a sum of money is paid **net**, it is paid after everything that should be subtracted from it has been subtracted.

> *Interest is paid gross, rather than having tax deducted.*
> *…a father earning £20,000 gross a year.*
> *Balances of £5,000 and above will earn 11 per cent gross, 8.25 per cent net.*
> *All bank and building society interest is paid net.*

> **Common Collocations**
>
> gross/net income   gross/net profit
> gross/net sales   gross/net earnings
> gross revenues   net assets
> net worth   net loss

● **break even** (breaks even, breaking even, broke even, broken even) PHRASE

When a company or a person running a business **breaks even**, they make enough money from the sale of goods or services to cover the cost of supplying those goods or services, but not enough to make a profit.

> *The airline hopes to break even next year and return to profit the following year.*

● **break-even point** N-SING

When a company reaches **break-even point**, the money it makes from the sale of goods or services is just enough to cover the cost of supplying those goods or services, but not enough to make a profit.

> *I've just heard that 'Terminator 2' finally made $200 million a couple of weeks ago, and $200 million was considered to be the break-even point for the picture.*

● **ROCE** ABBREVIATION

ROCE is a measure of the profit that a company makes and represents the efficiency with which the capital invested in a business is used to generate revenue. **ROCE** is an abbreviation for 'Return on Capital Employed'.

> *The ROCE formula is a very popular financial analysis indicator and is used widely in comparisons of the various profits of different firms and industries.*

● **capital employed** N-UNCOUNT

Capital employed is the value of a company's assets minus its liabilities and represents the investment required to enable a business to operate.

> *Our marketing and refining business continues to make less than acceptable returns on capital employed.*
> *Return on capital employed was 12 per cent.*

● **return** (returns) N-COUNT

The **return** on an investment is the profit that you get from it.

> *Profits have picked up but the return on capital remains tiny.*
> *Higher returns and higher risk usually go hand in hand.*

➲ **non-profit-making**: Topic 4.2; **asset**: Topic 8.3

PRACTISE YOUR VOCABULARY

1 Put each of the terms in the box into the correct place in the text.

mark-up   profit margin   break-even   profitability   gross

When companies talk about a _____ margin they usually mean the difference between the selling price of goods and their production cost, without taking into account other costs such as marketing and general overheads. The _____ is the difference between total costs and sales revenues. Margin is expressed as a percentage of the selling price, or as a percentage of the total cost of goods, in which case it is referred to as the _____. Both profit margin and the mark-up are measures of a business's _____. When sales reach a level where revenues match costs, a company or product reaches the _____ point.

2 Read the newspaper headlines and answer the questions.

1 **ABC achieves higher profit margins**

2 **ABC announces excellent sales figures, but higher manufacturing costs**

3 **ABC announces its Mexican operation breaks even at last**

4 **ABC's mark-ups are too high**

5 **ABCs annual report details its unprofitable activities**

a Which story is likely to tell you that the company has increased its revenue this year?
b Which story is likely to tell you that gross profit has fallen?
c Which story is likely to tell you about the closure of the company's unsuccessful American subsidiary?
d Which story is likely to tell you that profits can be expected soon?
e Which story is likely to tell you that consumers are unhappy with ABC's prices?

3 Look at the information in the box and answer the questions.

RATE OF RETURN ON CAPITAL EMPLOYED
The rate of return on capital employed (ROCE) is a good indicator of how well a company is performing. It allows a company to assess its performance by comparing its profit with the amount of capital in the business.

$$\text{ROCE (\%)} = \frac{\text{net profit}}{\text{capital employed (fixed assets and net current assets)}} \times 100$$

a What does ROCE stand for?
b What two factors does ROCE compare?
c Why do companies use ROCE?

Topic 8

FINANCE

● **credit** (credits, crediting, credited)

1 N-UNCOUNT

If you are allowed **credit**, you are allowed to pay for goods or services several weeks or months after you have received them.

The group can't get <u>credit</u> to buy farming machinery.
You can ask for a discount whether you pay cash or buy on <u>credit</u>.

2 N-UNCOUNT

If someone or their bank account is in **credit**, their bank account has money in it. [mainly BRIT]

I made sure the account stayed in <u>credit</u>.

3 VERB

When a sum of money **is credited** to an account, the bank adds that sum of money to the total in the account.

She noticed that only $80,000 <u>had been credited</u> to her account.

4 N-COUNT

A **credit** is a sum of money which is added to an account.

The statement of total debits and <u>credits</u> is known as a balance.

● **debit** (debits, debiting, debited)

1 VERB

When your bank **debits** your account, money is taken from it and paid to someone else.

We will always confirm the amount before <u>debiting</u> your account.

2 N-COUNT

A **debit** is a record of the money taken from your bank account, for example when you write a cheque.

The total of <u>debits</u> must balance the total of credits.

● **trade credit** (trade credits) N-VAR

Trade credit is when a supplier allows a business or customer to pay for goods or services some time after they were supplied.

It might be that the business is able to sell its finished goods before having to pay off the <u>trade credit</u>.
It is often normal practice within the industry for <u>trade credit</u> to be given, especially to larger customers.

● **invoice** (invoices, invoicing, invoiced)

1 N-COUNT

An **invoice** is a document that lists goods that have been supplied or services that have been done, and says how much money you owe for them.

His £700 <u>invoice</u> was settled immediately in cash.

2 VERB

If you **invoice** someone, you send them a bill for goods or services you have provided them with.

The agency <u>invoices</u> the client who then pays.

● **bill** (bills, billing, billed)

1 N-COUNT

A **bill** is a written statement of money that you owe for goods or services.

They couldn't afford to pay the <u>bills</u>.

2 VERB

If you **bill** someone for goods or services you have provided them with, you give or send them a bill stating how much money they owe you for these goods or services.

Are you going to <u>bill</u> me for this?

● **billing** N-UNCOUNT
invoicing N-UNCOUNT

Billing is the process of preparing and sending someone a bill. **Invoicing** is the process of preparing and sending someone an invoice.

More customers have been asking for itemised <u>billing</u>.
A machine capable of carrying out sales <u>invoicing</u>, letter writing and payroll applications.

● **revenue** (revenues) N-VAR

Revenue is money that a company, organization, or government receives from people.

Sales <u>revenue</u> was £7.9 million in the 3 months to September.
The only way to improve profits is to lift sales <u>revenues</u>.

● **letter of credit** (letters of credit) N-COUNT

1 A **letter of credit** is a letter written by a bank authorizing another bank to pay someone a sum of money. Letters of credit are often used by importers and exporters.

The organization has yet to secure any of the required £250,000 that must be deposited by <u>letter of credit</u> to secure the deal.

2 A **letter of credit** is a written promise from a bank stating that they will repay bonds to lenders if the borrower is unable to pay them.

The project is being financed through bonds and backed by a <u>letter of credit</u> from Lasalle Bank.

● **accounts payable** N-PLURAL
accounts receivable N-PLURAL

A company's **accounts payable** is all the money it owes to other companies for goods or services received, or a list of these companies and the amounts owed to them. A company's **accounts receivable** is all the money it is owed by other companies for goods or services it has supplied, or a list of these companies and the amounts they owe.

<u>Accounts payable</u> were understated by approximately $20 million that year.
The customer's record is updated, the company's <u>accounts receivable</u> ledger is debited and its cash ledger is credited.

● **cash flow** N-UNCOUNT

The **cash flow** of a firm or business is the movement of money into and out of it.

The company ran into <u>cash flow</u> problems and faced liquidation.

⮑ **order**: Topic 6.3; **on order**: Topic 6.3; **liability**: Topic 8.3; **debt**: Topic 8.4; **interest rate**: Topic 8.4; **creditor**: Topic 8.4; **turnover**: Topic 10.2

PRACTISE YOUR VOCABULARY

1 Use the terms in the box to complete the paragraph.

accounts payable   bills   accounts receivable   sales revenue   invoicing   trade credit   cash flow

The money received by a company from selling its goods or services is known as _____ or turnover. A company supplying goods or services to another company does not usually expect to be paid immediately, but after an agreed period. This arrangement is known as _____. Amounts that a business is waiting to be paid by its customers are _____. Money that a business owes to its suppliers are _____. When a customer orders goods from a supplier, the supplier invoices or _____ the customer for these goods. Producing and sending invoices is known as _____ or billing. The movement of money into and out of a business, independently of how much it owes and is owed, is the _____.

2 Put the heading 'money owed to the company' or 'money the company owes' into the correct place in the table.

19 accounts receivable £100,000 of trade credit given £250.00 letter of credit payable	32 accounts payable 34 invoices to be paid

3 What type of information is likely to be on an invoice? Choose from this list:

a price
b an itemized list of the products
c the date when the customer can expect to receive the goods
d information about the company's other goods/services

4 Match each of the terms relating to payment with the correct definition.

debit card   credit card   letter of credit   invoice

a A document sent with goods sold on trade credit, telling the purchaser that payment is due.
b A convenient, flexible and secure method of paying without cash, some time after you receive the goods.
c A card whose use results in money being removed from your bank account and sent to the seller's account.
d A secure method of overseas payment.

- **costs** N-PLURAL
  fixed costs N-PLURAL
  variable costs N-PLURAL
  direct costs N-PLURAL
  indirect costs N-PLURAL

A company's **costs** are the total amount of money involved in operating the business. **Fixed costs** or **direct costs** are expenses such as maintenance that do not vary with the level of output. **Variable costs** or **indirect costs** are expenses such as labour or materials that vary with the level of output.

> Costs have been cut by 30 to 50 per cent.
> The company admits its costs are still too high.
> Fixed costs have been reduced and work practices are changing to meet the demands of a much more competitive publishing environment.
> As a firm reaches full capacity, variable costs may start to increase at a faster rate than output.
> Revised working practices need to be implemented as a way to improve the quality of care and reduce direct and indirect costs.

Common Collocations
to cut costs   to reduce costs   to incur costs
rising costs

- **cost structure** (cost structures) N-COUNT

An organization's **cost structure** is all its different costs and the way these costs relate to and affect each other.

> The commission will look closely at the local cost structure to see whether we suffer from unnecessary costs which may mean tourists choose other overseas destinations.
> I agree in principle with the minimum wage, but the government fails to understand that businesses like mine need to change their entire cost structure to cope.

- **economies of scale** N-PLURAL

Economies of scale are the financial advantages that a company gains when it produces large quantities of products.

> Car firms are desperate to achieve economies of scale.
> Most centres have been created by individual companies which means that manufacturers cannot benefit from economies of scale.
> During the period when the Model T Ford dominated the US motor industry the only real difference between it and the Chevrolet was the low price Ford could charge because of his massive economies of scale.

- **unit cost** (unit costs) N-COUNT

Unit cost is the amount of money that it costs a company to produce one article.

> They aim to reduce unit costs through extra sales.

- **overheads** N-PLURAL

The **overheads** of a business are its regular and essential expenses, such as salaries, rent, electricity and telephone bills.

> We are having to cut our costs to reduce overheads and remain competitive.
> With lower overheads, small toy shops are in a better position to lower prices.

- **profit margin** (profit margins) N-COUNT

A **profit margin** is the difference between the selling price of a product and the cost of producing and marketing it.

> The group had a net profit margin of 30% last year.
> Are there ways to use technology to increase profit margins by lowering operating costs?

- **expenses** N-PLURAL
  expenditure (expenditures) N-VAR
  planned expenditure N-UNCOUNT

Expenses are amounts of money that you spend while doing something in the course of your work, which will be paid back to you afterwards. **Expenditure** is the spending of money on something, or the money that is spent on something. A company's or organization's **planned expenditure** is the amount of money it expects to spend over a particular period of time.

> As a member of the International Olympic Committee her fares and hotel expenses were paid by the IOC.
> Can you claim this back on expenses?
> Policies of tax reduction must lead to reduced public expenditure.
> An expenditure for clothing will qualify as a trade or business expense.
> …a £5 million reduction in planned expenditure.
> This 2.4 percent planned expenditure for capital may be too high.

Common Collocations
to increase expenditure   to reduce expenditure
to cut expenditure   to control expenditure

PRACTISE YOUR VOCABULARY

1 Use the terms in the box to complete the paragraph.

| cost structures   fixed costs   indirect costs   overheads   costs   direct costs |

A business's _____ are the money that it spends in order to produce goods or services. Businesses of different kinds have different _____ and define, calculate and refer to their costs in different ways. _____ do not vary in relation to output, whereas variable costs do. _____ are directly related to the things produced, e.g. raw materials and wages. _____ may include things like social security charges on top of wages. Overhead costs, or _____, usually cover the non-production costs of running a business, such as telephone bills, and can be extended to cover R & D activities, for example.

2 Which of the following refer to the cost of producing goods, and which refer to non-production costs?

   a direct costs   **b** indirect costs   **c** overheads   **d** variable costs

3 Which of the above terms refers to costs that change according to the level of output?

4 Match each word/phrase on the left with a definition from the right.

   a variable/indirect costs   **i** costs that are not related directly to production
   b overheads   **ii** spending by buyers on products and services
   c fixed costs/direct costs   **iii** the difference between the production cost and the selling price of a commodity
   d expenditure   **iv** costs which do not change when the level of production changes
   e economies of scale   **v** costs which change with changes in the level of production
   f profit margin   **vi** savings made by the fact that costs reduce as production increases

5 Look at FD&E Ltd's planned expenditure for the year and answer the questions.

FD&E Ltd Annual Cost Breakdown	
	£
Factory heating	15,000
Insurance	50,000
Equipment	12,000
Wages/labour costs	500,000
Rent of premises	50,000
Raw materials	400,000
Staff canteen	10,000
Miscellaneous expenses	13,000

   How much does the company expect to spend on each of the following:
   a Direct/fixed costs?
   b Indirect/variable costs?

6 Are these statements true/false?

	True	False
a If the production costs fall and the selling price remains the same, the profit margin will increase.	☐	☐
b If the production costs fall and the selling price increases, the profit margin will increase.	☐	☐
c If the production costs rise and the selling price remains the same, the profit margin will increase.	☐	☐
d To achieve economies of scale it is necessary to increase production.	☐	☐
e Economies of scale are achieved because unit costs fall as production increases.	☐	☐

● **account** (accounts) N-COUNT
profit and loss account (profit and loss accounts) N-COUNT
P&L ABBREVIATION

Accounts are detailed records of all the money that a person or business receives or spends. A company's **profit and loss account** is a financial record, published at the end of each financial year, that shows whether it has made a profit or a loss. The abbreviation **P&L** is also used.

> He kept detailed <u>accounts</u>.
> The net profit shown in the <u>profit and loss account</u>.
> ...the previous year's <u>P&L</u> figures.

● **balance sheet** (balance sheets) N-COUNT

A **balance sheet** is a written statement of the amount of money and property that a company or person has, including amounts of money that are owed or are owing. **Balance sheet** is also used to refer to the general financial state of a company.

> If you're in business for yourself, you'll be filing an income and expense statement and, in most cases, a <u>balance sheet</u>.
> Rolls-Royce needed a strong <u>balance sheet</u>.

● **international accounting standards (IAS)**
N-PLURAL
international standard (IS) account
(international standard accounts) N-COUNT
GAAP ABBREVIATION

International accounting standards are a set of internationally-agreed principles and procedures relating to the way that companies present their accounts. The abbreviation **IAS** is also used. **International standard accounts**, or **IS accounts**, are accounts that follow international accounting standards. **GAAP** is an accounting system based on generally-accepted methods of accounting. **GAAP** is an abbreviation for 'generally accepted accounting principles'.

> The World Bank is making its loans to some companies conditional on their adoption of <u>international accounting standards</u>.
> Should we have our own national standards or just use <u>IAS</u>?
> Quoted companies now understand that if they don't produce <u>international standard accounts</u>, they won't find support from foreign investors.
> All figures are based on US <u>GAAP</u>.

● **results** N-PLURAL
interim results N-PLURAL

A company's **results** are the set of figures, published at regular times, that show whether it has made a profit or a loss. When the figures are published outside these regular times, they are referred to as **interim results**.

> CGU is due to report its annual <u>results</u> to shareholders this week.
> He pleased the City on Thursday by announcing first-quarter <u>results</u> ahead of expectations.
> <u>Interim results</u> released last month showed a 6% rise to £256m.

● **audit** (audits, auditing, audited)

1 VERB
When an accountant **audits** an organization's accounts, he or she examines the accounts officially in order to make sure that they have been done correctly.

> They <u>audit</u> our accounts and certify them as being true and fair.

2 N-COUNT
An **audit** is an official examination of an organization's accounts.

> The bank first learned of the problem when it carried out an internal <u>audit</u>.

● **auditor** (auditors) N-COUNT

An **auditor** is an accountant who officially examines the accounts of organizations.

> An inquiry by the company's <u>auditors</u> revealed a series of fundamentally incorrect accounting entries over several years.
> Most corporations aren't public and don't require auditing; the corporations that do often select a major firm as an <u>auditor</u>.

● **bottom line** (bottom lines) N-COUNT

The **bottom line** is the total amount of money that a company has made or lost over a particular period of time.

> These small promotions were costly and they did nothing to increase his <u>bottom line</u>.
> ...to force chief executives to look beyond the next quarter's <u>bottom line</u>.

● **asset** (assets) N-COUNT
liability (liabilities) N-COUNT

The **assets** of a company are all the things that it owns. A company's or organization's **liabilities** are the sums of money which it owes.

> The company had <u>assets</u> of $138 million and <u>liabilities</u> of $120.5 million.

● **tangible asset** (tangible assets) N-COUNT
intangible asset (intangible assets) N-COUNT
current asset (current assets) N-COUNT
fixed asset (fixed assets) N-COUNT

Tangible assets are assets which are physical in nature, such as factories and offices. **Intangible assets** are assets which are non-physical in nature, such as patents and trademarks. **Current assets** are assets which a company does not use on a continuous basis, such as stocks and debts, but which can be converted into cash within one year. **Fixed assets** are assets which a company uses on a continuous basis, such as property and machinery.

> Capital, in the form of <u>tangible assets</u> such as machinery or <u>intangible assets</u> such as money, can be a key consideration.
> The company listed its <u>current assets</u> at $56.9 million.
> Investment in <u>fixed assets</u> is an important vehicle for ensuring that the latest technology is available to business.

➲ **return**: Topic 7.5; **revenue**: Topic 8.1; **turnover**: Topic 10.2

PRACTISE YOUR VOCABULARY

1 Divide these four words into two pairs of opposites.

profit   asset   liability   loss

2 Match each term on the left with the correct definition on the right.

a audit

i An accounting statement at the end of the financial year of a firm's sales revenue and costs.

b balance sheet

ii The audited financial statement of an organization which systematically records transactions.

c profit and loss account

iii An accounting statement of a firm's assets and liabilities.

d interim results

iv A legally required review of a company's accounts to establish their validity.

e accounts

v An unaudited progress report issued by a company to keep investors up to date.

f the bottom line

vi The most important part of the accounts telling how much profit the firm has made.

3 Put these events in the financial year into the correct order.

a Company accounts published   b Interim report published   c Audit

4 Read the paragraph and put the terms in the box into the correct place.

> *interim   profit and loss account   auditors   balance sheet   liabilities   accounting standards   results   assets*

Public Limited Companies (PLCs) are required by law to publish end-of-year financial statements. This report on the financial performance, or _____ of the company must include at least a _____ and a _____, so that shareholders can assess the performance of the company. _____ check the accuracy of the accounts and often apply national or internationally recognised _____. The balance sheet shows the firm's _____ and _____, whilst the profit and loss account tells shareholders what kind of return to expect on their investment. Companies often publish half-yearly or _____ results, especially if they need to warn shareholders of poor results. If a firm is doing well it can report a strong balance sheet, however.

5 Read this section from the minutes of a meeting to discuss the Westland takeover bid and answer the question.

> **ABC GROUP**
>
> **MINUTES**
>
> **Meeting of the Board of Directors, 19 June 2002**
>
> 5.1 Valuation of Assets:
>
> The Westland takeover offers a fair price for our current assets, but undervalues our fixed assets and seriously undervalues our intangible assets.

Which of these assets are fairly priced, which are undervalued, and which are seriously undervalued?

a premises   c brand names   e cash   g equipment   i know-how
b goodwill   d land   f stock   h copyrights   j machinery

● **interest** N-UNCOUNT
interest rate (interest rates) N-COUNT

Interest is extra money you receive if you have invested a sum of money. **Interest** is also the extra money that you pay if you have borrowed money or are buying something on credit. The **interest rate** is the amount of interest that must be paid on a loan or investment. It is expressed as a percentage of the amount that is borrowed or gained as profit.

> *Does your current account pay <u>interest</u>?*
> *The Finance Minister has renewed his call for lower <u>interest rates</u>.*
> *Our ISA Saver offers a variable <u>rate of interest</u> starting at 4%.*

Common Collocations
an interest rate <u>rise</u>/<u>fall</u>   interest rates <u>go up</u>/<u>come down</u> a <u>cut in</u> interest rates   an <u>increase in</u> interest rates <u>rising</u>/<u>falling</u> interest rates

● **borrow** (borrows, borrowing, borrowed) VERB
borrower (borrowers) N-COUNT
borrowing N-UNCOUNT

If you **borrow** money from someone or from a bank, they give it to you and you agree to pay it back at some time in the future. A **borrower** is a person or organization that borrows money. **Borrowing** is the activity of borrowing money.

> *Morgan <u>borrowed</u> £5,000 from his father to form the company.*
> *It's so expensive to <u>borrow</u> from finance companies.*
> *After six months, <u>borrowers</u> pay the standard rate of 9.4%.*
> *We have allowed <u>borrowing</u> to rise in this recession.*

● **lend** (lends, lending, lent) VERB
lender (lenders) N-COUNT
lending N-UNCOUNT

When people or organizations such as banks **lend** you money, they give it to you and you agree to pay it back at a future date, often with an extra amount as interest. A **lender** is a person or an institution that lends money to people. **Lending** is the activity of lending money to businesses or private individuals. It is also used to talk about the amount of money being lent.

> *Banks may be slow to <u>lend</u> money to the new company because of the uncertainty about its operating costs.*
> *…financial de-regulation that led to institutions being more willing to <u>lend</u>.*
> *…the six leading mortgage <u>lenders</u>.*
> *…a financial institution that specializes in the <u>lending</u> of money.*
> *…a slump in bank <u>lending</u>.*

● **loan** (loans, loaning, loaned)

① N-COUNT
A **loan** is a sum of money that you borrow.

> *The president wants to make it easier for small businesses to get bank <u>loans</u>.*
> *…<u>loan</u> repayments.*

② VERB
If you **loan** something to someone, you lend it to them.

> *Would it help if I <u>loaned</u> you some money?*

● **principal** (principals) N-COUNT

The **principal** of a loan is the original amount borrowed, excluding any interest payments.

> *They will eventually want to see payments being made to reduce the <u>principal</u> of the loan.*
> *I demand immediate payment of the <u>principal</u> of $60,000 and outstanding interest.*

● **debt** (debts)

① N-VAR
A **debt** is a sum of money that you owe someone.

> *Three years later, he is still paying off his <u>debts</u>.*
> *Shrinking economies mean falling tax revenues and more government <u>debt</u>.*
> *…reducing the country's $18 billion foreign <u>debt</u>.*

② N-UNCOUNT
Debt is the state of owing money.

> *<u>Debt</u> is a main reason for stress.*
> *They see foreign investment as a way of avoiding any more foreign <u>debt</u>.*

● **in/into debt** PHRASE
out of debt PHRASE

If you are **in debt** or get **into debt**, you owe money. If you are **out of debt** or get **out of debt**, you succeed in paying all the money that you owe.

> *He was already deeply <u>in debt</u> through gambling losses.*
> *The bank will make it easy for you to get <u>into debt</u>.*
> *How can I accumulate enough cash to get <u>out of debt</u>?*

● **debtor** (debtors) N-COUNT

A **debtor** is a country, organization, or person who owes money.

> *The United States holds the status of the No. 1 <u>debtor</u> to the United Nations, owing $1.1billion of the $1.85 billion owed to the world body.*
> *<u>Debtors</u> are sometimes embarrassed about getting help from more public sources of advice such as the Citizens Advice Bureau.*
> *…important improvements in the situation of <u>debtor</u> countries.*

● **creditor** (creditors) N-COUNT

Your **creditors** are the people who you owe money to.

> *The company said it would pay in full all its <u>creditors</u> except Credit Suisse.*

➲ **start-up**: Topic 2.3; **venture capitalist**: Topic 2.3; **default**: Topic 7.1; **insolvency**: Topic 7.4; **credit**: Topic 8.1; **liability**: Topic 8.3; **venture capital**: Topic 8.5

PRACTISE YOUR VOCABULARY

1 Which of these words do you associate with 'creditor' and which with 'debtor'?

borrow   lend   owe   repay

2 Ajax 6, a venture capital company, lends money to different start-up companies. Look at the table and answer the questions.

AJAX 6			
Company name	**Amount lent**	**Number of years of loan**	**Interest rate**
Allways Co. Ltd.	£500,000	5	10% pa
Bright Brothers	£100,000	7	15% pa
Chris Ltd.	£250,000	2	10% pa
Delaware Inc.	£300,000	4	20% pa
Eva Co. Ltd.	£600,000	6	10% pa

a Which borrower has 'Ajax 6' lent the most to?
b Which company has borrowed money at the highest interest rate?
c Which company will take longest to pay off the loan?
d What is the principal in the loans from Ajax 6 to Chris Ltd. and to Eva Co. Ltd.?
e How much interest will Allways Co. Ltd. pay to Ajax 6 this year?
f Which company will be out of debt to Ajax 6 first?

3 Are the following sentences true or false?

	True	False
a If the bank lends money to a company, the bank is one of the company's debtors.	☐	☐
b If you borrow money from the bank at a variable rate of interest, you might have to pay back more than you think you will.	☐	☐
c Creditors prefer low interest rates.	☐	☐
d Debtors prefer high interest rates.	☐	☐

4 Which of the following benefit most if interest rates are high, and which benefit most if they are low? Fill in the table below.

a banks   c manufacturing industry   e people with savings
b loan companies   d consumers   f credit card companies

high interest rates	low interest rates

● **all-cash deal** (all-cash deals) N-COUNT

An **all-cash deal** is a financial transaction such as a takeover in which the payment is made entirely in money and not, for example, in shares or share options.

...an _all-cash deal_ worth $9 million.
Shareholders are entitled to demand a proper _all-cash deal_.

● **equity** N-UNCOUNT

Equity is the money a company gets from selling the shares it owns.

It may be difficult to raise _equity_ from local private sources.

● **financing** N-UNCOUNT

The **financing** for something such as a business venture or a loan is the money that is needed for the venture or loan, and the way in which this money is provided.

Proper _financing_ was needed to put the business on a surer footing and speed up payments.
It's not unusual, as a matter of convenience, to have salesmen arrange _financing_ for home improvement loans.

● **management buyout** (management buyouts)
N-COUNT
MBO (MBOs) ABBREVIATION

A **management buyout** is the buying of a company by its managers. The abbreviation **MBO** is also used.

It is thought that a _management buyout_ is one option.
She joined the company full time in 1978, and following an _MBO_ in 1989 she became joint managing director.

● **raise** (raises, raising, raised) VERB

If a person or company **raises** money that they need, they manage to get it, for example by selling their property or borrowing.

They managed to _raise_ £50,000 to set up the company and McGregor sold his house to _raise_ capital.

● **rights issue** (rights issues) N-COUNT

A **rights issue** is when a company offers shares at a reduced price to people who already have shares in the company.

The _rights issue_ will depress earnings per share in the short term.
The acquisition will be financed mainly by a _rights issue_ raising £354 million.

● **flotation** (flotations) N-VAR
share flotation (share flotations) N-COUNT
share issue (share issues) N-COUNT
share offering (share offerings) N-COUNT
public offering (public offerings) N-COUNT

The **flotation** of a company is the selling of shares in a company to the public. When there is a **share flotation**, a **share issue**, a **share offering** or a **public offering**, shares in a company are made available for people to buy.

He said letsbuyit.com was considering _flotation_ on the London Stock Exchange.
Flotations this quarter are at their lowest level in over a decade.
...a _share flotation_ which aims to raise £32 million.
A group called Dreamworld Ltd proposed to buy the park and float it on the stock exchange with a $75 million _share issue_.
Last year the employees rejected a further _share offering_.
The subsequent electric-utility sale, expected to fetch $13billion, will mark the world's largest _public offering_.

● **takeover** (takeovers) N-COUNT
takeover bid (takeover bids) N-COUNT

A **takeover** is the act of gaining control of a company by buyng more of its shares than anyone else. A **takeover bid** is an attempt to do this.

...the proposed £3.4 billion _takeover_ of Midland Bank by the Hong Kong and Shanghai.
...a hostile _takeover bid_ for NCR, America's fifth-biggest computer-maker.

● **venture capital** N-UNCOUNT

Venture capital is capital that is invested in projects that have a high risk of failure, but that will bring large profits if they are successful.

Successful _venture capital_ investment is a lot harder than it sometimes looks.
The model isn't all that complicated: develop a good idea, raise _venture capital_, grow rapidly, and then go public or sell out.

● **working capital** N-UNCOUNT

Working capital is money which is available for use immediately, rather than money which is invested in land or equipment.

The cash raised will be used for _working capital_ and to settle some bank debts.
A second problem is that, as long as land law is uncertain, banks will be unwilling to lend to farmers, and no farm can survive without access to _working capital_.

● **liquidity** N-UNCOUNT

A company's **liquidity** is the amount of cash or liquid assets it has easily available.

The company maintains a high degree of _liquidity_.
...serious _liquidity_ problems.

➲ **backer**: Topic 2.3; **grow**: Topic 2.5; **shareholder**: Topic 7.2; **share**: Topic 7.2; **return**: Topic 7.5; **ROCE**: Topic 7.5; **cash flow**: Topic 8.1; **unit cost**: Topic 8.2; **asset**: Topic 8.3; **liability**: Topic 8.3; **loan**: Topic 8.4

PRACTISE YOUR VOCABULARY

1 Look at these newspaper headlines and decide which of the sentences which follow relates to which headline.

1   **Westland Bank in takeover bid for ABC Group**

4   **Takeover may be an all-cash deal worth £1.5 billion**

2   **Eastern Brothers flotation to go ahead**

5   **ThinkBIG.com in rights issue**

3   **Xceed technology hope to raise venture capital**

6   **Management buyout at Clipper Co.**

a The firm, which has been in the family for 25 years, will sell shares in order to raise long-term finance.
b The banks were unwilling to take a risk on their revolutionary new designs.
c The hostile bid for control will be resisted by the group's board.
d Existing shareholders will be able to buy the shares at a 15% discount on current prices.
e Senior executives hope to resist the hostile takeover bid by raising institutional backing to take over the company themselves.
f The proposed takeover will be paid for in cash, rather than in shares.

2 The senior executives of ABC Group hope to resist Westland's hostile takeover bid by financing a management buyout to take over the company themselves. Read the list of ways they could do this and choose a term in the box that means the same as one of the underlined terms.

> *raise capital   by arranging a bank loan   share issue/flotation   participate in a rights issue*

a They will <u>get financial support</u> from a venture capital company.
b They will invite existing shareholders to <u>acquire additional shares in the company</u> to raise new capital.
c They will raise equity from private investors or a <u>public offering on the stock market.</u>
d They will raise money <u>through debt,</u> from a lender.

3 Use the terms in the box to complete the paragraph.

> *liquidity   working capital   financing   takeover*

Most businesses increase in size through internal growth, i.e. they produce more and take on more workers. Businesses also grow in size through external growth, though, such as buying another business in a _____. Sometimes growing the business may be the only way it can survive. Increasing production can lower unit costs, for example. In order to survive, it is necessary to have enough working capital to pay for day-to-day expenses such as wages or bills. _____ is money used to bridge the gap between the time products are planned, materials are paid for and the goods produced, and the time payment is received for them from customers when they are sold. A firm without sufficient working capital has _____ problems, and needs to find some form of _____.

Topic 9

MARKETING

● **primary data** N-UNCOUNT
secondary data N-UNCOUNT

Primary data is information about a subject that is collected at first-hand, for example by means of interviews. **Secondary data** is information about a subject that has already been written or published.

> *A large number of published books and articles, plus various newspaper reports, are used to supplement his <u>primary data</u>. <u>Secondary data</u> sources – for example, various national and international statistical publications – were used to supplement the main body of information.*

● **field research** N-UNCOUNT
desk research N-UNCOUNT

Field research is research that is done in a real, natural environment, for example by interviewing people, rather than in a theoretical way. **Desk research** is research that is done in a theoretical way, by reading what has already been written about a subject.

> *We must ensure that <u>field research</u> finds its way back into practice, within British industry and commerce.*
> *He states that <u>desk research</u> cannot "fulfil the <u>field research</u> role of putting the supplier in direct touch with the consumer."*

● **market research** N-UNCOUNT

Market research is the activity of collecting and studying information about what people want, need, and buy.

> *Saturn carried out extensive <u>market research</u> to decide how to sell its cars.*
> *A new all-woman <u>market research</u> company has been set up to find out what women think about major news and issues.*

Common Collocations

to <u>conduct</u> market research   to <u>do</u> market research
to <u>carry out</u> market research

● **survey** (surveys, surveying, surveyed)

① N-COUNT
If you carry out a **survey**, you try to find out detailed information about a lot of different people or things, usually by asking people a series of questions.

> *According to the <u>survey</u>, overall world trade has also slackened.*

② VERB
If you **survey** a number of people, companies, or organizations, you try to find out information about their opinions or behaviour, usually by asking them a series of questions.

> *Business Advisers <u>surveyed</u> 211 companies for the report.*
> *Only 18 percent of those <u>surveyed</u> opposed the idea.*

Common Collocations

to <u>conduct</u> a survey   to <u>do</u> a survey
a survey <u>finds</u>   a survey <u>shows</u>
a survey <u>reveals</u>   a survey <u>says</u>

● **respondent** (respondents) N-COUNT

A **respondent** is a person who replies to something such as a survey or set of questions.

> *There were more than 300 <u>respondents</u> to the survey.*

● **consumer panel** (consumer panels) N-COUNT
focus group (focus groups) N-COUNT

A **consumer panel** is a specially selected group of people who are intended to represent the likely users of a particular product or service. **Consumer panels** try out the product or service and give their opinions on it. A **focus group** is a specially selected group of people who are intended to represent the general public. **Focus groups** have discussions in which their opinions are recorded as a form of market research.

> *Our <u>consumer panel</u> tasted both homemade chocolate cakes and cakes made from mixes.*
> *He put together a business plan and tested it with a <u>focus group</u>.*

● **market test** (market tests, market testing, market tested)
test market (test markets, test marketing, test marketed)

① N-COUNT
If a company carries out a **market test**, it asks a group of people to try a new product or service and give their opinions on it. A **test market** is an area or a group of people that tries a new product or service so that its qualities can be evaluated.

> *The new product performed well in a <u>market test</u> in Las Vegas.*
> *From 1983 to 1985, Minneapolis alone served as the <u>test market</u> for 110 products.*

② VERB
If a company **market tests** a new product or service, or if they **test market** it, a group of people are asked to try it and are then asked for their opinions on it.

> *These nuts <u>have been market tested</u> and found to be most suited to the Australian palate.*
> *Adolph Coors Co. said its Coors Brewing Co. unit will <u>test market</u> a new line of bottled water in the West early next year.*

● **market-led** ADJ
market-oriented ADJ
market-orientated ADJ

A company that is **market-led**, **market-oriented** or **market-orientated** aims to develop products or services in order to fill gaps in the existing market.

> *…moving away from an old-style textiles industry towards international companies that are <u>market-led</u>.*
> *…some <u>market-oriented</u> solutions for the problems of the elderly.*
> *Service industries like banking and insurance have also become more <u>market-orientated</u>.*

➲ **market**: Topic 1.4; **product-led**: Topic 5.2

PRACTISE YOUR VOCABULARY

1 Use the terms in the box to complete the paragraph.

> primary data   desk research   market-led   field research   market research
> consumer panels   secondary data   surveys   market test

A market for a product is the people or organizations who buy it, or an area where it is sold. Companies quick to respond to the needs of a market are _____, or market-oriented. The gathering of information about what consumers want and need, and what makes them buy, is known as _____. There are two ways of collecting information – _____ and _____. Desk research involves the use of _____ and field research involves the collection of _____. Secondary data includes information from sources such as the media or trade associations. Primary data is collected through the use of _____, (i.e. questioning individuals), _____, (i.e. questioning groups of people, for example) or by carrying out a _____ to see how successful the product is before launching it more widely.

2 Match a type of data collected on the left with a research method on the right.

primary data   field research
secondary data   desk research

3 Which of the following are examples of primary data and which are examples of secondary data?

		Primary	Secondary
i	published sales figures	☐	☐
ii	reports from the sales force	☐	☐
iii	information published by the competition	☐	☐
iv	data from telephone interviews	☐	☐
v	data from consumer panels	☐	☐
vi	focus groups	☐	☐

4 Match the two halves of the sentences.

a A company which is market-oriented	**i** finding out what customers want and need, and what makes them buy.
b Market research is the process of	**ii** no-one has yet collected.
c Primary data is information which	**iii** tries to find out what consumers want before developing a product.
d Secondary data is information which	**iv** is already available, both inside and outside the organization.
e Carrying out a survey involves	**v** test marketing.
f New products can be tested on consumer panels. This process is called	**vi** asking questions of respondents, either by filling in a questionnaire or by interview.

● **life cycle** (life cycles) N-COUNT

The **life cycle** of a product is the time period from when it is first purchased until the end of its usefulness.

> Each new product would have a relatively long _life cycle_.
> The _life cycle_ of new products in the highly competitive consumer electronics field is becoming ever shorter.

● **development** (developments) N-VAR

Development is the process or result of making a basic design gradually better and more advanced.

> …the _development_ of new and innovative telephone services.

● **launch** (launches, launching, launched)

① VERB

If a company **launches** a new product, it makes it available to the public.

> Crabtree & Evelyn _has_ just _launched_ a new jam, Worcesterberry Preserve.
> Marks & Spencer recently hired model Linda Evangelista to _launch_ its new range.

② N-COUNT

The **launch** of a new product is the act of making it available to the public.

> The company's spending has also risen following the _launch_ of a new Sunday magazine.
> …the most important product _launch_ from Microsoft in six years.

Common Collocations

a launch _party_   an _official_ launch
a _product_ launch

● **growth** N-COUNT

The **growth** of something such as an industry, organization, or market is its development in size, wealth, or importance.

> Littlewoods, which has seen underlying sales _growth_ of 10 percent at its high street stores, said that it would continue as a value retailer.
> We experienced strong sales _growth_, partially a result of good market _growth_.

● **maturity** N-UNCOUNT

Maturity is the state of being fully developed.

> The market will have reached _maturity_ within two or three years at the most.

● **saturation** N-UNCOUNT
　saturated ADJ

The **saturation** of a market is the process or state that occurs when so many similar products are already available within the market that any new products are unlikely to sell well. If a market is **saturated**, so many similar products are already available within the market that any new products are unlikely to sell well.

> I don't think that we have reached market _saturation_ yet.
> As the market became more _saturated_, firms began to export the product.

● **decline** (declines, declining, declined)

① VERB

If something **declines**, it becomes less in quantity, importance, or strength.

> The number of staff _has declined_ from 217,000 to 114,000.
> Hourly output by workers _declined_ 1.3% in the first quarter.
> After five years of _declining_ sales, Boeing says the airline industry is poised for a turnaround.

② N-VAR

If there is a **decline** in something, it becomes less in quantity, importance, or quality.

> The _decline_ in sales means that advisers at Natwest Life are completing on only a handful of endowments each year.
> The essential problem is the relative _decline_ of manufacturing.
> The first signs of economic _decline_ became visible.

○ **research and development**: Topic 5.2; **R&D**: Topic 5.2; **product-orientated**: Topic 5.2; **test market**: Topic 9.1; **market research**: Topic 9.1

PRACTISE YOUR VOCABULARY

1 Use the terms in the box to complete the paragraph.

| product life cycle   decline   growth   maturity   saturated   launched |

New products are often the outcome of research and development projects. When the development stage is complete, the project is ready to be _____. This stage is usually backed up by a marketing campaign to make consumers aware of it. In the _____ phase of the product life cycle, sales and profits rise, as the product reaches _____. At this stage, sales of the product reach a peak and profits are at their maximum. Many companies try to extend this phase of the product life cycle and use extension strategies such as finding new uses or new markets for the product, or changing its appearance. When the market becomes _____ with competing products, sales start to _____. At this stage the company needs to have a new product ready to begin a new _____.

2 Use the terms below to label the diagram showing the product life cycle.

a product launch   **c** product development stage   **e** market saturation
b product decline   **d** product growth   **f** product maturity

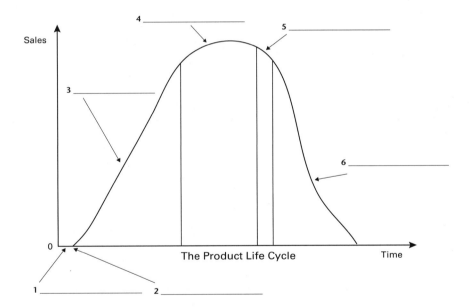

The Product Life Cycle

3 The Airlie Motor Company is one of the world's largest car manufacturers. The company has to regularly bring out new models in order to stay competitive. Read the sentences below describing the life cycle of the Airlie Rapide, and put them into the right order.

a Airlie carries out market research to test market the model.
b Airlie's competitors bring out cars which are technologically superior to the Rapide.
c Airlie builds up to world production levels of 800,000 cars per year.
d Airlie spends $6 billion and 6 years developing the model.
e Airlie's competitors are now producing models that can successfully compete with the Rapide.
f Airlie launches the model at motor shows in Europe and the USA.
g Airlie pays off the $6 billion development costs and uses profits to start developing other cars in the range.

● **advertising** N-UNCOUNT

Advertising is the activity of creating advertisements and making sure people see them.

> ...the sums spent on _advertising_ by Internet companies.
> ...a well-known _advertising_ slogan.

● **advertisement** (advertisements) N-COUNT
  advert (adverts) N-COUNT
  ad (ads) N-COUNT

An **advertisement** is an announcement in a newspaper, on television, or on a poster about something such as a product, event, or job. The forms **advert** and **ad** are also used.

> Miss Parrish recently placed an _advertisement_ in the local newspaper.
> I saw an _advert_ for a transport job with a large steel and engineering company.
> She replied to an _ad_ she saw in the New York Times.

● **promotion** (promotions) N-VAR

A **promotion** is an attempt to make a product or event popular or successful, especially by advertising.

> During 1984, Remington spent a lot of money on advertising and _promotion_.
> Ask about special _promotions_ and weekend deals too.

● **print** ADJ
  billboard (billboards) N-COUNT

The **print** media consists of newspapers and magazines, but not television or radio. A **billboard** is a very large board on which posters are displayed.

> I have been convinced that the _print_ media are more accurate and more reliable than television.
> ...a huge _billboard_ on Sunset Boulevard advertising her singing talents.

● **junk mail** N-UNCOUNT
  spam (spams) N-VAR

Junk mail is advertisements and publicity materials that you receive through the post, which you have not asked for and which you do not want. **Spam** is unwanted e-mail sent to a large number of people, usually as advertising.

> ...the growth in _junk mail_.
> My American e-mail account gets 5 or 6 _spam_ messages every day.
> ...a program that will automatically delete _spams_.

● **tag line** (tag lines) N-COUNT

The **tag line** of something such as a television commercial is the phrase that comes at the end and that is meant to be amusing or easy to remember.

> The _tag line_ was changed from "Bacardi Breezer, there's Latin spirit in every one" to "Breezer, there's Latin soul in every one".

● **tailor** (tailors, tailoring, tailored) VERB

If you **tailor** something such as a product or activity to someone's needs, you make it suitable for a particular person or purpose by changing parts of it.

> Marriott is a good example of such a business, as it has huge information databases on its customers allowing it to _tailor_ its hotel chains to their needs.
> A computer system can only answer yes or no, but we _tailor_ our response to fit the individual customer.

● **advertising agency** (advertising agencies) N-COUNT

An **advertising agency** is a company whose business is to create advertisements for other companies or organizations.

> _Advertising agencies_ are losing their once-powerful grip on brand marketing.

● **advertising campaign** (advertising campaigns) N-COUNT

An **advertising campaign** is a planned series of advertisements.

> The Government has launched a mass _advertising campaign_ to reduce the nation's electricity consumption.

● **advertising standards** N-PLURAL

Advertising standards are the standards of honesty and decency that advertisements are expected to follow.

> The _Advertising Standards_ Authority is the body to write to if you find an advertisement which is unacceptable in some way. This is an independent body which keeps _advertising standards_ high.

● **budget** (budgets) N-COUNT

The **budget** for something is the amount of money that a person, organization, or country has available to spend on it.

> Some companies have a _budget_ for external training, at others all training is handled on the job.
> Like any other small-business owner trying to make such improvements, Gibbins had to do it on a tight _budget_.

● **account** (accounts) N-COUNT

A regular customer of a company can be referred to as an **account**, especially when the customer is another company.

> Biggart Donald, the Glasgow-based marketing agency, has won two Edinburgh _accounts_.

● **account executive** (account executives) N-COUNT

An **account executive** is a person who works at a fairly senior level for a company such as an advertising agency or a marketing firm and who deals with regular customers.

> ...an _account executive_ in marketing for IBM.
> ..._account executives_ from their ad agency.

➲ **strategy**: Topic 2.5; **point of sale**: Topic 6.4; **direct mail**: Topic 6.4; **direct selling**: Topic 6.4; **market share**: Topic 12.1

PRACTISE YOUR VOCABULARY

1 **Which of the following is true?**

   a   **i** Promotion is an example of advertising.   **ii** Advertising is an example of promotion.

   b   **i** A tag line usually comes at the start of an ad.   **ii** A tag line usually comes at the end of an ad.

2 **Use the terms in the box to complete the paragraph.**

> *tailor advertisements*   *advertising campaign*   *advertising standards*   *advertisement*   *advertising budget*
> *advertising agencies*   *print*   *account executive*

Advertising tells people about products through a variety of media types, e.g. TV, _____, billboards etc.

An _____ may use more than one media type, with TV ads supported by a print advertisement in a

magazine, for example. Most campaigns are designed and managed by _____, or more specifically by an

_____. The cost of using an advertising agency comes out of the company's _____.

Agencies are often asked to design a global advertisement that can be used in various countries. They will often

_____, or adapt them to a market's particular needs. Agencies need to take care when designing an

_____ that it meets each country's _____.

3 **Put these four media types into the correct place in the table.**

   a junk mail   **b** TV   **c** newspapers   **d** billboards   **e** spam

Media type	Advantages	Disadvantages
1 _____	very good for short sharp messages	can be affected by the weather
2 _____	can be targeted	may be totally ignored by recipient
3 _____	can provide a lot of detail/information	a company's advertisement may be 'lost' amongst many others, possibly those of its rivals
4 _____	can demonstrate the product in use	consumers may not pay attention
5 _____	can reach a lot of people very quickly	can be deleted before it reaches customer

● **branding** N-UNCOUNT

Branding refers to the image or impression that a company creates for its products, usually through advertising.

> *As we enter the 21st century, companies are placing greater emphasis on <u>branding</u> and marketing.*
> *Williamson points to French Connection, the fashion retailer, as another example of how skilful <u>branding</u> can invigorate trading.*

Common Collocations

a branding <u>strategy</u>	a branding <u>exercise</u>
<u>corporate</u> branding	<u>global</u> branding

● **brand** (brands) N-COUNT
own brand (own brands) N-COUNT
own label (own labels) N-COUNT

A **brand** of a product is the version of it that is made by one particular manufacturer. **Own brands** or **own labels** are products which have the trademark or label of the shop which sells them, especially a supermarket chain. They are normally cheaper than other popular brands.

> *I bought one of the leading <u>brands</u>.*
> *This range is substantially cheaper than any of the other <u>own brands</u> available.*
> *People will trade down to <u>own labels</u> which are cheaper.*

● **generic** (generics)

① ADJ

A **generic** drug or other product is one that does not have a trademark and that is known by a general name, rather than the manufacturer's name.

> *Barry Zeigler says <u>generic</u> products can make a big dent in name brand sales only when the generic is much less expensive.*

② N-COUNT

A **generic** is a drug or other product that does not have a trademark and that is known by a general name, rather than the manufacturer's name.

> *The program saved $11 million in 1988 by substituting <u>generics</u> for brand-name drugs.*

● **brand name** (brand names) N-UNCOUNT

The **brand name** of a product is the name the manufacturer gives it and under which it is sold.

> *Drugs can be sold under different <u>brand names</u> across the EU.*
> *When it comes to soft drinks, Coca-Cola is the biggest selling <u>brand name</u> in Britain.*

● **brand awareness** N-UNCOUNT

Brand awareness is how much people know about a particular brand, and the ideas they have about it.

> *<u>Brand awareness</u> provides customers with a degree of reassurance.*
> *Norwich Union have got to buy their way into this market. They've got to create <u>brand awareness</u>.*

● **brand image** (brand images) N-UNCOUNT

The **brand image** of a particular brand of product is the image or impression that people have of it, usually created by advertising.

> *Few products have <u>brand images</u> anywhere near as strong as Levi's.*

● **brand loyalty** N-UNCOUNT

Brand loyalty is the way some people always buy a particular brand of a product, and are not likely to start buying a different brand.

> *Suddenly perfume is losing its luxury cachet and becoming an everyday purchase and buyers are no longer showing <u>brand loyalty</u>.*
> *Since the Netscape browser allowed Web-page designers to use features that could not be seen by any other browser, a great deal of <u>brand loyalty</u> was guaranteed.*

● **brand recognition** N-UNCOUNT

Brand recognition is when a person knows what a product is or knows something about it as soon as they see it or hear its name.

> *The strategic linchpin of Sun-Rype's marketing plans is the strong <u>brand recognition</u> enjoyed by their products.*

● **brand stretching** N-UNCOUNT

Brand stretching is when a company uses an existing brand name to sell a new product. They do this because they think that people who buy the existing products with that brand name will also buy the new ones.

> *…new developments such as <u>brand stretching</u>, in which tobacco companies use non-tobacco products such as the Marlboro Classics clothing range to promote a particular brand of cigarette.*

● **diversification** N-UNCOUNT

① **Diversification** is when a company starts to produce new and different goods or services.

> *He joined NWW in 1990 and was seen as the driving force behind <u>diversification</u> into areas such as water and sewerage projects in the Far East and Mexico.*

② **Diversification** is when people start to invest their money in more than one place or type of product. This can reduce the amount of risk involved.

> *PEP regulations allow you to invest in overseas funds within certain limits. With an election coming up in Britain in the next couple of years, international <u>diversification</u> makes sense.*
> *…a simple illustration of how portfolio <u>diversification</u> works.*

● **USP** (USPs) N-COUNT

The **USP** of a product or service is a particular feature of it which can be used in advertising to show how it is different from, and better than, other similar products or services. **USP** is an abbreviation for 'Unique Selling Point'.

> *With Volvo, safety was always the <u>USP</u>.*
> *The ease of purchase was the <u>USP</u> and it made the products especially attractive.*

⊃ **product mix**: Topic 3.4; **core values**: Topic 3.4

PRACTISE YOUR VOCABULARY

1 Use the terms in the box to complete the paragraph.

| generic products   brand awareness   brand image   own brand   brand name   USP |

A brand of a product is a version of it made by one particular manufacturer. Consumers may or may not recognize a
particular _____. This knowledge, or lack of it, is measured in terms of brand recognition and
_____. A product sold by a retailer, under the retailer's own name rather than the manufacturer's, is an
_____ product. Products that are not sold under a brand name are _____. Companies try
hard to show consumers how their products are different from their competitor's products and what the
_____ is. Part of the process of making a product different from other similar ones requires a company to
develop a strong _____ for the products in its product mix.

2 Look at the seven word partners with the word 'brand', then match each one to one of the comments below.

```
                        name
                        awareness
                        recognition
  own ——  brand  ——    image
                        loyalty
                        stretching
```

a   'When ice-cream bars were first launched I could
    pick out the Jupiter ice-cream bar straight away
    because the packaging was so familiar.'

b   'I always buy Worthit shampoo because it's just as
    good as a branded product, but much cheaper.'

c   'I always buy their jeans. I would never buy any
    other brand.'

d   'Cool-Cola is the most famous one I can think of.'

e   'I love the adverts. I think they've made the drink
    seem really appealing.'

f   'I don't know anything about the different mobile
    phones on the market, I'm afraid.'

g   'I think companies that use a famous name on lots
    of products just make the brand seem cheap.'

3 Are these statements true or false?

	True	False
a Own label products sell at higher prices than branded products.	☐	☐
b The purpose of developing a brand image is to enable consumers to identify with a product.	☐	☐
c Memorable brand names are often long and complicated.	☐	☐
d The diversification of a brand name can be a failure if it weakens the brand's core values.	☐	☐

● **price** (prices) N-VAR
list price (list prices) N-COUNT

The **price** of something is the amount of money that you have to pay in order to buy it. The **list price** of something is its official price, before any discounts are included.

> …a sharp increase in the _price_ of petrol.
> They expected house _prices_ to rise.
> They haven't come down in _price_.
> I ended up saving 50% on the holiday _list price_.

Common Collocations

a _market_ price	a _purchase_ price	_cut_ price
a price _tag_	a price _rise_	

● **cost** (costs, costing, cost)

☐ N-COUNT

The **cost** of something is the amount of money that is needed in order to buy, do, or make it.

> The _cost_ of a loaf of bread has increased five-fold.
> Badges are also available at a _cost_ of £2.50.

② VERB

If something **costs** a particular amount of money, you can buy, do, or make it for that amount.

> This course is limited to 12 people and _costs_ £50.
> It's going to _cost_ me over $100,000 to buy new trucks.

Common Collocations

low-cost	cost-_cutting_	cost-_effective_	cost _savings_

● **pricing strategy** (pricing strategies) N-COUNT

A company's **pricing strategy** is the system of prices it sets for the goods it produces or the service it provides.

> This leads us to the conclusion that The Economist has different _pricing strategies_ in different markets.

● **market price** (market prices) N-COUNT
market value (market values) N-COUNT

If you talk about the **market price** or **market value** of something, you mean that its price or value depends on how many of the items are available and how many people want to buy them.

> …the _market price_ of cocoa.
> He must sell the house for the current _market value_.

● **price-sensitive** ADJ

If the market for a product or service is **price-sensitive**, it is affected by changes in price.

> …Matrix Essentials hair salon products, aimed at younger _price-sensitive_ consumers.
> The visitor attraction market is already crowded and is _price sensitive_.

● **competition-based pricing** N-UNCOUNT
cost-based pricing N-UNCOUNT
market-orientated pricing N-UNCOUNT
penetration pricing N-UNCOUNT

Competition-based pricing is the policy of setting a price for goods or services based on the price charged by other companies for similar goods or services. **Cost-based pricing** is the policy of setting a price for goods or services based on how much it costs to produce, distribute and market them. **Market-orientated pricing** is the policy of setting a price for goods or services based on an analysis of the market and consumer requirements. **Penetration pricing** is the policy of setting a relatively low price for goods or services in order to encourage sales.

> _Competition-based pricing_ is easily implemented on the internet.
> A _cost-based pricing_ strategy had caused this company to lose orders it should have won.
> We will also maintain a _market-orientated pricing_ strategy and a firm grip on our cost base.
> A policy broadly akin to _penetration pricing_ was adopted to achieve maximum penetration in this sector.

● **discount** (discounts, discounting, discounted)

☐ N-COUNT

A **discount** is a reduction in the usual price of something.

> They are often available at a _discount_.
> All full-time staff get a 20 per cent _discount_ on goods up to £1,000 each year.

② VERB

If a shop or company **discounts** an amount or percentage from something that they are selling, they take that amount or percentage off the usual price.

> This has forced airlines to _discount_ fares heavily in order to spur demand.
> Tour prices are being _discounted_ as much as 33%.

● **discounting** N-UNCOUNT

Discounting is the practice of offering a reduction in the usual price of something.

> …heavy _discounting_ of football shirts.
> …a vicious period of _discounting_ led by Esso's 2p per litre voucher promotion.

➲ **rival**: Topic 3.3; **marketing mix**: Topic 3.5

PRACTISE YOUR VOCABULARY

1 **Use the terms in the box to complete the paragraph.**

cost   pricing strategies   market price   price-sensitive (2)   discounting   list price

Price is part of the marketing mix, and all businesses must decide how to price their products or services. This can be quite difficult, as consumers are heavily influenced by the _____ of something. A product may have a published _____ but this price may rarely be charged because of _____ by sellers. When a price has been 'decided' by the market, it is known as the _____. The market for a particular product can be easily affected by changes in price, in which case it is _____, and consumers, too, if they are very aware of prices are also _____. If the company is able to set its own price there are several _____ or policies that it can choose.

2 **Match a pricing strategy on the left with a reason the right.**

a Company A is using penetration pricing		**i** because they think a careful analysis of the market will help them set the best price.
b Company B is using competition-based pricing		**ii** to get its products into a new market.
c Company C uses cost-based pricing		**iii** because adding a percentage profit margin to the production costs is a quick and easy way of setting a price.
d Company D uses market-orientated pricing		**iv** so consumers won't think their products are more expensive than those of their competitors.

3 **Read the information about the four companies and select the pricing strategy they are most likely to use when setting the price of their product.**

cost-based pricing   penetration pricing   competition-based pricing   market-orientated pricing

a Qualfast are a new company and are very concerned to establish a large customer base. They hope to get their products into the market rapidly so that consumers will become familiar with their name.

b Hall & Co. spend a lot of money each year analysing the market and carrying out market research to make sure they know what their customers want.

c Anderton Ltd. are one of many companies offering a similar service. They are concerned not to set their prices any higher than those of their main rivals.

d Carlo Inc. is a small company with small profit margins. They are very aware of how much they spend on production, distribution and marketing.

Topic 10

INCREASING SALES

● **rise** (rises, rose, risen)

1 VERB

If something **rises**, it it becomes greater in number, level, or amount.

> *Pre-tax profits rose from £842,000 to £1.82m.*
> *Tourist trips in Britain rose by 10.5% between 1977 and 1987.*
> *The number of business failures has risen.*

2 N-COUNT

If there is a **rise** in the number, level, or amount of something, it becomes greater.

> *...the prospect of another rise in interest rates.*
> *Book sales totalled £886 million, a rise of 1.6%.*

Common Collocations

to rise <u>sharply</u>   to rise <u>rapidly</u>   to rise <u>dramatically</u>

● **increase** (increases, increased, increased)
decrease (decreases, decreasing, decreased)

1 VERB

If something **increases** or if you **increase** it, it becomes greater in number, level, or amount. If something **decreases** or if you **decrease** it, it becomes less in quantity, size, or intensity.

> *Japan's industrial output increased by 2%.*
> *The company has increased the price of its cars.*
> *The increased investment will help stabilise the economy.*
> *The number of independent firms decreased from 198 to 96.*
> *Raw-steel production decreased 2.1% last week.*
> *We've got stable labor, decreasing interest rates, low oil prices.*

2 N-COUNT

If there is an **increase** in the number, level, or amount of something, it becomes greater. A **decrease** in the quantity, size, or intensity of something is a reduction in it.

> *...a sharp increase in productivity.*
> *He called for an increase of 1p on income tax.*
> *There has been a decrease in the number of people out of work.*
> *...a decrease of 40 per cent.*

Common Collocations

to increase <u>sharply</u>   a <u>marked</u> increase
to <u>significantly</u> increase/decrease
a <u>dramatic</u> increase/decrease
a <u>significant</u> increase/decrease

● **improve** (improves, improving, improved) VERB
improvement (improvements) N-VAR

If something **improves** or if you **improve** it, it gets better. If there is an **improvement** in something, it becomes better. If you make **improvements** to something, you make it better.

> *The euro's rate against the dollar will also improve.*
> *...a restructuring programme to improve its UK performance.*
> *They were warned they were in danger of losing their franchises unless they made vast improvements to services.*
> *If there is room for improvement in employment regulations or human resources, the software will show this.*

● **fall** (falls, falling, fell, fallen)
drop (drops, dropping, dropped)

1 VERB

If something **falls**, it decreases in amount, value, or strength. If a level or amount **drops** or if someone or something **drops** it, it quickly becomes less.

> *As the service sector has grown, the importance of oil to the economy has fallen.*
> *...a time of falling living standards.*
> *The price of used cars dropped by 9.3 per cent.*
> *He had dropped the price of his London home by £1.25m.*

2 N-COUNT

If there is a **fall** in something, it decreases in amount, value, or strength. If there is a **drop** in the level or amount of something, it decreases quickly.

> *There was a sharp fall in the value of the pound.*
> *He was prepared to take a drop in wages.*

Common Collocations

to drop/fall <u>sharply</u>   a <u>significant</u> drop/fall
to drop/fall <u>dramatically</u>   a <u>dramatic</u> drop/fall

● **level off** (levels off, levelling off, levelled off)
PHRASAL VERB
stabilize (stabilizes, stabilizing, stabilized) VERB

If a changing number or amount **levels off**, it stops increasing or decreasing at such a fast speed. If something **stabilizes** or **is stabilized**, it becomes stable.

> *There are predictions that prices will level off in the new year.*
> *Officials hope the move will stabilize exchange rates.*
> *Through this mechanism the price of the commodity can be stabilized over time, avoiding short-term fluctuations in price.*

● **peak** (peaks, peaking, peaked)

1 VERB

When something **peaks**, it reaches its highest value or its highest level.

> *British unemployment is likely to peak in the winter of 2002–03.*

2 N-COUNT

The **peak** of a process or an activity is the point at which it is at its strongest, most successful, or most fully developed.

> *In the North East, for example, there are twice as many vacancies as there were at the peak of the last boom in 1988.*
> *Skiing prices normally reach a peak at February half-term.*

● **constant** ADJ

If an amount or level is **constant**, it stays the same over a particular period of time.

> *Earnings have remained constant despite the strength of sterling.*
> *It says more than one-hundred-thousand immigrants would be needed annually to keep the workforce at a constant level.*

➲ **decline**: Topic 9.2; **grow**: Topic 10.2; **growth**: Topic 10.2

PRACTISE YOUR VOCABULARY

1 Put each of the verbs showing change into the correct place in the table.

| to rise   to increase   to decrease   to improve   to fall   to drop   to level off |
| to stabilize   to reach a peak   to peak   to remain constant |

↑	→	↓

2 Wordbuilding:

a True or false? The following terms do not have a corresponding noun:

to level off   to reach a peak   to remain constant

b Write the noun form, where appropriate, of the verbs in the table above (be careful with improve and grow!).

3 The eight graphs describe the trading performance of Manton Inc. Choose one of the terms in the box to describe each graph.

| grew rapidly   fell slightly   rose sharply   levelled off   remained constant   peaked dramatically |
| increased gradually   improved steadily |

1 Turnover   2 Costs   3 Sales   4 Output

5 Prices   6 Profits   7 Overheads   8 Demand

4 Look at the bar chart and circle the correct word in each sentence to describe it.

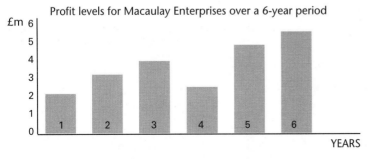

Profit levels for Macaulay Enterprises over a 6-year period

a Profit has increased/remained constant/decreased over the 6-year period.

b There was a levelling off/temporary fall/peak in profits in year 4.

c Profit over the period has increased steadily/slightly.

111

● **business objective** (business objectives)
N-COUNT
sales objective (sales objectives) N-COUNT

A company's **business objectives** are the things that it is trying to achieve. A company's **sales objectives** are the number of sales that it is trying to achieve.

> The key *business objectives* of commercial and charitable organizations are essentially the same – to bring in as much money as possible and to make the most effective use of available resources.
> *Sales objectives* have surpassed expectations.

● **maximize** (maximizes, maximizing, maximized)
VERB
maximization N-UNCOUNT

If you **maximize** something, you make it as great in amount or importance as you can. The **maximization** of something is the act of making it as great in amount or importance as possible.

> In order to *maximize* profit the firm would seek to *maximize* output.
> The manufacturer's interest is in developing effective distribution in order to *maximize* sales to consumers.
> Profit *maximization* is seen as one of the major objectives of a business.
> …share-holders whose goal is the *maximization* of profits.

● **grow** (grows, growing, grown) VERB

① If the economy or a business **grows**, it increases in wealth, size, or importance.

> The economy continues to *grow*.
> …a fast-*growing* business.

② If someone **grows** a business, they take actions that will cause it to increase in wealth, size, or importance.

> A lot of smaller enterprises have problems raising capital to *grow* their business.

● **growth** N-UNCOUNT

The **growth** of something such as profits, sales, or turnover is the increase in it.

> It has restructured its American operations and is now experiencing *growth* in sales of established products.
> …the very rapid *growth* in profits and revenues achieved by most high-tech companies.
> The market has shown annual *growth* of 20 per cent for several years.
> His business has had a *growth* in turnover of 15–20% since the 1980s.

● **turnover** (turnovers) N-VAR

The **turnover** of a company is the value of the goods or services sold during a particular period of time.

> The company had a *turnover* of £3.8 million.
> The association represents 98 percent of Australian companies in the industry, which has an estimated total annual sales *turnover* of $4.7 billion.

● **expand** (expands, expanding, expanded) VERB
expansion N-UNCOUNT

If a company **expands** something such as its product range, it increases the number of different products that it makes. The **expansion** of a product range is the act of increasing it.

> …a successful strategy of *expanding* its product range into clothing and financial services.
> Like the other designers, Doran moved into wallpaper as a way of *expanding* an existing product range.
> Tesco is to speed up the *expansion* of its Internet home delivery service, creating 7,000 full-time jobs.
> …a team which was responsible for a rapid *expansion* of the car range, the Imp being followed by the Hillman Hunter and Avenger models.

● **new market** (new markets) N-COUNT

If a company develops a **new market** for its products, it tries to sell its products to a group of people that has not previously bought them.

> The lack of national boundaries on the internet offers a huge opportunity to reach *new markets*.
> There are ambitious plans for expanding beyond that into *new markets*.

Common Collocations

to open up new markets	to break into new markets
to expand into new markets	to move into new markets
to find new markets	to develop new markets

● **mission statement** (mission statements)
N-COUNT

A company or organization's **mission statement** is a document which states what they aim to achieve and the kind of service they intend to provide.

> Parts of Levi's *mission statement* look a trifle unrealistic – particularly abroad.
> A *mission statement* should say who you are, what you do, what you stand for and why you do it.

➲ **shareholder**: Topic 7.2; **dividend**: Topic 7.2; **profit**: Topic 7.5; **break even**: Topic 7.5; **revenue**: Topic 8.1; **market share**: Topic 12.1

PRACTISE YOUR VOCABULARY

1 Use the terms in the box to complete the paragraph.

| new markets   mission statement   maximize profit   growth in sales turnover   market share |

An important objective for most businesses is to stay in business, and to at least break even. Most companies want to do more than survive, however, and their prime objective is often to _____. This profit maximization benefits the owners or the shareholders of the company, as they receive a better dividend at the end of the year. Companies frequently set themselves other objectives, though, and these are often an indication of how well the business is performing. Sales objectives may include selling into _____, _____, growth in profits, expansion of the product range and increase in _____. Sometimes these sales objectives may be more important than profit objectives. Many companies describe their overall aims in a _____.

2 Match the two halves of each sentence.

a At the moment our firm has 25% of the available sales, but we want to increase this to 30% over the next 5 years;

b Other businesses seem to have a growth rate of about 5% per year and we want to achieve the same level;

c We've never sold our software range in Asia before this year;

d As well as clothes, our company is moving into footwear;

e We need to sell more products. We're aiming to increase our sales by 10% this year;

f Despite the possible long-term disadvantages we are operating at the level which brings in the most money now;

i in other words, we're expanding the product range.

ii in other words, we're selling into new markets.

iii in other words, we want to increase our market share.

iv in other words, we're maximizing profits.

v in other words, we're focusing on a growth in profits.

vi in other words, we're trying to increase our sales turnover.

3 Match each of the three sales objectives a–c with the correct description.

a growth in sales turnover   **b** expansion of the product range   **c** selling into new markets

i Having a wider range of markets should lead to more profit.

ii Selling more should lead to higher turnover.

iii Selling a wider variety of products should increase profits.

4 Are the following sentences true or false?

	True	False
a Sales maximization is the same as expansion.	☐	☐
b If sales increase then turnover increases.	☐	☐
c If a company is successful in finding a new market for its products, turnover will increase.	☐	☐
d A mission statement gives product details.	☐	☐
e A mission statement may include broad sales objectives such as growth.	☐	☐

● **predatory pricing** N-UNCOUNT

If a company practises **predatory pricing**, it charges a much lower price for its products or services than its competitors in order to force them out of the market.

> *Predatory pricing by large supermarkets was threatening the livelihood of smaller businesses in Queensland shopping centres.*
> *Utah Pie charged that the defendants had engaged in predatory pricing by selling pies below cost.*

● **price cutting** N-UNCOUNT
price war (price wars) N-COUNT

If a company engages in **price cutting**, it reduces the price of its products or services in order to try to sell more of them. If competing companies are involved in a **price war**, they each try to gain an advantage by lowering their prices as much as possible in order to sell more of their products or services and damage their competitors financially.

> *An understandable reluctance to travel, shared by many people following the terrorist attacks in the United States, has led to some drastic price cutting by holiday companies.*
> *...a price-cutting campaign.*
> *Their loss was partly due to a vicious price war between manufacturers that has cut margins to the bone.*

● **price fixing** N-UNCOUNT

If competing companies practise **price fixing**, they agree to charge the same price as each other for similar products or services.

> *...companies that have engaged in price-fixing.*
> *...allegations of price fixing.*

● **price discriminate** (price discriminates, price discriminating, price discriminated) VERB
price discrimination N-UNCOUNT

If a company **price discriminates**, it charges different prices to different consumers or in different markets for the same products or services. **Price discrimination** is the practice of charging different prices to different consumers or in different markets for the same products or services.

> *The firm must identify how much its customers are willing to pay before it can effectively price discriminate.*
> *...the government's past efforts to prevent price discrimination.*

● **undercut** (undercuts, undercutting, undercut) VERB

If you **undercut** someone or **undercut** their prices, you sell a product more cheaply than they do.

> *The firm will be able to undercut its competitors whilst still making a profit.*
> *...promises to undercut air fares on some routes by 40 per cent.*
> *Prices were undercut and profits collapsed.*

● **cartel** (cartels) N-COUNT

A **cartel** is an association of similar companies or businesses that have grouped together in order to prevent competition and to control prices.

> *Since RTZ has no agreements with other producers, it cannot be accused of running a cartel.*
> *Since 1993 OPEC, the oil cartel dominated by Saudi Arabia, has kept its output constant at around 25m barrels a day.*

● **restrictive practice** (restrictive practices) N-COUNT

Restrictive practices are ways in which people involved in an industry, trade, or profession protect their own interests, rather than having a system which is fair to the public, employers, and other workers. [BRIT]

> *The Act was introduced to end restrictive practices in the docks.*
> *We had further plans to tackle restrictive practices and other inefficiencies in the medical profession.*

● **loss leader** (loss leaders) N-COUNT

A **loss leader** is an item that is sold at such a low price that it makes a loss in the hope that customers will be attracted by it and buy other goods at the same shop.

> *Economy sliced bread became a loss leader and the supermarkets turned to new premium products to recoup their margins.*
> *Firms such as Gillette and Kodak have long pushed loss leaders like razors and cameras so as to make a killing out of the blades and film that go with them.*

● **collude** (colludes, colluding, colluded) VERB
collusion N-UNCOUNT

If one person, company, or organization **colludes** with another, they co-operate with them illegally or secretly. **Collusion** is secret or illegal co-operation between companies or organizations.

> *Staff were colluding with tourist bus drivers and using the same ticket five or six times.*
> *He found no evidence of collusion between record companies and retailers.*
> *Some stockbrokers, in collusion with bank officials, obtained large sums of money for speculation.*

⊃ **market leader**: Topic 3.3; **monopoly**: Topic 3.3; **rival**: Topic 3.3

PRACTISE YOUR VOCABULARY

1 **Use the terms in the box to complete the paragraph.**

undercuts	*predatory pricing*	*collude*	*restrictive practice*	*price wars*	*price fixing*	*cartel*

When a business sells a product at a lower price than its competitors it _____ them. Companies
responding to each others' price cuts by cutting prices further engage in _____. Firms which use price
cutting to hurt their rivals or to drive them out of the market practise _____. When there are many
businesses in a particular market but only a few companies dominate it, many companies follow the price set by the
market leader. In extreme cases firms might even _____ with other companies, and practise
_____. This activity is often illegal and is an example of a _____. A group of suppliers who
agree to fix a price for their products are known as a _____. Often a cartel will exploit the consumer by
overpricing their goods, because they are able to suppress competition.

2 **Tick (✓) a column to show who benefits first in each case:**

	the seller	the consumer
predatory pricing		
price cutting/price wars		
price discrimination		
cartels		
restrictive practices		
loss leaders		

3 **What are the following examples of? Choose from the terms listed in the box above.**

a Company A, a supermarket, buys milk at 15p per litre and sells it at 12p per litre in the hope that customers will buy
other more expensive products.

b Company B manufactures all kinds of household electrical appliances. It has just come into competition with a new
company that makes only food mixers. Company X has cut the price of its mixers by 25%.

c Company C is a bank. It charges its business customers 40p for each cheque they write, but this service is free to
individual account holders.

d Company D has just reduced the price of its newspapers by 5p after its main rival announced that it was reducing its
price by 3p.

e Company E, a French perfume maker, refuses to allow their products to be sold at HIPLIE, the budget supermarket.

f Companies F, G and H have got together to set up an agency to coordinate the marketing of their products.

4 **Choose the correct term in each sentence.**

a If a government is keen to increase competition it might pass laws against:
  i undercutting prices   **ii** the operation of cartels   **iii** price wars

b Which of the following is likely to lead to higher prices?
  i selling loss leaders   **ii** price fixing   **iii** undercutting competitors' prices

c Which strategy focuses on selling increased numbers of the product?
  i price cutting   **ii** price fixing   **iii** collusion

● **relocate** (relocates, relocating, relocated) VERB
relocation (relocations) N-VAR

If people or businesses **relocate** or if someone **relocates** them, they move to a different place. **Relocation** is the act of moving a person or business to a different place.

> If the company was to <u>relocate</u>, most employees would move.
> Its headquarters will soon <u>be relocated</u> from Westminster to the Greenwich site.
> The company says the cost of <u>relocation</u> will be negligible.
> …the <u>relocation</u> to Bristol of financial institutions like Lloyds TSB.

Common Collocations	
to relocate <u>to</u>/<u>from</u> somewhere	relocation <u>costs</u>
relocation <u>expenses</u>	a relocation <u>package</u>
<u>forced</u> relocation	<u>proposed</u> relocation

● **low-cost centre** (low-cost centres) N-COUNT
low-wage centre (low-wage centres) N-COUNT

A **low-cost centre** is a country or region where business costs are lower, for example because labour or materials are cheaper there. A **low-wage centre** is a country or region where labour is cheap.

> But as long as it remains a high-skill, relatively <u>low-cost centre</u> that is free from excessive red tape, the City will thrive.
> …well-educated, multilingual employees with specific process skills, who live in, or are able and prepared to move to, relatively <u>low-cost centres</u>.
> Yet poorer provinces can undercut that. 'Shenzhen is no longer a <u>low-wage centre</u>,' says Liu Shi Chao.

● **enterprise zone** (enterprise zones) N-COUNT

An **enterprise zone** is an area, usually a depressed or inner-city area, where the government offers incentives, for example lower taxes, in order to attract new businesses.

> …the implementation of <u>enterprise zones</u> in communities with high unemployment.
> Because it is in an <u>enterprise zone</u>, taxes on non-food items are 3.5% instead of the usual 7%.

● **greenfield site** (greenfield sites) N-COUNT
brownfield site (brownfield sites) N-COUNT

A **greenfield** site is an area of land that has not been built on before. A **brownfield site** is an area of land in a town or city where houses or factories have been built in the past, but which is not being used at the present time.

> The Government has ruled out the building of a new airport on a <u>greenfield</u> site.
> Most foreign investors in Britain have opted for <u>greenfield sites</u>.
> Obviously <u>greenfield sites</u> are cheaper and easier for builders to develop than brownfield ones.
> By 2005 he wants half of all new houses to be built on previously developed land: so-called <u>brownfield sites</u>.

● **manufacturing base** (manufacturing bases) N-COUNT

The **manufacturing base** of a country or area is all the factories or companies which produce goods there.

> Working with their foreign investors, they were beginning slowly to rebuild the country's <u>manufacturing base</u>.
> I think it's very important for Connecticut to maintain a <u>manufacturing base</u>.

● **drift** N-UNCOUNT

Drift refers to the tendency of some companies to move their manufacturing operations to sites where costs are lower, especially to less developed countries.

> The government is tackling the consequences of the <u>drift</u> of manufacturing to the Far East.
> After spotting the <u>drift</u> of chip manufacturing to countries with lower costs in Asia, Mr Uchiyama switched into bio-electronics.

➲ **partnership**: Topic 2.4; **inward investment**: Topic 3.2; **subsidy**: Topic 3.2; **raw materials**: Topic 4.3; **component**: Topic 6.3; **supplier**: Topic 12.2

PRACTISE YOUR VOCABULARY

1 Use the terms or phrases in the box to complete the paragraph.

enterprise zones   relocate   low-wage centre   manufacturing base

The decision about where to locate the company is an important one as it can affect sales, costs and profitability. Companies may need to move their _____ in order to expand, or move to more up-to-date premises in order to modernize. Often businesses choose to _____ in order to reduce their costs. Moving to government-assisted development areas, or _____, can save money on rent and taxes, and relocating to a _____ can make huge savings, too.

2 Which of the following might be regarded as low-cost and/or low-wage centres?

a Germany   **c** Bangladesh   **e** Canada
b The Philippines   **d** Denmark   **f** Romania

3 Look at the newspaper headlines a–e and match each extract i–v with the correct headline.

LargeCorp to relocate to enterprise zone	**SuperCom to relocate to greenfield site**

a _____   d _____

Low-wage centres attract UK firms	**Office block completed on former brownfield site**

b _____   e _____

Manufacturing drift to low-cost centres continues

c _____

 i Labour costs in Eastern Europe provide an incentive to relocate.
 ii The company will receive generous government subsidies and pay little tax for 5 years.
 iii Companies are relocating their manufacturing bases to the Far East.
 iv The out-of-town site will allow the company to build a state-of-the-art factory.
 v A new business development area near the city centre is popular.

4 Put these advantages in the appropriate column of the table:

a cheap   **b** close to customers   **c** space to expand

enterprise zone	greenfield site	brownfield site

5 Read this newspaper headline and answer the questions.

Inward investment increases to record levels

	True	False
a Firms are relocating.	☐	☐
b Fewer firms are moving than in the past.	☐	☐
c Foreign firms are moving to this country.	☐	☐
d The government is benefiting from foreign investment.	☐	☐

● **reposition** (repositions, repositioning, repositioned) VERB

To **reposition** a company, product, or service means to try to interest more people or different people in it, for example by changing certain things about it or changing the way it is marketed.

The sell-off is aimed at repositioning the company as a publisher principally of business information.

Mazda needs to reposition itself if it is to boost its sales.

● **rebrand** (rebrands, rebranding, rebranded) VERB
rebranding N-UNCOUNT

To **rebrand** a product or organization means to present it to the public in a new way, for example by changing its name or appearance. **Rebranding** is the process of giving a product or an organization a new image, in order to make it more attractive or successful.

There are plans to rebrand many Texas stores.

The £85m programme will involve an extensive rebranding of the airline, designed to accentuate Virgin's 'Britishness'.

● **re-evaluate** (re-evaluates, re-evaluating, re-evaluated) VERB

If you **re-evaluate** something such as a plan or an idea, you consider it again in order to make a judgement about it, for example about how good or bad it is.

However, it's vital to stand back occasionally and re-evaluate where a business is heading.

We are currently re-evaluating our strategy to increase the profile of this campaign.

● **public image** N-SING

The **public image** of a company, product, or person is the perception that the public has of them or of their values.

The low-key profile adopted by Sir Philip Beck, Mr Robinson's predecessor, exacerbated the company's bad public image.

It would be in the banks' best interests to participate in the UAR scheme because it might help to improve their public image.

● **facelift** (facelifts) N-COUNT

If you give a place or thing a **facelift**, you do something to make it look better or more attractive.

For the first time in years the factory is getting a facelift.

All BP's 19,800 petrol stations were given a facelift along with its fleet of tankers.

Common Collocations

to have a facelift	to get a facelift
to need a facelift	to undergo a facelift
to be given a facelift	

● **rejuvenate** (rejuvenates, rejuvenating, rejuvenated) VERB

If you **rejuvenate** an organization or system, you make it more lively and more efficient, for example by introducing new ideas.

The government pushed through schemes to rejuvenate the inner cities.

He has masterminded South Korea's new business links with the North, and has a record of rejuvenating fading businesses.

● **upmarket**
downmarket

① ADJ

Upmarket products or services are expensive, of good quality, and intended to appeal to people in a higher social class. If you describe a product or service as **downmarket**, you think that they are cheap and are not very good in quality.

…restaurants which years ago weren't quite so upmarket as they are today.

…K-Mart, the decidedly downmarket American chain.

② ADV

If a product or service moves **upmarket**, it tries to appeal to people in a high social class. If you say that a product or service has moved **downmarket**, you mean that it has become less expensive and poorer in quality.

Japanese firms have moved steadily upmarket.

Now that American sales are slowing, both firms are moving downmarket.

● **flagship brand** (flagship brands) N-COUNT

The **flagship brand** among a company's products is the one that the company considers most important.

Its single malt remains the flagship brand as the leading malt in Scotland and No. 2 in Britain.

They make the company's flagship brands, including Pepsi, 7UP and Mirinda drinks.

➲ **strategy**: Topic 2.5; **target market**: Topic 3.4; **core values**: Topic 3.4; **downturn**: Topic 7.3; **turn around**: Topic 7.4; **peak**: Topic 10.1

PRACTISE YOUR VOCABULARY

1 Read the text and answer the questions.

> In 1996 the company's turnover peaked at $7.1bn, but by 2000 sales had taken a dramatic downturn. At this point the firm considered moving its brand downmarket in an attempt to rejuvenate the brand. They planned to offer the range in supermarkets. Some analysts warned that the strategy to improve sales by appealing to discount shoppers could damage the brand's public image with existing customers.

  a Were the company pleased with sales figures in 2000 or worried by them?
  b What strategy to improve sales did the firm consider in 2000?
  c What effect did they hope this strategy would have?
  d What is the danger of this strategy, according to some business analysts?

2 Complete the table by placing these statements in the correct spaces:

  a New target market may not trust the product because of its old image.
  b Sales might increase.
  c The core values of the brand might become diluted.
  d Potential to increase profit per item.

	ADVANTAGE	DISADVANTAGE
Moving the brand upmarket		
Moving the brand downmarket		

3 Look at the reasons for rebranding on the left and match each one with the correct explanation on the right.

  a in response to a changing market
  b because of brand globalization

  i Companies selling the same product in different markets around the world need to re-evaluate the product's success in each market.

  ii The company needs to rejuvenate the look of its flagship brand.

4 Are these statements true or false?

	True	False
a Moving a brand upmarket never means putting the price up.	☐	☐
b One way to find a wider audience for a product is to move downmarket.	☐	☐
c A company only repositions a brand in order to sell it in a specific market.	☐	☐
d A company sometimes rebrands a product to change consumers' views of it relative to its competitors.	☐	☐
e Firms which re-evaluate their public image recognize the importance of a variety of stakeholders to their well-being.	☐	☐
f A company's flagship brand is any brand in its range that sells well.	☐	☐

Topic 11

CUSTOMER SERVICE

● **customer care** N-UNCOUNT

Customer care refers to the way that companies behave towards their customers, for example how well they treat them.

> ...very low standards of <u>customer care</u>.
> What has happened to our reputation for <u>customer care</u> and good service?

● **customer relations**

① N-PLURAL

Customer relations are the relationships that a business has with its customers and the way in which it treats them.

> Good <u>customer relations</u> require courtesy, professionalism and effective response.
> Senator Colston said he was satisfied Telstra had improved its services and <u>customer relations</u>.

② N-UNCOUNT

Customer relations is the department within a company that deals with complaints from customers.

> ...Tucson Electric's <u>customer relations</u> department.

● **emotional capital** N-UNCOUNT

When people refer to the **emotional capital** of a company, they mean all the psychological assets and resources of the company, such as how the employees feel about the company and how committed they are to it.

> "The study's findings illustrate that UK organisations are not nourishing their intellectual and <u>emotional capital</u>," says Mr Thomson.
> How many companies have paid the price of an alienated workforce with problems like poor customer service, labour disputes and low productivity – all hallmarks of low <u>emotional capital</u>?

● **service with a smile** PHRASE

If a person or company provides **service with a smile**, they treat their customers in a friendly and helpful way.

> Attention to details, substantial comfort and convenience, space, and <u>service with a smile</u> are what you can expect and count on.

● **loyal** ADJ
   customer loyalty N-UNCOUNT

A **loyal** customer is someone who continues to buy products from the same shop or company over a long period of time.
Customer loyalty is the state of being a loyal customer.

> ...the treatment of <u>loyal</u> customers by banks and building societies.
> Luckily our customers have remained <u>loyal</u> to us.
> For the supermarkets, these programs supposedly encourage <u>customer loyalty.</u>
> Julie Cunningham of Datamonitor says: "<u>Customer loyalty</u> is at an all-time low."

● **customer satisfaction** N-UNCOUNT

When customers are pleased with the goods or services they have bought, you can refer to **customer satisfaction**.

> "I really believe that it is possible to both improve <u>customer satisfaction</u> and reduce costs," Danon says.
> <u>Customer satisfaction</u> with their mobile service runs at more than 90 per cent.

● **corporate hospitality** N-UNCOUNT

Corporate hospitality is the entertainment that a company offers to its most valued clients, for example by inviting them to sporting events and providing them with food and drink.

> Marconi, the troubled telecoms equipment group, is cutting back on <u>corporate hospitality</u> at football grounds to save cash.
> ...executives in a <u>corporate hospitality</u> tent.

● **code of practice** (codes of practice) N-COUNT

A **code of practice** is a set of written rules which explains how people working in a particular profession should behave.

> The auctioneers are violating a <u>code of practice</u> by dealing in stolen goods.
> The Government hoped the housing industry would bring in a voluntary <u>code of practice</u> to protect purchasers.

● **serve** (serves, serving, served) VERB

① If something **serves** people or an area, it provides them with something that they need.

> This could mean the closure of thousands of small businesses which <u>serve</u> the community.
> ...Inter-City Gas Corp., which mainly <u>serves</u> customers in Ontario and Manitoba.
> ...a desire to make education <u>serve</u> the needs of politicians and business.

② Someone who **serves** customers in a shop or a bar helps them and provides them with what they want to buy.

> They wouldn't <u>serve</u> me in any pubs 'cos I looked too young.
> Auntie and Uncle suggested she <u>serve</u> in the shop.

● **repeat business** N-UNCOUNT

If a company gets **repeat business**, people who have bought thier goods and services before buy them again.

> Nearly 60% of our bookings come from <u>repeat business</u> and personal recommendation.

➲ **repeat customer:** Topic 11.2

PRACTISE YOUR VOCABULARY

1 Does the speaker in each sentence offer their client good customer care?

a 'Whenever I've had an unhappy client, I've dealt with the problem face-to-face rather than by telephone or in writing.'

b 'I had a difficult client who criticized me for something that wasn't my fault. I apologized for causing the problem because the customer is always right.'

c 'If a client asks me for help that I'm not really qualified to give, I tell them what I think they want to hear.'

d 'One of our distributors failed to deliver goods to a very important client. Because we had employed the distributor I took full responsibility for the problem.'

2 Complete each box in the flow chart with one of these terms:

a *customer needs*   b *customer satisfaction*   c *repeat business*   d *customer loyalty*   e *customer care*

| Good quality _____ or customer service | should meet _____ or wants. | If it does, this should lead to _____, because the customers are happy. | This can in turn lead to _____. | The company will then benefit from the customers' _____. |

3 Match each term on the left with a term on the right to make common word pairs associated with customer care, then use each one to complete the sentences.

a corporate   i business
b code of   ii capital
c repeat   iii hospitality
d emotional   iv practice

i   A _____ is devised by the firm itself.
ii _____ is a form of bribery and is therefore unacceptable.
iii If the level of _____ is low, productivity often suffers.
iv _____ is cheaper than new business.

4 Find four word partners with the word 'customer' on the opposite page and add them to the diagram.

customer

5 Use one of the word pairs above to complete each sentence.

i   The _____ department in any firm has a very important role in interfacing with the public.
ii Most firms prize _____ very highly, and often give these customers special treatment.
iii Most firms like to know how happy their customers are and have systems to find out their levels of _____.
iv Most consumers value good levels of _____ and will not return to a business which does not deliver it.

6 Use each term to complete the sentences.

| service with a smile   customer relations   code of practice   serve customers |

a Because of increased consumer expectations most companies try hard to promote good _____.
b They are giving their sales staff more customer care training and teaching them how to _____.
c In addition they encourage all their staff to offer _____.
d Many companies have developed a _____ for their firm.

● **client** (clients) N-COUNT
consumer (consumers) N-COUNT
customer (customers) N-COUNT

A **client** of a professional person or organization is a person or company that receives a service from them in return for payment. A **consumer** is a person who buys things or uses services. A **customer** is someone who buys goods or services, especially from a shop.

...a solicitor and his client.
The company required clients to pay substantial fees in advance.
...claims that tobacco companies failed to warn consumers about the dangers of smoking.
...improving public services and consumer rights.
Our customers have very tight budgets.
...the quality of customer service.
We also improved our customer satisfaction levels.

Common Collocations

client service	customer satisfaction
a client list	customer service
consumer confidence	to attract customers
consumer demand	to gain customers
consumer goods	to lose customers to somebody
consumer protection	
consumer spending	

● **customer base** (customer bases) N-COUNT
client base (client bases) N-COUNT

A business's **customer base** or **client base** is all its regular customers, considered as a group.

...Halifax's customer base of 21 million people.
Enviros Consulting has 250 staff and a client base of more than 2,000 organisations worldwide.
However, in recent years the group has struggled to expand its client base.

● **repeat customer** (repeat customers) N-COUNT

If a company gets **repeat customers**, people who have bought their goods or services before buy them again.

Over a third of the business comes from repeat customers.
Our quality craftsmanship has seen many repeat customers.

● **turn away** (turns away, turning away, turned away) PHRASAL VERB

If a business **turns** customers **away**, it is unable to provide them with what they want, for example because it does not have enough goods available.

They had to turn customers away and close the place down.
Last year we sold out in record time and had to turn away many customers.

● **after-sales service** (after-sales services) N-VAR

A company's **after-sales service** is all the help and information that it provides to customers after they have bought a particular product.

...a local retailer who offers a good after-sales service.
They are also attempting to keep the car buyer as a long-term customer by offering after-sales service.

● **warranty** (warranties) N-VAR

A **warranty** is a written promise by a company that, if you find a fault in something they have sold you within a certain time, they will repair it or replace it free of charge.

...a twelve month warranty.
The equipment is still under warranty.

● **guarantee** (guarantees, guaranteeing, guaranteed)

① N-COUNT

A **guarantee** is a written promise by a company to repair or replace a product free of charge if it has any faults within a particular time.

Whatever a guarantee says, when something goes wrong, you can still claim your rights from the shop.
It was still under guarantee.

② VERB

If a company **guarantees** its product or work, they provide a guarantee for it.

Some builders guarantee their work.
All Dreamland's electric blankets are guaranteed for three years.

○ **market research**: Topic 9.1; **code of practice**: Topic 11.1; **customer care**: Topic 11.1; **customer loyalty**: Topic 11.1; **repeat business**: Topic 11.1

PRACTISE YOUR VOCABULARY

1 Put each of the three terms into the correct place in the diagram below.

i customers   **ii** consumers   **iii** clients

a _____

b _____ (*people who buy professional services*)

c _____ (*people who buy products from a shop*)

2 Complete the paragraph with one of the terms from the box.

customer base   after-sales service   repeat customers   warranties and guarantees

Good Wheels, a company which sells motorbikes and scooters, has carried out extensive market research in an effort to improve sales. The results show that the company needs to improve two areas of its practice if it is to keep or increase its _____, namely its after-sales service and its advertising. They have decided to offer extended _____ as part of their _____. Good Wheels needs more _____, as it is more costly to find new customers than to satisfy current ones, and better customer care may help them achieve this.

3 Which of the following are aspects of Good Wheels' after-sales service, and which are other types of customer service? Put them into the right place in the table.

a length of warranty

b knowledgeable sales staff

c repair facilities at all dealerships

d sale of good quality accessories (e.g. helmets)

e 3-year guarantee

f test-drive service

g free advice

after-sales service	other types of customer service

4 Match each situation on the left with the correct explanation on the right.

a This company is turning customers away.		**i** It is only selling to its current customer base.
b This company is failing to attract new customers.		**ii** Satisfied customers are recommending them to friends.
c This company is attracting many new clients.		**iii** It is unable to meet demand.

5 Which of the statements describes which of the companies in Exercise 4?

a Its customer base is increasing.

b Its customer base is static.

c Its customer base is not increasing as much as it could.

● **training** N-UNCOUNT
staff training N-UNCOUNT
staff development N-UNCOUNT
retraining N-UNCOUNT

Training is the process of learning the skills that you need for a particular job or activity. **Staff training** is the process of teaching the employees of a company the skills they need for their job. **Staff development** is the process of teaching the employees of a company new skills that will help them to advance in their job. **Retraining** is the process of learning new skills, especially in order to get a new job.

> He called for much higher spending on education and _training_.
> The industry is anxious to improve _staff training_.
> ...a programme of systematic _staff development_.
> ...measures such as the _retraining_ of the workforce at their place of work.

Common Collocations	
<u>vocational</u> training	<u>management</u> training
<u>youth</u> training	a training <u>session</u>
a training <u>course</u>	a training <u>programme</u>

● **incentive** (incentives) N-VAR

If someone is provided with an **incentive** to do something, they are offered something that encourages them to do it.

> The latest staff _incentive_ comes on top of a £1,000 bonus that Murray has already promised staff if its takeover is successful.
> ..._incentives_ for good staff to stay, such as share options, more free time or extra training.

● **commit** (commits, committing, committed) VERB
committed ADJ

If you **commit** to something such as a purchase or an agreement, or if you **commit** yourself to it, you say that you will definitely buy it or agree to it. Someone who is **committed** to something has definitely agreed to do it or definitely wants to do it.

> You don't have to _commit_ to anything over the phone.
> Banks and retailers are expected today to _commit_ themselves to launching so-called smartcards by the end of 2004.
> All the staff are actively _committed_ to the process of continual improvement of the organisation.

● **induction** N-UNCOUNT

Induction is a procedure for introducing someone to a new job or organization.

> In our _induction_ programme, we mix graduates who will work in different disciplines to encourage them to work as a team.
> ...an _induction_ course for new members.

● **apprentice** (apprentices) N-COUNT
apprenticeship (apprenticeships) N-VAR

An **apprentice** is a young person who works for someone in order to learn their skill. Someone who has an **apprenticeship**

works for a fixed period of time for a person who has a particular skill in order to learn the skill. **Apprenticeship** is the system of learning a skill like this.

> I started off as an _apprentice_ and worked my way up.
> He left school at 15 and trained as an _apprentice_ carpenter.
> After serving his _apprenticeship_ as a toolmaker, he became a manager.

● **supervisor** (supervisors) N-COUNT

A **supervisor** is a person who is in charge of activities or people, especially workers.

> ...a full-time job as a _supervisor_ at a factory.
> This information is usually provided by the employee's _supervisor_.

● **head of department** (heads of department)
N-COUNT

In a company, the **head of department** is the most senior person in a particular department.

> My _head of department_ told me that doing good work was the only proper way of attracting business.

● **on-the-job training** N-UNCOUNT
off-the-job training N-UNCOUNT

On-the-job training is training that is given to employees while they are at work. **Off-the-job training** is training that takes place outside the workplace.

> Japanese companies provide _on-the-job training_ as well as access to technical education.
> A quarter had received _off-the-job training_ in their jobs.

● **mentor** (mentors, mentoring, mentored)

1 N-COUNT
A person's **mentor** is someone who gives them help and advice over a period of time, especially help and advice related to their job.

> To get your career back on track, seek help from a _mentor_ or a career coach.

2 VERB
To **mentor** someone means to give them help and advice over a period of time, especially help and advice related to their job.

> He _had mentored_ scores of younger doctors.

● **mentoring** N-UNCOUNT

Mentoring is the practice of assigning a junior member of staff to the care of a more experienced member of staff in order to provide the more junior employee with help and assistance.

> There will be a system of _mentoring_ where successful business people will become the applicants' mentors to help and advise them.
> The company's _mentoring_ programme focuses specifically on women and minorities.

➲ **co-worker**: Topic 14.3; **multi-skilled**: Topic 13.5

PRACTISE YOUR VOCABULARY

1 Match each job title on the left with the corresponding extract from a job advertisement on the right.

a   **Head of Staff Training**

i   …assess the effectiveness of technical training programmes and co-ordinate the activities of our young trainees to improve the effectiveness of on-the-job training in the company…

b   **Human Resource Manager (with special responsibility for mentoring scheme)**

ii   …helping the company to refocus its business without losing committed staff by offering them new roles in the company at this exciting time…

c   **Apprenticeship Scheme Supervisor**

iii   …you will have overall responsibility for a wide variety of programmes, both in-house and external, and for developing new systems to assess staff needs and the training programmes to meet them…

d   **Head of Retraining**

iv   …you will co-ordinate all aspects of the firm's relationship with its customers…

e   **Head of Customer Services Department**

v   …you will design and implement this new support initiative to help with induction of staff into the company, support staff in the medium term and give them an incentive to stay with us long-term…

2 Choose the correct answer.

a Who is more likely to be your mentor at work?

   i the Managing Director   **ii** an apprentice   **iii** a co-worker

b Which is likely to take the longest time to complete?

   i an apprenticeship   **ii** an induction programme   **iii** a staff training workshop

c Which of the following is not likely to be involved in developing other members of staff?

   i a mentor   **ii** an apprentice   **iii** a supervisor

d Which of the following is more likely to be conducted outside your place of work?

   i an apprenticeship scheme   **ii** an induction programme   **iii** off-the-job training

3 Match what these people say about their own staff training and development to the descriptions on the right.

Alan	– "No one makes any career progress in this department. There's no incentive to work harder."	a He's receiving off-the-job training.
Bill	– "I used to be a fitter in the factory but now I'm learning how to work with computers in the design department."	b They have poor staff development.
Colin	– "My firm sends me to the local technical college one day a week."	c The firm has an induction programme.
Doreen	– "At work we all take turns at doing a variety of jobs, which means we have to be trained to do more. It's much more interesting."	d He's retraining.
Edwina	– "Before we could work with customers we had to learn about how the firm wants us to treat the public."	e The firm has a multi-skilled workforce.

● **public relations**
PR ABBREVIATION

1 N-UNCOUNT
Public relations is the part of an organization's work that is concerned with obtaining the public's approval for what it does. The abbreviation **PR** is often used.

> The move was good _public relations_.
> George is a _public relations_ officer for The John Bennett Trust.
> The company's _public-relations_ department denied the story.
> Steve Martin, head of _PR_ for Adidas.
> ...a _PR_ company.

2 N-PLURAL
You can refer to the opinion that the public has of an organization as **public relations**.

> The club's _public relations_ are disastrous.
> ...a full-time media relations officer, with a brief to improve the _public relations_ of England teams abroad.

Common Collocations
a public relations/PR firm
a public relations/PR campaign
a public relations/PR exercise
a public relations/PR consultant
a public relations/PR coup
a public relations/PR offensive
a public relations/PR stunt
a public relations/PR disaster

● **publicity manager** (publicity managers) N-COUNT
publicity officer (publicity officers) N-COUNT

A **publicity manager** or a **publicity officer** is a person whose job is to make sure that a large number of people know about a company's activities so that it is successful.

> ...Bob Deuel, Disney's _publicity manager_.
> ...a _publicity officer_ for Granada TV.

● **press release** (press releases) N-COUNT

A **press release** is a written statement about a matter of public interest which is given to the press by an organization concerned with the matter.

> British Telecommunications, its single largest customer, issued a supportive _press release_.
> We sent _press releases_ to all the commercial and public radio and television stations.

● **press conference** (press conferences) N-COUNT

A **press conference** is a meeting held by a person or organization in which they answer journalists' questions about a matter of public interest.

> ...a Los Angeles _press conference_ for a new adventure drama.
> Mr Case, the Internet pioneer, attended the _press conference_ to announce the deal.

● **corporate image** (corporate images) N-COUNT

An organization's **corporate image** is the way that it presents itself to the public, and the way it is perceived.

> Telecom Eireann is changing its name to Eircom and has launched a £500,000 advertising campaign to promote its _corporate image_.
> ...the damaging effect the current scandal could have on their _corporate images_.

● **corporate values** N-PLURAL

The **corporate values** of a company are its attitudes and goals in relation to such things as its workforce, its customers, and society in general.

> The John Lewis Partnership, for example, has had the happiness of employees at the centre of its _corporate values_ since the 1920s.
> ...changes in traditional _corporate values_ and behaviour, particularly in relation to environmental and social performance.

● **corporate advertising** N-UNCOUNT

Corporate advertising is advertising that aims to promote a company's name and image rather than a particular product.

> ..._corporate advertising_ for a giant multinational trying to create a favourable climate for the firm's operations.
> Philip Morris Co. is launching a massive _corporate advertising_ campaign.

● **below-the-line promotion** (below-the-line promotions) N-VAR
above-the-line promotion (above-the-line promotions) N-VAR

Below-the-line promotion is the use of promotional methods that can be controlled by the company selling the goods or service, such as in-store offers and direct selling.
Above-the-line promotion is the use of promotional methods that the company cannot directly control, such as television or press advertising.

> The above-the-line advertising campaign will be supported by a PR and _below-the-line promotion_.
> The developments in own label products come at a time when traditional in-store and _below-the-line promotion_ are back in vogue.
> For all maternity clothing retailers, most _above-the-line promotion_ is conducted through focused sources such as mother and baby magazines.

○ **direct marketing**: Topic 3.5; **corporate responsibility**: Topic 4.2; **corporate culture**: Topic 13.3

PRACTISE YOUR VOCABULARY

1 Which of the following are examples of below-the-line promotion and which are examples of public relations activities?

	Below-the-line promotion	Public relations activities
a offering the public tours of company premises		
b holding exhibitions at trade fairs		
c holding press conferences		
d making donations to the community		
e direct marketing		
f issuing press releases		

2 Are these statements true or false?

	True	False
a The PR department of a company mainly deals with customer complaints.	☐	☐
b Below-the-line promotion uses media advertising as its main tool.	☐	☐
c Below-the-line promotion gives the firm more control over the distribution of its message than does above-the-line promotion.	☐	☐
d Press releases are written by the public relations department and given to the media.	☐	☐
e It is the role of the Publicity Manager to establish a strong corporate image with the public.	☐	☐

3 What are the advantages and disadvantages of below-the-line promotion and corporate advertising? Put these phrases into the appropriate places in the table.

a allows the firm to target its message at interested groups
b many companies share the same values so the public may not be able to differentiate them
c allows the company to promote itself as a whole
d events such as trade fairs may have an impact for a limited period. Some consumers dislike direct mail.

	below-the-line promotion	corporate advertising
ADVANTAGE		
DISADVANTAGE		

4 Which of the following are examples of below-the-line promotion and which are examples of corporate advertising?

a promotion through direct mail, exhibitions and trade fairs, merchandising, packaging, personal selling, PR
b promotion through television, newspapers and magazines, cinema, radio, posters, the Internet

5 Word pairs – corporate. Match each word pair to the correct definition.

corporate — values
corporate — advertising
corporate — image

a the promotion of the firm's image to the public
b the perception that people have of a corporation
c the attitudes, beliefs and goals of a company

● **consumer laws** N-PLURAL
   consumer protection N-UNCOUNT

Consumer laws are laws that are designed to protect people's rights when they buy something. **Consumer protection** is the protection provided by such laws.

> ...Internet companies, which feared that the Parliament would force them to adhere to the <u>consumer laws</u> of 15 different nations.
> Queensland's lonely and loveless will be be protected soon from unscrupulous dating agencies by tough new <u>consumer laws</u>. Many consumer groups welcomed the move, saying it would enhance <u>consumer protection</u>.
> ...new <u>consumer protection</u> legislation.

● **caveat emptor** CONVENTION

Caveat emptor means 'let the buyer beware', and is a warning to someone buying something that it is their responsibility to identify any faults in it.

> Of course, <u>caveat emptor</u> should apply in the housing market as it does in anything else.
> But cyberspace is exactly like the real world when it comes to personal finance: <u>Caveat emptor</u> is the most important rule.

● **consumer rights** N-PLURAL

Consumer rights are the legal rights that people have when they buy something.

> Returning the tribunal's powers is a major step forward for <u>consumer rights</u> in this country.
> ...an organisation campaigning for <u>consumer rights</u>.

● **customer data** N-UNCOUNT

Customer data is information about a company's customers, especially information about their shopping habits, that is stored in a database.

> IT allows networks of car dealers to collect, store and analyse <u>customer data</u>.
> The company will generate revenues by selling <u>customer data</u> to financial-services providers, removal companies and other groups.

● **Trade Descriptions Act** N-SING
   Trades Descriptions Act N-SING

In Britain, the **Trade Descriptions Act** or the **Trades Descriptions Act** is a law designed to prevent companies from presenting their goods or services in a dishonest or misleading way.

> ...the section of the <u>Trade Descriptions Act</u> that makes it an offence to mark things in such a way that they hide the real price.
> Last year it was convicted and fined under the <u>Trades Descriptions Act</u> for placing For Sale boards on empty homes in the area.

● **Data Protection Act** N-SING

In Britain, the **Data Protection Act** is a law designed to protect people against the misuse of information about them stored on computer.

> Under the new <u>Data Protection Act</u>, organisations have to be careful how they disseminate information gained as a result of processing personal data.
> Using names from a computer without permission breaches the <u>Data Protection Act</u>.

● **Internet security** N-UNCOUNT

Internet security is the use of measures to improve the security of a website, especially in order to safeguard personal and financial information.

> ...a breach of <u>Internet security</u>.
> And there is no need to worry about <u>internet security</u>. totopools.com follows strict procedures to ensure that your personal and credit card details are securely stored.
> ...an <u>Internet security</u> company.

➲ **big business:** Topic 2.1

PRACTISE YOUR VOCABULARY

1 Use the words in the box to complete the paragraph.

| consumer rights consumer protection caveat emptor consumer laws |

In recent years there has been a lot of interest in consumer protection. In the past it was the consumer's responsibility to make sure that the goods they bought were satisfactory. This approach is based on the phrase _____, or 'let the buyer beware'. Today, however, many people think that consumers are at the mercy of big business, and that governments should pass legislation, or _____ to protect consumers. There are several reasons why this _____ is necessary, including the fact that competitive markets may lead firms to take advantage of consumers, by reducing the quality of the goods they offer, for example. Laws have been passed to protect _____ in relation to safety of goods, buying on credit, food labelling, and much more.

2 Match the newspaper headlines on the left with the extracts from the story on the right.

a **Government promises new powerful data protection act**

i …people's credit card details have been misused and their personal details have been passed on to other businesses without their authorisation…

b **Judges reject new consumer protection legislation**

ii …here, rights are especially strong on door-to-door selling and Internet security…

c **Huge questions raised over Internet security**

iii …in the absence of meaningful consumer rights, the rule for anyone buying anything is still 'caveat emptor'…

d **Megastores prosecuted under Trade Descriptions Act**

iv …all citizens will have the right to see all information held by most government departments…

e **'Consumer protection' the strongest in Europe says Government minister**

v …labelling was incorrect on 32 items, and weights were wrong on 17 out of 20 fresh items purchased by inspectors…

3 Answer the following questions.

a Which of the following is used to protect customer data?

  i the Trade Descriptions Act   **ii** the Data Protection Act   **iii** caveat emptor

b Which of the following is the Trade Descriptions Act an example of?

  i the Data Protection Act   **ii** caveat emptor   **iii** consumer laws

c Which of the following protects the seller from faults in their products?

  i the Data Protection Act   **ii** the Trade Descriptions Act   **iii** caveat emptor

4 Are the following true or false?

	True	False
a Consumer laws are designed to protect businesses from dissatisfied customers.	☐	☐
b Customer data is the information consumers need to decide what to buy.	☐	☐
c The Data Protection Act prohibits companies from misusing data about their customers.	☐	☐
d The Trades Descriptions Act protects consumers.	☐	☐
e The warning caveat emptor applies to sellers of goods.	☐	☐

131

Topic 12

SERVICES

market (markets)

1 N-COUNT

The **market** for a particular type of thing is the number of people who want to buy it, or the area of the world in which it is sold.

> The foreign *market* was increasingly crucial.
> …the Russian *market* for personal computers.

2 N-SING

The **market** refers to the total amount of a product that is sold each year, especially when you are talking about the competition between the companies who sell that product.

> The two big companies control 72% of the *market*.
> Ben & Jerry's conquered the *market* and in a few years owned their own giant corporation.
> The actions of a country's competition authority can affect foreign companies' ability to enter its *market*.

Common Collocations
to *enter* a market   an *emerging* market

market economy (market economies) N-COUNT
market forces N-PLURAL

If you talk about a **market economy**, you are referring to an economic system in which the prices of things depend on how many are available and how many people want to buy them, rather than prices being fixed by governments. If you talk about **market forces**, you mean the economic factors that affect the availability of goods and the demand for them, without any help or control by governments.

> Their ultimate aim was a *market economy* for Hungary.
> …opening the economy to *market forces* and increasing the role of private enterprise.

market conditions N-PLURAL

Market conditions are the economic situation that exists within a market, especially the stock market.

> Investors need every bit of wile and guile they can acquire to perform well in these *market conditions*.

marketplace (marketplaces) N-COUNT
market sector (market sectors) N-COUNT

The **marketplace** refers to the activity of buying and selling products. A **market sector** is one part of a market, consisting of related products or services.

> It's our hope that we will play an increasingly greater role in the *marketplace* and, therefore, supply more jobs.
> It achieved this growth by identifying a *market sector*, and moving quickly to become the market leader in that sector.

segment (segments, segmenting, segmented)

1 N-COUNT

A **segment** of a market is one part of it, considered separately from the rest.

> Three-to-five day cruises are the fastest-growing *segment* of the market.
> Women's tennis is the market leader in a growing market *segment* – women's sports.

2 VERB

If a company **segments** a market, it divides it into separate parts, usually in order to improve marketing opportunities.

> The big six record companies are multinational, and thus can *segment* the world market into national ones.
> Perhaps the greatest value of this approach is that it is capable of generating new ways of *segmenting* the market.

market segmentation N-UNCOUNT

Market segmentation is the division of a market into separate parts.

> …increasing *market segmentation*, with specialist builders constructing dwellings aimed at the young singles market and elderly persons.

market share (market shares) N-VAR

A company's **market share** in a product is the proportion of the total sales of that product that is produced by that company in relation to other companies.

> Ford has been gaining *market share* this year at the expense of GM and some Japanese car manufacturers.
> Littlewoods, which is one of Liverpool's major employers, is being hit too by loss of *market share* in its mail-order business.

Common Collocations
to *lose* market share   to *gain* market share
to *increase* market share   to *grab* market share

market entry N-UNCOUNT

A company's **market entry** is its entry into a market where it has not done business before.

> Digital delivery will certainly lower the cost of *market entry*.

PRACTISE YOUR VOCABULARY

1 Use the terms in the box to complete the paragraph.

market forces   marketplace   segment   market share   market segmentation   market economy   market

A _____ for a product is the people or organizations who buy it, or an area where it is sold. A
_____ is one where things are bought and sold freely and not under government control. In a market
economy, prices are decided by _____, the factors that influence the demand for things, their availability,
and consequently their price. _____ means the same as market. A market sector or _____
is part of a larger market, and 'segment' is also used to refer to a particular category of customer. When companies try to
identify specific groups of customers they talk about segmenting the market or _____. The proportion of
sales that a company or product has in a particular market is the _____.

2 Use one of the word pairs with the word 'market' to complete the sentences.

```
        economy
                    entry
forces
                  conditions
place      market
                    sector
segmentation
          share
```

a _____ are the 'laws' of supply and demand that determine price and quantity bought and sold in a
market.
b In the soft drinks market, Cool-Cola have the biggest _____ in many regions of the world.
c Many companies use _____ to classify their customers by shared characteristics such as age or income.
d The factors that affect the performance of the market are the _____.
e A _____, or a free market economy, is a method of organizing the economy to produce goods and
services.
f When a new company joins the market this is known as _____.
g A _____ is part of a larger market.
h The _____ is the activity of buying and selling products or services.

3 Which of the following are characteristics of a market economy?

a government control of manufacturing industry
b profit
c floating prices
d fixed wages and salaries
e private ownership of industry
f high levels of state regulation
g fixed exchange rates

4 Match what the people say to the descriptions on the right.

Pat – 'Our company is selling proportionally less than we were last year. Our main competitor has launched very successful new products and is selling much more.'	**a** He's talking about market segmentation.
Jordan – 'We focus the products our shops stock on the general population type that live in the area, different areas have different groups living there and we stock according to this factor.'	**b** He's talking about market share.

● **service industry** (service industries) N-COUNT
tertiary industry (tertiary industries) N-VAR

A **service industry** or **tertiary industry** is an industry such as banking or insurance that provides a service, but does not produce anything.

> Although shops and <u>service industries</u> are doing reasonably well, manufacturing output is falling.
> Loans to <u>tertiary industry</u> grew by $171 million over the year.

● **supplier** (suppliers) N-COUNT

A **supplier** is a person, company, or organization that sells or supplies something such as goods or equipment to customers.

> …Hillsdown Holdings, one of the UK's biggest food <u>suppliers</u>.
> Japan is Asia's dominant <u>supplier</u> of imports and technology.

Common Collocations

a <u>leading</u> supplier	a <u>major</u> supplier
a <u>sole</u> supplier	a <u>preferred</u> supplier

● **supplier partnership** (supplier partnerships) N-COUNT

A **supplier partnership** is a relationship between a company and a supplier.

> …the practical implementation of <u>supplier partnerships</u> in manufacturing industry.
> Villadsen is responsible for reducing manufacturing cycle time, strengthening <u>supplier partnerships</u>, overseeing quality assurance and streamlining purchasing procedures.

● **supplier base** N-SING

A company's **supplier base** consists of all the companies that are its suppliers, considered as a group.

> Most retailers have narrowed their <u>supplier base</u> over the past decade, though Marks and Spencer, for example, is careful to maintain a spread of competing suppliers for its products.
> We needed to dramatically reduce our <u>supplier base</u>.

● **outsource** (outsources, outsourcing, outsourced) VERB
outsourcing N-UNCOUNT

If a company **outsources** goods or services, it pays workers from outside the company to supply the goods or provide the services. **Outsourcing** is the use of outside companies to supply goods or services.

> Increasingly, corporate clients are seeking to <u>outsource</u> the management of their facilities.
> The difficulties of <u>outsourcing</u> have been compounded by the increasing resistance of trade unions.

● **service business** (service businesses) N-COUNT
service organization (service organizations) N-COUNT

A **service business** or **service organization** is a business or an organization that provides a service but does not produce anything.

> Still more significant was the formal announcement on June 25th that <u>service businesses</u> such as retailing, transport and banking will be opened to foreign investors.
> …<u>service organizations</u> that deliver repeated services of a common kind, such as car-hire businesses, transport firms, restaurants and so on.

● **virtual company** (virtual companies) N-COUNT

A **virtual company** is a company which outsources all of its activities, and which uses IT to communicate with clients or customers.

> It is a <u>virtual company</u>, outsourcing everything from manufacture to logistics and sales.
> One reason it is so competitive is that it has established itself as a <u>virtual company</u>, buying in all distribution and other services from outside suppliers, rather than operating its own facilities.

➲ **IT**: Topic 1.1; **virtual integration**: Topic 1.1; **service sector**: Topic 2.2; **lean production**: Topic 5.1; **JIT manufacturing**: Topic 5.1; **customer base**: Topic 11.2; **service**: Topic 12.3; **service provider**: Topic 12.3

PRACTISE YOUR VOCABULARY

1 Read the text and answer the questions.

> In an attempt to cope with the demands of a changing market, many companies are attempting to make themselves more flexible. To do this they are adopting new production methods, such as lean production methods and JIT manufacturing. For JIT manufacturing to be successful a company must have reliable suppliers. Suppliers are businesses that provide resources that allow other companies to produce goods and services. Companies are making greater use of outsourcing, or forming supplier partnerships to supply components and carry out some of the company's processes, leaving the company free to focus on its core areas. Outsourcing requires quick and effective communication with suppliers and workers, and a high degree of co-operation. Other companies join together in short-term collaborations, using IT to communicate. They are known as virtual companies, and have outsourced all of their activities. Their supplier base is far greater than that of a more traditional company.

Are the sentences true or false?

	True	False
a Suppliers produce goods or services which the public buy.	☐	☐
b Supplier partnerships result in the company employing fewer people.	☐	☐
c Virtual companies use modern technology and outsourcing to be efficient.	☐	☐
d A company's supplier base is its warehouse.	☐	☐

2 Look at the chart and answer the questions.

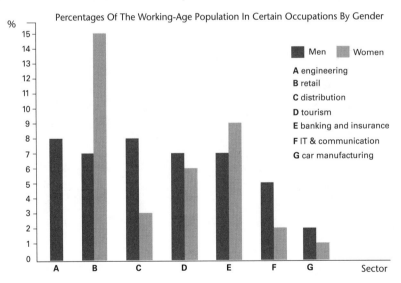

Percentages Of The Working-Age Population In Certain Occupations By Gender

■ Men ▨ Women

A engineering
B retail
C distribution
D tourism
E banking and insurance
F IT & communication
G car manufacturing

a Which service industry employs the most men?

b Which service industry employs the most women?

c Which manufacturing industry employs the most people?

d Does manufacturing employ more men or more women?

e What is the total percentage of men in manufacturing?

f What is the total percentage of men in the service sector?

g What is the total percentage of women in manufacturing?

h What is the total percentage of women in the service sector?

3 Match each of the four service businesses to the products they get from suppliers.

a HairLight hairdressers	**i** tools, plants and pesticides
b Rococo Chanel's Garden Design	**ii** computer software, printers
c Clean Up Office Cleaners	**iii** shampoo and hair products
d Glen's Graphic Designers	**iv** detergents, overalls, dusters

● **service** (services)

① N-COUNT

If an organization or company provides a particular **service**, they can do a particular job or a type of work for you.

> The kitchen maintains a twenty-four hour _service_ and can be contacted via Reception.
> Iberia's main objective is to provide an excellent _service_ to its customers.

② N-UNCOUNT

The level or standard of **service** provided by an organization or company is the amount or quality of the work it can do for you.

> First Technology is proud of its commitment to excellence and its high standard of _service_.
> The current level of _service_ will be maintained except that the evening 'Network Express' trains will be withdrawn.

Common Collocations

to _provide_ a service
to _offer_ a service
a _mail-order_ service

● **services** N-PLURAL

Services are activities such as tourism, banking, and selling things which are part of a country's economy, but are not concerned with producing or manufacturing goods.

> In the 25 years to 1998, Scotland's _services_ sector grew by 2.2% a year.
> Mining rose by 9.1%, manufacturing by 9.4% and _services_ by 4.3%.

Common Collocations

goods and services
public services
financial services

● **customer service** N-UNCOUNT

Customer service refers to the way that companies behave towards their customers, for example how well they treat them.

> …a mail-order business with a strong reputation for _customer service_.
> The firm has an excellent _customer service_ department.

Common Collocations

to _provide_ customer service
to _improve_ customer service
a customer service _representative_
a customer service _centre_

● **service provider** (service providers) N-COUNT

A **service provider** is a company that provides a service, especially an Internet service.

> Just under 50 per cent of all home users switched to another _service provider_ last year, compared to 24 per cent of business users.

● **criterion** (criteria) N-COUNT

A **criterion** is a factor on which you judge or decide something.

> Location used to be the most important _criterion_ in buying petrol but people are showing a tendency to drive further and further for lower and lower prices.
> We believe our proposals do meet the BBC's core public service _criteria_ of distinctiveness and quality.

Common Collocations

selection criteria   _performance_ criteria
to _meet_ a criterion _for_ something
to _set_ a criterion _for_ something

● **consumer choice** N-UNCOUNT

Something that increases **consumer choice** increases the number of different products or services that are available for people to buy.

> Really, there ought to be _consumer choice_ operating here and the competitive pressures of the marketplace ought to be allowed to take effect.
> The experts say health service reform means higher taxes and less _consumer choice_.

➲ **service business**: Topic 12.2; **service industry**: Topic 12.2

PRACTISE YOUR VOCABULARY

1 **Use the terms in the box to complete the paragraph.**

service   services   customer service   service providers   service criteria

The service industry provides a range of _____, both to individuals and to other businesses. Successful companies in this sector know that there's a direct link between _____ and revenues, and understand the need to offer good _____. Consumers judge individual _____ on _____ such as friendliness of staff, quality of literature, flexibility, efficiency of response to telephone calls, letters and emails and competitiveness. If they receive shoddy service from a company, they often transfer their custom to another provider.

2 **Use each word pair to complete the sentences.**

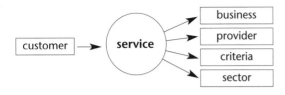

a Customers use _____ such as how knowledgeable the staff are to assess how good a company's customer service is.

b The _____ consists of companies which engage in activities which provide services.

c In a competitive market offering excellent _____ is just as important as having a good product.

d Banks, hairdressing salons and car-hire firms are all examples of _____es.

e A _____ is an organization which provides services either to the public or to other businesses.

3 **Which of the following refer to providing a service and which refer to the services sector?**

a 'I always go back to that company because the staff are so knowledgeable and helpful.'

b Industries like tourism now employ more people than mining and engineering.

c The sales representative was brilliant and really helped us to make a good decision.

d The arrival of foreign competition on the British high street has forced many long-established stores to re-evaluate the way they treat their customers.

e As these industries expand, consumer choice is increasing.

4 **Read the text and answer the questions.**

Women will make up 50% of business travellers within 5 years, but British hotels are still unsure how to treat them. A survey of hotel guests and owners shows some improvements such as well-lit parking spaces close to the main entrance exclusively for women.

a Do women account for a significant share of the business travel market?

b Why do you think hotels offer reserved parking spaces to women guests?

● leisure revolution N-SING

People sometimes refer to the recent increase in tourism and other leisure-time activities as the **leisure revolution**.

By 1970 the canal was ready to play its part in the new <u>leisure revolution</u> that was giving canals an unexpected lease of life.
The BBC has been slow to respond to the <u>leisure revolution</u>, relying on tried and tested subjects like cooking and gardening.

● work-life balance N-UNCOUNT

Your **work-life balance** is how you organize your days, for example, how many hours you spend at work, and how much time you spend with friends and family or doing things you enjoy.

Young people, in particular, expect <u>work-life balance</u>.
Middle-ranking and senior managers unanimously stipulated <u>work-life balance</u> as their main criterion when choosing jobs.

● social chapter N-SING

The **social chapter** is an agreement between countries in the European Union concerning workers' rights and working conditions.

Britain's rejection of the <u>social chapter</u> of the Maastricht treaty preserves employers' freedom from over-regulation and under-flexibility of labour.
...the 11 governments which signed the <u>social chapter</u>.

● body (bodies) N-COUNT

A **body** is an organized group of people who deal with something officially.

...the Chairman of the policemen's representative <u>body</u>, the Police Federation.
...the main trade union <u>body</u>, COSATU, Congress of South African Trade Unions.

> #### Common Collocations
> a <u>review</u> body   a <u>regulatory</u> body
> an <u>independent</u> body

● public sector N-SING

The **public sector** is the part of a country's economy which is controlled or supported financially by the government.

...Carlos Menem's policy of reducing the <u>public sector</u> and opening up the economy to free-market forces.
Questions were raised about whether a <u>public sector</u> body should have been investing taxpayers' money in this way.

> #### Common Collocations
> a public sector <u>worker</u>   public sector <u>pay</u>
> public sector <u>borrowing</u>   a public sector <u>union</u>
> a public sector <u>employee</u>   a public sector <u>organization</u>

● trade association (trade associations) N-COUNT

A **trade association** is a body representing organizations within the same trade. It aims to protect their collective interests, especially in negotiations with governments and trade unions.

...one of the two main <u>trade associations</u> for antiques dealers.
...a comprehensive list of <u>trade associations</u> covering home energy efficiency.

● core sector (core sectors) N-COUNT

The **core sectors** of a company or industry are the most important or most profitable areas of its activity.

In the UK it could be argued that we have neglected production as a <u>core sector</u>, subsequently losing in world trade terms to Germany, Japan, Korea.
Hagstrom believes that Buffett's <u>core sectors</u> – advertising, consumer products, financial services, healthcare and media – have the scope to out-perform the S&P 500 in forthcoming years.

● service quality N-UNCOUNT

Service quality is the level or standard of service provided by an organization or company.

Improvements in efficiency and in <u>service quality</u> may well require substantial changes.
To ensure security for our customers and staff, and to help maintain <u>service quality</u>, phone calls may be recorded.

➲ **market share**: Topic 12.1; **service industry**: Topic 12.2; **service**: Topic 12.3

PRACTISE YOUR VOCABULARY

1 Use the terms in the box to complete the paragraph about the international tourism industry.

| service quality | core sectors | leisure revolution |

Tourism is often called the 'world's biggest industry', and many people view growth in this sector as part of the so-called
_____. The suppliers of travel services include many firms that operate in the _____ of the
tourism industry, including hotels, transport companies and destination marketing organizations. In the global marketplace,
south Asia, the Pacific Rim and the Americas are gaining market share of international tourist arrivals and Europe's share is
steadily declining. Improvements to _____ may help to reverse this trend.

2 Put each of the bodies (a–i) under the correct heading in the table below.

   a World Tourism Organization   **f** local tourist associations
   b national tourism organizations (NTOs)   **g** British Airways
   c European Union (EU)   **h** International Air Transport Association (IATA)
   d Holiday Inn International   **i** Hertz Car Rental
   e Pacific-Asia Travel Association

Public sector bodies	Trade associations	Companies

3 Match each of the newspaper headlines with an extract from the appropriate story.

  a | **Service sector trade associations use their collective strength**   **b** | **Work-life balance worst in Europe**   **c** | **Social chapter increases workers' rights**

   i Amongst the benefits for working people will be a guaranteed holiday entitlement and a limit to the length of the
      working week.
  ii ...especially in the leisure industry, where employment has increased dramatically. These groups are increasingly able to
      put pressure on the government.
 iii Statistics show that new technology has not freed us from work as we now have the longest average working week and
      it is increasing not shrinking.

● **financial service** (financial services) N-COUNT
financial product (financial products) N-COUNT

A company or organization that provides **financial services** is able to help you do things such as make investments or buy a pension or mortgage. A **financial product** is something such as an investment, a pension, or a mortgage.

> ...voluntary organisations that provide independent advice to consumers on <u>financial services</u>.
> ...<u>financial service</u> companies.
> Sites such as moneyextra allow consumers to compare <u>financial products</u>, such as car insurance, from several different companies.

● **financial services provider** (financial services providers) N-COUNT

A **financial services provider** is a company or organization that offers financial services.

> ...one of the fastest-growing <u>financial services providers</u> in the country.

● **financial consultant** (financial consultants) N-COUNT
financial adviser (financial advisers) N-COUNT

A **financial consultant** or **financial adviser** is someone whose job is to advise people about financial products and services.

> They have agreed to provide the services of a qualified <u>financial consultant</u> to help you analyse your current investment, pension, mortgage and insurance needs.
> ...an independent <u>financial adviser</u>.

● **cashpoint** (cashpoints) N-COUNT

A **cashpoint** is a machine built into the wall of a bank or other building, which allows people to take out money from their bank account using a special card. [BRIT]

> Chris couldn't find a <u>cashpoint</u> to get the money for a taxi home.
> You are issued with a personal identification number that allows you to withdraw money from more than 400,000 <u>cashpoint</u> machines worldwide.

> ### Common Collocations
> a cashpoint <u>card</u>　　　a cashpoint <u>network</u>
> a cashpoint <u>machine</u>

● **telephone banking** N-UNCOUNT

Telephone banking is banking services that are available to customers over the telephone.

> One reason for the relatively slow adoption of online banking is that it is not yet much more convenient than <u>telephone banking</u>.

● **electronic trading** N-UNCOUNT
online banking N-UNCOUNT

Electronic trading is the buying or selling or stocks and shares by means of the Internet. **Online banking** is banking services that are available to customers by means of the Internet.

> <u>Electronic trading</u> is cheaper than traditional floor trading.
> Two of the world's biggest investment banks have teamed up with a rival of the New York Stock Exchange to offer a new <u>electronic trading</u> system.
> This move to <u>online banking</u> has been partly driven by the move to flexible working.

● **personal banking** N-UNCOUNT

Personal banking is the part of a bank's activities that is concerned with bank accounts belonging to individual customers rather than to businesses.

> What they don't understand is that consumers who use PCs for <u>personal banking</u> today used to be those institutions' most profitable customers.
> Services are confined to a range of <u>personal banking</u> products, such as mortgages.

● **call centre** (call centres) N-COUNT

A **call centre** is an office where people work answering or making telephone calls for a particular company.

> I phoned Dell's <u>call centre</u> and spoke to an operator, who patiently answered some of my queries.
> Andrew is one of 204,000 <u>call-centre</u> employees in Britain.

PRACTISE YOUR VOCABULARY

1 Use the terms in the box to complete the paragraph.

> cashpoints   personal banking   call centres   telephone banking   financial services
> financial services providers   online banking

New technology is widely used in _____, and the personal relationship that customers used to have with

their bank manager has been replaced by _____ and _____, for example, as well as the

use of _____ to withdraw money without ever going into the bank. Banks, and other companies which

provide _____ often use _____ to handle enquiries from customers. These anonymous

centres are often unpopular with callers who do not feel they are treated like valued individual customers.

_____ are now attempting to re-establish a 'personal' service using customer data stored on their

computers.

2 Which word is missing from these three word pairs? Complete the sentences using the word pairs.

a _____ services   _____ services providers   _____ adviser

b i A _____ is an investment consultant who may operate independently or be the representative of a
   particular company.

  ii Most banks offer a range of _____ including mortgages, loans and investment advice.

  iii Examples of _____ include banks, insurance companies, investment companies and financial advisers.

3 Match the comments to the service they are talking about.

Alex "I love it because it means I can do all my banking when I'm at work and no one knows that I'm not working." ☐

Benny "I always use them, it's better than queuing up for ages at the counter just to get some cash and they're there when the bank is closed, too." ☐

Carl "I can't stand them. It's so impersonal." ☐

Derek "It's really convenient. I do all my banking in this way. A quick call is all it takes." ☐

Edward "It's great to get advice from somebody who doesn't get commission on a sale – someone really neutral." ☐

Paul "I've made money on my share investments, all on my PC, from the comfort of my own home." ☐

a He's talking about cashpoints.
b He's talking about telephone banking.
c He's talking about online banking.
d He's talking about financial consultants.
e He's talking about call centres.
f He's talking about electronic trading.

Topic 13

MANAGERS

● **senior** ADJ

The **senior** people in an organization or profession have the highest and most important jobs.

> *Each group presents its findings to senior managers.*
> *…the company's senior management.*

● **executive** (executives)

[1] N-COUNT

An **executive** is someone who is employed by business at a senior level. Executives decide what the business should do, and ensure that it is done.

> *Several top executives subsequently resigned.*
> *…an advertising executive.*

[2] ADJ

The **executive** sections and tasks of an organization are concerned with the making of decisions and with ensuring that decisions are carried out.

> *A successful job search needs to be as well organised as any other executive task.*
> *I don't envisage I will take an executive role, but rather become a consultant on merchandise and marketing.*

Common Collocations	
an executive director	an executive officer
an executive chairman	an executive committee

● **non-executive** ADJ

Someone who has a **non-executive** position in a company or organization gives advice but is not responsible for making decisions or ensuring that decisions are carried out.

> *Mr Margetts is a non-executive director of Anglo American.*
> *The issue became whether he should leave altogether or remain as chairman in a non-executive role.*

Common Collocations	
a non-executive director	a non-executive officer
a non-executive chairman	a non-executive committee

● **director** (directors) N-COUNT

The **directors** of a company are its most senior managers, who meet regularly to make important decisions about how it will be run.

> *…Karl Uggerholt, the financial director of Braun UK.*
> *There were two female directors employed at the station.*

● **board of directors** (boards of directors) N-COUNT
board (boards) N-COUNT

A company's **board of directors** is the group of people elected by its shareholders to manage the company. The **board** of a company or organization is the group of people who control it and direct it.

> *The Board of Directors has approved the decision unanimously.*
> *He wants her to put it before the board at a special meeting.*
> *…the agenda for the September 12 board meeting.*

● **company secretary** (company secretaries) N-COUNT

A **company secretary** is a person whose job within a company is to keep the legal affairs, accounts, and administration in order.

> *…David Jackson, company secretary of Powergen.*

● **chairman** (chairmen) N-COUNT
chairwoman (chairwomen) N-COUNT
chairperson (chairpersons) N-COUNT
chair (chairs) N-COUNT

[1] The **chairman** of a company is the head of it.

> *I had done business with the company's chairman.*

[2] The **chairman**, **chairwoman**, **chairperson** or **chair** of a meeting, committee, or organization is the person in charge of it.

> *The chairman declared the meeting open.*
> *I hear you, Mr. Chairman.*
> *Primakov was in Japan meeting with the chairwoman of the Socialist Party there.*
> *As chairperson and party president, she'll be in charge.*
> *She is the chair of the Committee on Women in the Military.*

● **managing director** (managing directors) N-COUNT
MD (MDs) N-COUNT

The **managing director** of a company is the most important working director, and is in charge of the way the company is managed. The abbreviation **MD** is also used.

> *…Nick Webb, managing director of Simon & Schuster UK.*
> *He's going to be the MD of the Park Lane company.*

● **chief executive officer** (chief executive officers) N-COUNT
CEO (CEOs) N-COUNT

The **chief executive officer** of a company is the person who has overall responsibility for the management of that company. The abbreviation **CEO** is often used.

> *Dr Fredrik C Verkroost has been appointed chief executive officer of the Domain Dynamics Group.*
> *…Geoffrey Paterson, CEO of Teamphone.*

● **annual general meeting** (annual general meetings) N-COUNT
AGM (AGMs) ABBREVIATION

The **annual general meeting** of a company or organization is a meeting which it holds once a year in order to discuss the previous year's activities and accounts. The abbreviation **AGM** is also used.

> *The club has its annual general meeting at the end of this month.*
> *The CCBA is holding its AGM at 3pm on January 8.*

➲ **limited company**: Topic 2.4; **shareholder**: Topic 7.2

PRACTISE YOUR VOCABULARY

1 The diagram shows who controls a public limited company. Use the terms in the box to complete it.

| board of directors   managers   shareholders |

a _____ (owners of the company)

↓

b _____ (responsible to the shareholders)

↓

c _____ (appointed by the board to run the company)

2 Use the terms in the box to complete the paragraph.

| board of directors   board   senior executives   chief executive officer   managing director   company secretary   chair |

People at the head of an organization are _____ or senior managers. The _____ is the

person who has overall responsibility for the day-to-day running of an organization. In the case of a limited company the

CEO is normally the _____, appointed by the _____ on the authority of its members. The

same person is usually the _____ of meetings of the _____, i.e. the people who are legally

responsible for a company. The person responsible for keeping the minutes of board meetings is the

_____.

3 Which of the following people are likely to be on the board of directors of a company?

a company secretary   c CEO   e executive directors
b non-executive directors   d managers   f members of staff

4 Match each of the roles (i–iv) to the correct definition (a–d).

i *director*   ii *executive director*   iii *non-executive director*   iv *board of directors*

a A company director with a seat on the board who is also a salaried employee of the company, and actively involved in
the running of the company.

b A director with a seat on the board who is not a working employee of the company, sometimes brought onto the board
for his or her specialist knowledge. He or she takes no part in the running of the company.

c The management committee of a limited company, the members of which are appointed by the shareholders whose
interests they represent. They meet under the company chairman to decide on major policy matters and the
appointment of key managers.

d A person who is appointed an elected officer of the company at the annual general meeting (AGM) and manages the
company on behalf of the shareholders. He or she acts by resolutions made at meetings of the board.

● **management style** (management styles)

N-COUNT

● **management ability** (management abilities)

N-COUNT

A person's **management style** or **management ability** is the way they behave as a manager or the qualities they have as a manager.

Ware became increasingly unhappy at the new <u>management style</u> and he left to join Dunlop.
The only hard questions directed at the group concerned its poor <u>management ability</u>.
At Courtaulds Textiles, Martin Taylor has demonstrated outstanding <u>management abilities</u>.

● **hierarchy** (hierarchies) N-VAR

A **hierarchy** is a system of organizing people into different ranks or levels of importance, for example in society or in a company.

Like most other American companies with a rigid <u>hierarchy</u>, workers and managers had strictly defined duties.
...those lower down the management <u>hierarchy</u>.

Common Collocations

<u>corporate</u> hierarchy   a <u>strict</u> hierarchy
a <u>rigid</u> hierarchy

● **collective** ADJ

Collective actions, situations, or feelings involve or are shared by every member of a group of people.

It was a <u>collective</u> decision.
...a more <u>collective</u> style of leadership.

● **decision-making** N-UNCOUNT

Decision-making is the process of reaching decisions, especially in a large organization or in government.

Much of the pioneering work was based on <u>decision-making</u> models borrowed from the social sciences.
She wants to see more women involved in <u>decision making</u>.

● **crisis management** N-UNCOUNT

People use **crisis management** to refer to a management style that concentrates on solving the immediate problems occurring in a business rather than looking for long-term solutions.

Today's NSC is overcome, through no fault of its own, by day-to-day <u>crisis management</u>.
...a <u>crisis-management</u> team.

● **change management** N-UNCOUNT

Change management is a style of management that aims to encourage organizations and individuals to deal effectively with the changes taking place in their work.

She is hoping to go into <u>change management</u> or IT management when she graduates.
A key part of <u>change management</u> is making sure the right information is available for people to make informed choices.

● **leader** (leaders) N-COUNT

The **leader** of a group of people or an organization is the person who is in control of it or in charge of it.

...the <u>leader</u> of a great marketing team.
But he never won much praise as a manager, nor as a team <u>leader</u>.

● **autocratic** ADJ
● **democratic** ADJ
● **laissez-faire** ADJ

An **autocratic** person or organization has complete power and makes decisions without asking anyone else's advice. Something that is **democratic** is based on the idea that everyone should have equal rights and should be involved in making important decisions. A **laissez-faire** style or approach is based on the idea that people should be allowed to make decisions themselves, without interference from those in authority.

Weston's <u>autocratic</u> style at the family firm had its critics.
NBBJ also prides itself on an open and <u>democratic</u> management culture.
He's quite <u>democratic</u> in that he'll listen to ideas from anybody really.
"Technically, we have <u>laissez-faire</u> management," says Droege. "We all talk a lot over the Internet about what we might do."

● **subordinate** (subordinates) N-COUNT

If someone is your **subordinate**, they have a less important position than you in the organization that you both work for.

Haig tended not to seek guidance from <u>subordinates</u>.
Nearly all her <u>subordinates</u> adored her.

● **delegate** (delegates, delegating, delegated) VERB
● **delegation** N-UNCOUNT

If you **delegate** duties, responsibilities, or power to someone, you give them those duties, those responsibilities, or that power so that they can act on your behalf. The **delegation** of responsibility is the act of giving the responsibility for something to another person.

He talks of travelling less, and <u>delegating</u> more authority to his deputies in Britain and Australia.
Many employers find it hard to <u>delegate</u>.
A key factor in running a business is the <u>delegation</u> of responsibility.

➲ **staff**: Topic 13.4; **entrepreneur**: Topic 13.5; **entrepreneurial**: Topic 13.5

PRACTISE YOUR VOCABULARY

1 Put these four terms into the correct place in the table:

a laissez-faire   **b** democratic   **c** autocratic

management style	method
i	Leader makes decisions. Others are informed and carry them out.
ii	Leader discusses with others before the decision is made. The group can influence the decision that is made.
iii	There is no formal structure to make decisions. The leader does not force his or her views on others.

2 Choose the correct answer to each question.

a If management delegate responsibility, to whom is it given?

i superiors   **ii** subordinates   **iii** no one

b Which of the following is least likely to delegate responsibility?

i an autocratic leader   **ii** a democratic leader   **iii** a laissez-faire leader

c Which of these leaders is most likely to develop a strong hierarchy?

i an autocratic leader   **ii** a democratic leader   **iii** a laissez-faire leader

d Which of these leaders is most likely to involve staff in collective decision-making?

i an autocratic leader   **ii** a democratic leader   **iii** a laissez-faire leader

e Which of these leaders is most likely to leave decision-making to individual members of staff?

i an autocratic leader   **ii** a democratic leader   **iii** a laissez-faire leader

3 Which book would be useful for each of these people?

| a **Democratic Management: You Can Reap the Rewards** | b **Delegate: The Way to Clear Your Desk and Your Head** | c **Crisis Management Systems: Planning to Cope** | d **Change Management: The Manager's Handbook for Interesting Times** |

Bob 'There are lots of new developments in our field. We need to be prepared to cope with their effect on our firm.'

Ian 'My boss finds it very hard to accept ideas. I need to convince her that this can be good for the firm.'

Sally 'I'm always worrying that something might go wrong at the factory, or with our delivery system. What would happen if it did?'

Geoff 'I'm simply overloaded. I spend all day making decisions and meeting all kinds of people so I never have any time to actually manage the firm.'

4 Read the text about management ability and answer the questions.

> In a competitive environment being able to cope with change is very important. A good leader needs to know what direction the company should be going in and be able to lead it through change. They need to plan how to achieve their goals and be able to persuade others that their decisions are the right ones. A person with management ability will be able to do all of these things and be able to motivate their staff.

a The text lists five management abilities. What are they?

b Can you add any other management abilities that you think are important?

● **corporate culture** (corporate cultures) N-COUNT
organizational culture (organizational cultures) N-COUNT

A **corporate culture** or **organizational culture** is the set of values and attitudes within a company or organization that influences the general behaviour of its employees, for example how efficient or friendly they are.

> *Passion, freedom and autonomy are all part of French <u>corporate culture</u>.*
> *The entire <u>organizational culture</u> must be prepared to change by embracing diversity.*

● **bureaucratic culture** (bureaucratic cultures) N-COUNT
performance culture (performance cultures) N-COUNT

If you talk about the **bureaucratic culture** in a workplace, you mean that there is a lot of emphasis on complicated rules and procedures. If you talk about a **performance culture**, you mean that the emphasis is on being successful and achieving results.

> *Devine admits GM's <u>bureaucratic culture</u> is a problem.*
> *Keith Brookes, an assistant secretary at Bifu, said that the group's <u>performance culture</u> is putting intense pressure on staff.*

● **facilitate** (facilitates, facilitating, facilitated) VERB

To **facilitate** an action or process, especially one that you would like to happen, means to make it easier or more likely to happen.

> *The new airport will <u>facilitate</u> the development of tourism.*
> *He argued that the economic recovery had been <u>facilitated</u> by his tough stance.*

● **dress code** (dress codes) N-COUNT

The **dress code** in a workplace is the rules about what kind of clothes employees are allowed to wear there.

> *Three months ago the Boots Company relaxed its <u>dress code</u> in certain areas of its business.*

> ### Common Collocations
> a <u>strict</u> dress code   a <u>relaxed</u> dress code
> to <u>adhere to</u> a dress code

● **dress-down Friday** (dress-down Fridays) N-COUNT

In some companies employees are allowed to wear clothes that are less smart than usual on Fridays. This day is known as a **dress-down Friday**.

> *But is it really feasible to don sportswear to the office without the excuse of <u>dress-down-Friday</u>?*

● **hot-desking** N-UNCOUNT
hot-desk (hot-desks, hot-desking, hot-desked) VERB

Hot-desking is the practice of not assigning particular desks to particular employees in a workplace, so that employees can work at any desk that is available. If an employee works in this way, you can say that they **hot-desk**.

> *I think that very few employees prefer <u>hot-desking</u> to having a fixed desk.*
> *…a sales manager who worked from the car between <u>hot-desking</u> in offices in Bristol, Birmingham and London.*

● **empower** (empowers, empowering, empowered) VERB
empowerment N-UNCOUNT

To **empower** someone means to give them the means to achieve something, for example to become stronger or more successful. The **empowerment** of a person or group of people is the process of giving them power and status in a particular situation.

> *<u>Empowering</u> the underprivileged lies in assuring them that education holds the real source of power.*
> *The new law <u>empowers</u> people to challenge wrongdoing in the workplace.*
> *This government believes very strongly in the <u>empowerment</u> of women.*
> *Phil is committed to employee <u>empowerment</u> and enlightened management.*

➲ **corporate**: Topic 2.1; **corporate values**: Topic 11.4

PRACTISE YOUR VOCABULARY

1 One of the word pairs refers to an organization's beliefs and values, and the other three word pairs are examples. Which are which?

bureaucratic culture   facilitating culture   organizational culture   performance culture

2 Choose the correct answer:

a If a company pursues a policy of empowerment, who is empowered?
   i staff/workers   **ii** customers   **iii** suppliers

b If a company has a dress code, how will staff normally be expected to appear?
   i casual   **ii** smart   **iii** however they like

c If a company introduces 'dress-down Friday', how will staff be expected to appear on Fridays?
   i in fancy dress   **ii** casual   **ii** smart

d If a company expects its staff to hot-desk, will they
   i always have the same desk   **ii** find a desk on arrival at work   **iii** never have a desk

3 Another way of describing corporate cultures is by looking at the solidarity and sociability in an organization. Sociability is the relationship between individuals who see each other as friends. Solidarity describes cooperation between individuals which takes place when the need arises or when there is a shared interest.

Read the information in the table and decide which one of the four types of organization would most suit each of the following people:

a Steven is a journalist and spends most of his time at work in front of a computer screen.

b Gail is very task-orientated. She thinks that the only thing that really matters at work is getting results.

c Mary enjoys feeling that she really fits in at work. She wants to be liked and to feel proud of the company she works for. She greatly admires her boss.

d Rupert thinks it is important to enjoy his work, and most of his friends are work colleagues. He is keen on business lunches, and is often out of the office in the afternoons.

Type of Organization	Sociability/ Solidarity	Features of the Culture	Associated Problems
Networked organization	High sociability/ low solidarity	Teamwork, creativity, openness. Workers enjoy working.	Discipline difficult due to friendships. Productivity may suffer.
Mercenary organization	Low sociability/ high solidarity	Clearly defined roles, getting things done, setting targets. Business has strong focus and can respond to threats.	Workers only work together if they have to. As roles are clearly defined, there may be conflict over 'grey' areas of work.
Fragmented organization	Low sociability/ low solidarity	Form of culture best suited to organizations where individuals do not need to work together e.g. law firms.	
Communal organization	High solidarity/ high sociability	Similar to networked businesses but more goal-orientated (though less mercenary than mercenary organizations). Concerned with shared values. Leaders guide the business.	Shared goals may stifle individual creativity. Need to recruit those who fit in with the culture of the business.

● **human resource management** N-UNCOUNT
  HRM ABBREVIATION

Human resource management is the work within a company that involves the recruitment, training and welfare of staff. The abbreviation **HRM** is also used.

> *Before this time supervisors handled nearly all aspects of human resource management.*
> *...areas in which HRM can demonstrate measurable cost savings.*

● **human resources** N-UNCOUNT
  HR ABBREVIATION

Human resources is the department in a company or organization that deals with employees, keeps their records, and helps with any problems they might have. The abbreviation **HR** is also used.

> *RAM has also appointed Mark Molloy from Gartmore as head of human resources.*
> *We are a small firm so there is no HR department for me to go to.*

● **human resource planning** N-UNCOUNT
  HRP ABBREVIATION

Human resource planning is the work within a company that involves identifying the future employment needs of the company and recruiting the staff to meet those needs. The abbreviation **HRP** is also used.

> *Finally, a realistic understanding of current workforce capabilities is essential for effective human resource planning.*
> *Since HRP was instituted, vacancies at this level have been reduced by roughly 50 percent.*

● **staff** (staffs)

⒈ N-COUNT-COLL
The **staff** of an organization are the people who work for it.

> *The staff were very good.*
> *The outpatient program has a staff of six people.*
> *...members of staff.*
> *Many employers seek diversity in their staffs.*

⒉ N-PLURAL
People who are part of a particular staff are often referred to as **staff**.

> *10 staff were allocated to the task.*
> *He had the complete support of hospital staff.*

● **personnel** N-PLURAL

The **personnel** of an organization are the people who work for it.

> *There has been very little renewal of personnel in higher education.*

● **workforce** (workforces) N-COUNT

The **workforce** is the total number of people in a country or region who are physically able to do a job and are available for work. The **workforce** is also the total number of people who are employed by a particular company.

> *...a country where half the workforce is unemployed.*
> *...an employer of a very large workforce.*

● **employee** (employees) N-COUNT

An **employee** is a person who is paid to work for an organization or for another person.

> *He is an employee of Fuji Bank.*
> *Many of its employees are women.*

● **line manager** (line managers) N-COUNT

Your **line manager** is the person at work who is in charge of your department, group, or project.

> *He claimed his line manager, a woman, had bullied him so relentlessly that the stress caused a mental breakdown.*
> *Mr Ezra was line manager to Mr Archer, 24.*

● **management philosophy** (management philosophies) N-COUNT

A company's **management philosophy** is the set of ideas it has about how the business should be run.

> *Second, Bertelsmann's management philosophy dictates that divisional chiefs should run their bits of the business independently.*
> *...alternative management philosophies that were intended to foster work-force commitment.*

● **theory X** N-UNCOUNT
  theory Y N-UNCOUNT

Theory X is the idea that employees work better when they are closely supervised and when their work is strictly controlled. **Theory Y** is the idea that employees work better when they are given responsibility for their own work and when their personal needs are satisfied.

> *Some managers certainly hold a Theory X point of view about some of the people in the business and a Theory Y point of view about the others.*

● **hierarchical** ADJ
  flat ADJ

A **hierarchical** system or organization is one in which people have different ranks or positions, depending on how important they are. Companies with a **flat** structure are organized in a less hierarchical way than traditional companies, with the aim of giving all employees a relatively equal status within the company.

> *They claim that the hierarchical structure of schools replicates the hierarchical structure of the workplace.*
> *The management structure remains flat rather than hierarchical to make everyone feel they have an important role to play.*

➲ **induction**: Topic 11.3; **organizational culture**: Topic 13.3; **recruit**: Topic 14.1; **wage**: Topic 14.2; **co-worker**: Topic 14.3

Managers – Human Resource Management

PRACTISE YOUR VOCABULARY

1 Put each of the words under the correct heading.

a employee   **b** staff   **c** worker   **d** workforce   **e** personnel

Individual in an organization	Collective term for people in an organization

2 Match each term to the correct definition.

a human resources   **b** human resource planning   **c** human resource management

i Deciding how to use a company's human resources most effectively.

ii The people employed in an organization, also known as personnel.

iii Deciding how many, and what type of workers are needed in the organization, and at what salary.

3 Which of the following does the HR department deal with?

a career development   **d** training   **g** discipline

b recruitment   **e** payments to suppliers

c wage negotiating   **f** induction

4 Which type of workplace relationship, shown by the diagrams, is most likely to include line managers?

HIERARCHICAL STRUCTURE   FLAT STRUCTURE

A ⟷ B ⟷ C ⟷ D

5 Theory X and theory Y are management philosophies which describe the reasons why people work, based on opposing views of people's motivation. Put the reasons into the correct place in the table.

a Workers can enjoy work.

b Workers are selfish, ignore the needs of organizations, avoid responsibility and lack ambition.

c Management should create a situation where workers can show creativity and apply their knowledge to the job.

d Workers are motivated by money.

Theory X	Theory Y
	Workers have many different needs which motivate them.
Workers are lazy and dislike work.	
	If motivated, workers can organize themselves and take responsibility.
Workers need to be controlled and directed by management.	

● **entrepreneur** (entrepreneurs) N-COUNT
entrepeneurial ADJ

An **entrepreneur** is a person who sets up businesses and business deals. **Entrepreneurial** means having the qualities that are needed to succeed as an entrepreneur.

…Martha Lane Fox, the 26-year-old entrepreneur who set up lastminute.com.
…her prodigious entrepreneurial flair.
We feel that we have the entrepreneurial skills to build a major business in this area.

> ### Common Collocations
> entrepreneurial spirit   entrepreneurial skills
> entrepreneurial culture   entrepreneurial activity

● **talent** (talents) N-VAR
flair N-SING

Talent is the natural ability to do something well. If you have a **flair** for a particular thing, you have a natural ability to do it well.

This is one of the few places where the talent for business has been allowed to blossom without hindrance.
He was an unusual man with great business talents coupled with deep political convictions.
He showed a flair for business when he was just six years old, selling juice for two cents a glass.
…a bid that would primarily have been about injecting new management flair into the organisation.

● **tycoon** (tycoons) N-COUNT

A **tycoon** is a person who is successful in business and so has become rich and powerful.

…a self-made Irish property tycoon.
The media tycoon had illegally shifted money out of his workers' pension funds to support his crumbling business empire before he died.

> ### Common Collocations
> a media tycoon   a property tycoon
> a business tycoon   a publishing tycoon

● **skill** (skills)

☐ N-COUNT
A **skill** is a type of work or activity which requires special training and knowledge.

…methods of developing the management skills needed to create the environment for innovation within a business.
Commercial, entrepreneurial and financial skills will need to be in place to implement any long term business strategies.
…when a person who has prided himself on a technical skill discovers that his job can be done better by a machine.

☐ N-UNCOUNT
Skill is the knowledge and ability that enables you to do something well.

Last year's IT installation problems raise questions about the quality and depth of management skill.

● **guru** (gurus) N-COUNT

A **guru** is a person who some people regard as an expert or leader.

He treasures the advice he was given by business guru Sir John Harvey-Jones.
Management gurus are among the most powerful opinion formers of the modern age.

> ### Common Collocations
> a design guru   an advertising guru
> an investment guru   a marketing guru

● **self-employed** ADJ

If you are **self-employed**, you organize your own work and taxes and are paid by people for a service you provide, rather than being paid a regular salary by a person or a firm.

There are no paid holidays or sick leave if you are self-employed.
…a self-employed builder.

● **multi-skilling** N-UNCOUNT
multi-skilled ADJ

Multi-skilling is the practice of training employees to do a number of different tasks. **Multi-skilled** employees have a number of different skills, enabling them to do more than one kind of work.

He said restructuring at the station would lead to increased multi-skilling among staff.
…the development of a more adaptable, multi-skilled workforce, capable of moving with the times.

● **run** (runs, running, ran, run) VERB

If you **run** a business, you are in charge of it or you organize it.

His stepfather ran a prosperous business.
…a well-run organization.

➲ **high-tech sector**: Topic 1.2; **small business**: Topic 2.1; **start-up**: Topic 2.3; **factors of production**: Topic 4.3

PRACTISE YOUR VOCABULARY

1 Use the terms in the box to complete the paragraph.

flair   run their own business   technical skills   self-employed   entrepreneur

An _____ is a person who owns and manages his or her own business. An individual might be able to see a gap in the market and exploit it more flexibly than a large company, and many people would like to _____. An individual hoping to start up a new company needs to have entrepreneurial _____ or talent, as well as good _____ and financial skills, because they make a profit through risk-taking or initiative. They are _____, and often work longer hours for less pay than they would if they were an employee of another company.

2 Re-order the sentences to make a paragraph with a logical sequence.

a The entrepreneur has no guarantee that this new business venture will be successful, and often invests his or her own savings in the business, meaning that the entrepreneur needs to be a risk taker.

b The entrepreneur's flair or talent ensures that the business becomes successful.

c An entrepreneur begins with an idea and then forms a new business.

d The new organization begins producing goods or services.

3 Are the sentences true or false?

	True	False
a A successful entrepreneur is likely to be multi-skilled.	☐	☐
b A tycoon is likely to have good financial skills.	☐	☐
c An entrepreneur is likely to be self-employed.	☐	☐
d A good guru can help managers to develop new managerial skills.	☐	☐

4 Read the text and answer the questions.

> It is estimated that there are about 20,000 former students from India's Institutes of Technology living in America. These entrepreneurs are working in the booming US hi-tech sector, where Indian-born software inventors are having enormous success. A recent survey found that the IITs have produced more millionaires than any other university-level institution.

a The paragraph describes the 'brain drain,' or emigration of technologists for better pay and conditions, from which country to which country?

b What kind of entrepreneurial activity are the IIT graduates engaged in?

c How successful are these Indian entrepreneurs?

Topic 14

EMPLOYEES

● **hire** (hires, hiring, hired) VERB
fire (fires, firing, fired) VERB

If you **hire** someone, you employ them or pay them to do a
particular job for you. If an employer **fires** you, they dismiss you
from your job.

The rest of the staff <u>have been hired</u> on short-term contracts.
If he wasn't so good at his job, I probably would <u>have fired</u> him.

● **headhunt** (headhunts, headhunting,
headhunted) VERB

If someone who works for a particular company **is
headhunted**, they leave that company because another
company has approached them and offered them another job
with better pay and higher status.

He <u>was headhunted</u> by Barkers last October.
They may <u>headhunt</u> her for the position of Executive Producer.

● **recruit** (recruits, recruiting, recruited) VERB
dismiss (dismisses, dismissing, dismissed) VERB

If you **recruit** people for an organization, you select them and
persuade them to join it or work for it. When an employer
dismisses an employee, the employer tells the employee that
they are no longer needed to do the job they have been doing.

The police are trying to <u>recruit</u> more black and Asian officers.
...the power to <u>dismiss</u> civil servants who refuse to work.

● **headhunter** (headhunters) N-COUNT
recruitment consultant (recruitment
consultants) N-COUNT

A **headhunter** or **recruitment consultant** is a person or
service that helps professional people to find work by
introducing them to potential employers.

*...a top international <u>headhunter</u> who places chairmen and chief
executives in private companies, with salaries of up to £1 million.
<u>Recruitment consultants</u> and employment agencies may help to
locate opportunities more effectively, but there are pitfalls.*

● **notice** N-UNCOUNT
give somebody notice PHRASE
hand in your notice PHRASE
give in your notice PHRASE

If you give **notice** about something that is going to happen,
you give a warning in advance that it is going to happen. If an
employer **gives** an employee **notice**, the employer tells the
employee that he or she must leave his or her job within a fixed
period of time. If you **hand in** your **notice** or **give in** your
notice, you tell your employer that you intend to leave your job
soon within a set period of time.

*Employers and employees often do not expressly agree on the
length of <u>notice</u> required to terminate employment.
The next morning I telephoned him and <u>gave</u> him his <u>notice</u>.
He <u>handed in</u> his <u>notice</u> at the bank and ruined his career.
He sold his house and <u>gave in</u> his <u>notice</u>.*

● **constructive dismissal** N-UNCOUNT
unfair dismissal N-UNCOUNT

If an employee claims **constructive dismissal**, they begin a
legal action against their employer in which they claim that they
were forced to leave their job because of the behaviour of their
employer. If an employee claims **unfair dismissal**, they begin a
legal action against their employer in which they claim that they
were dismissed from their job unfairly.

*The woman claims she was the victim of <u>constructive dismissal</u>
after being demoted from her job as senior supervisor.
His former chauffeur is claiming <u>unfair dismissal</u> on the grounds
of racial discrimination.*

● **severance** ADJ

Severance pay is a sum of money that a company gives to its
employees when it has to stop employing them.

*We were offered 13 weeks' <u>severance</u> pay.
More than 170 workers opted for a voluntary <u>severance</u> package
of four to 12 months' pay, plus travel and education vouchers.*

● **redundant** ADJ
redundancy (redundancies) N-VAR

If you are made **redundant**, your employer tells you to leave
because your job is no longer necessary or because your
employer cannot afford to keep paying you. **Redundancy**
means being made redundant.

*My husband was made <u>redundant</u> late last year.
Thousands of bank employees are facing <u>redundancy</u>.
Last week, 15 <u>redundancies</u> were announced.*

● **sack** (sacks, sacking, sacked) VERB
give someone the sack PHRASE
get the sack PHRASE

If your employers **sack** you, they tell you that you can no longer
work for them. If someone is **given the sack**, or if they **get
the sack**, they are sacked.

*Earlier today the Prime Minister <u>sacked</u> 18 government officials.
People who make mistakes can <u>be given</u> the <u>sack</u> the same day.
52 managers <u>got</u> the <u>sack</u> in one year.*

● **reference** (references) N-COUNT
referee (referees) N-COUNT

A **reference** is a letter that is written by someone who knows
you and which describes your character and abilities. When you
apply for a job, an employer might ask for references. A **referee**
is a person who gives you a reference, for example when you are
applying for a job.

*The firm offered to give her a <u>reference</u>.
One problem that frequently arises is that you do not wish to
give your present employer as a <u>referee</u> when applying for a job.*

➲ **compensation**: Topic 14.2; **interview**: Topic 14.4

PRACTISE YOUR VOCABULARY

1 Which of the terms are associated with hiring, or appointing new employees, and which with firing or terminating an employee's contract? Complete the table.

a to headhunt   **e** to fire   **i** to write (someone) a reference

b to recruit   **f** to interview   **j** to give (someone) notice

c to offer a severance package   **g** to dismiss   **k** to hire

d to give (someone) the sack   **h** to make (someone) redundant

finding and appointing new employees	the termination of an employee's contract

2 When a worker is made redundant, the firm is obliged to make a payment to the employee. What is this payment called?

a compensation   **b** severance payment

3 Use the terms below to complete the job advertisement.

a recruit   **b** length of notice   **c** referees

Scot, Sinclair, Murdoch (UK)
LEGAL OFFICER

Due to expansion of the firm, we need to _____ a new legal officer to join our established legal team. Please check our website at Scotsim.co.uk for full details. Application is by letter, with the names of three _____ and you should indicate the _____ you must give your current employer.

---

4 Use the terms in the box to complete the paragraph.

> *headhunted*   *constructive dismissal*   *recruitment consultant*

It is very flattering when a _____ telephones you and tells you that you are being _____.
Sometimes they call you because your employer has asked them to find you another role with another firm, however. This happens because companies find it easier and cheaper to dump a difficult employee rather than risk being sued for unfair or _____.

- **pay** N-UNCOUNT
  salary (salaries) N-COUNT
  wage (wages) N-COUNT
  remuneration (remunerations) N-VAR
  income (incomes) N-VAR

Your **pay** is the money that you get from your employer as wages or salary. A **salary** is the money that someone is paid each month by their employer, especially when they are in a profession such as teaching, law, or medicine. Someone's **wages** are the amount of money that is regularly paid to them for the work that they do. Someone's **remuneration** is the amount of money that they are paid for the work that they do. A person's **income** is the money that they earn or receive, as opposed to the money that they have to spend or pay out.

> ...their complaints about their _pay_ and conditions.
> ...the workers' demand for a twenty per cent _pay_ rise.
> The lawyer was paid a huge _salary_.
> The government decided to increase _salaries_ for civil servants.
> His _wages_ have gone up.
> ...the continuing marked increase in the _remuneration_ of the company's directors.
> $31,000 is a generous _remuneration_.
> Many families on low _incomes_ will be unable to buy their own homes.
> Average _income_ is now higher here than in most of Europe.

Common Collocations
a pay _rise_   a pay _cut_   a _rate of_ pay
a salary _increase_   a wage _demand_

- **golden handshake** (golden handshakes) N-COUNT

A **golden handshake** is a large sum of money that a company gives to an employee when he or she leaves, as a reward for long service or good work.

> He was given the _golden handshake_ after losing his post as boss of the University of Wales when it merged with another hospital.

- **bonus** (bonuses) N-COUNT

A **bonus** is an extra amount of money that is added to someone's pay, usually because they have worked very hard.

> Workers in big firms receive a substantial part of their pay in the form of _bonuses_ and overtime.
> The BBC's 23 most senior managers shared £800,000 in _bonus_ payments last year.

Common Collocations
a bonus _scheme_   an _annual_ bonus   to _receive_ a bonus

- **benefit** (benefits) N-COUNT
  fringe benefit (fringe benefits) N-COUNT

Benefits or **fringe benefits** are extra things that some people get from their job in addition to their salary, for example a car.

> The parents were working but all were employed at jobs which paid little, did not guarantee hours and did not provide _benefits_. They also want job security, increased _fringe benefits_ and more rights for part-time workers.

- **benefits package** (benefits packages) N-COUNT

A **benefits package** is a set of benefits, such as health insurance and parental leave, that some people get from their job in addition to their salary.

> New West Consultants pays staff high wages and has an excellent _benefits package_.
> ...a _benefits package_ that included maternity leave, parental leave, adoption aid, flexible schedules, part-time work, job sharing and support for care of elderly dependents.

- **perk** (perks) N-COUNT

Perks are special benefits that are given to people who have a particular job or belong to a particular group.

> ...a company car, private medical insurance and other _perks_.
> One of the _perks_ of being a student is cheap travel.

- **share option** (share options) N-COUNT
  stock option (stock options) N-COUNT

A **share option** or **stock option** is an opportunity for the employees of a company to buy shares in the company at a special price.

> Only a handful of firms offer _share option_ schemes to all their employees.
> He made a huge profit from the sale of shares purchased in January under the company's _stock option_ program.

- **minimum wage** N-SING

The **minimum wage** is the lowest wage that an employer is allowed to pay an employee, according to a law or agreement.

> I think that the introduction of a national _minimum wage_ for the first time ever will help millions of low-paid people.

- **performance-related pay** N-UNCOUNT

Performance-related pay is a rate of pay which is based on how well someone does their job.

> Teachers will fight Ministers' plans to introduce _performance-related pay_ in schools.

- **compensation** N-UNCOUNT

Compensation is money that someone who has experienced loss or suffering claims from the person or organization responsible, or from the state.

> He received one year's salary as _compensation_ for loss of office.
> Executives are increasingly willing to change companies for _compensation_ packages that offer the possibility of big bonuses.

⮎ **social chapter**: Topic 12.4; **working conditions**: Topic 14.3

PRACTISE YOUR VOCABULARY

1 Which of the following forms of remuneration involve the employee receiving cash and which do not? Tick the appropriate column.

Remuneration	cash	other		cash	other		cash	other
a golden handshake b bonus c fringe benefit			d perks e share/stock options f performance-related 　pay award			g compensation h benefits package i wage		

2 Which of the following are examples of fringe benefits or perks?

a stock options

b rapid promotion

c free health insurance

d overseas travel on company business

e use of a subsidized canteen

f relocation package to cover moving expenses

g company car

h attendance at board meetings

i supply of company stationery

3 Which of the following two employees do you think is most likely to prefer performance-related pay?

a Keith is 42 years old, married with 3 small children. He's been with the firm for 12 years. He's good at his job, but he has never applied for a promotion and he has a poor sick-leave record.

b Carolina is 26. She's just joined the firm on its new fast-track graduate program. She's single, often puts in unpaid extra work and loves travelling.

4 The European Union's Social Chapter is designed to establish minimum wages and working conditions in member countries. Look at the details of the Chapter on the left and match each section with what workers say on the right.

a Equal rights for part-time and full-time workers	Julia	– 'They used to be able to force us to work longer hours. Now they can't it means I can get home for when the kids come home from school.'
b Reduction of inequality between the pay of men and women	Florence	– 'My work has its rewards but traditionally it's been poorly paid. I'm not rich now, but I'm better off.'
c Most employees to work a maximum of 48 hours per week	Carlos	– 'It's meant that we all get the same wage for the same job.'
d Workers' rights to paid holidays	Anna	– 'Just because I'm only there for 15 hours a week shouldn't mean I get treated differently to full-timers.'
e Setting of a minimum wage	Gianfranco	– 'Getting away with my family used to be more difficult.'

5 Look at the table and answer the questions.

UK minimum wage (1999) per hour		Sterling equivalent		
UK		Portugal	Canada	Belgium
£3.60		£2.10	£3.80	£4.56

Are the following statements true or false?

	True	False
a Workers on the minimum wage in Portugal have a better income than those in Canada.	☐	☐
b Workers on the minimum wage in Belgium have the best salary shown here.	☐	☐
c Workers on the minimum wage in European countries shown here have higher wages than their North American counterparts shown here.	☐	☐

● **industrial relations** N-PLURAL

Industrial relations refers to the relationship between employers and employees in industry, and the political decisions and laws that affect it.

> *The offer is seen as an attempt to improve <u>industrial relations</u>.*
> *New <u>industrial relations</u> legislation curbed the power of the unions.*

● **trade union** (trade unions) N-COUNT

A **trade union** is an organization that has been formed by workers in order to represent their rights and interests to their employers, for example in order to improve working conditions or wages.

> *You can ask the tribunal to declare that your employer is infringing the regulations or get your <u>trade union</u> to take this up.*

● **works council** (works councils) N-COUNT

A **works council** is an elected body of workers within a company, which negotiates with management over such things as working conditions, holiday and safety.

> *…a European directive calling for <u>works councils</u> for all companies with more than 50 employees.*

● **staff representative** (staff representatives)
   N-COUNT
   rep (reps) N-COUNT

A **staff representative** or **rep** is a worker who is elected by other workers to represent their interests to management.

> *The company yesterday began the process of electing <u>staff representatives</u> to fulfil the legal requirements for consultation.*
> *He called for <u>staff representatives</u> on the boardroom committees that control directors' earnings.*
> *If your employer has procedures to deal with bullying, follow them, taking a colleague or union <u>rep</u> for support.*

● **arbitration** N-UNCOUNT

Arbitration is the judging of a dispute between people or groups by someone who is not involved.

> *The matter is likely to go to <u>arbitration</u>.*

● **blue-collar** ADJ
   white-collar ADJ

Blue-collar workers work in industry, doing physical work, rather than in offices. **White-collar** workers work in offices rather than doing physical work.

> *By 1925, <u>blue-collar</u> workers in manufacturing industry had become the largest occupational group.*
> *…corporate lawyers, accountants and other <u>white-collar</u> workers.*

● **colleague** (colleagues) N-COUNT
   co-worker (co-workers) N-COUNT

Your **colleagues** or **co-workers** are the people you work with, especially people on the same job or project as you.

> *Without consulting his <u>colleagues</u> he flew from Lisbon to Split.*
> *A <u>co-worker</u> of mine mentioned that she leaves her computer on all the time.*

● **strike** (strikes, striking, struck)

1 N-COUNT

When there is a **strike**, workers stop doing their work for a period of time, usually in order to try to get better pay or conditions for themselves.

> *French air traffic controllers have begun a three-day <u>strike</u> in a dispute over pay.*
> *…a call for <u>strike</u> action.*

2 VERB

When workers **strike**, they take part in a strike.

> *…their recognition of the workers' right to <u>strike</u>.*
> *The government agreed not to sack any of the <u>striking</u> workers.*

● **go on strike** PHRASE

When workers **go on strike**, they strike.

> *Staff at the hospital <u>went on strike</u> in protest at the incidents.*

● **industrial action** N-UNCOUNT

If workers take **industrial action**, they join together and do something to show that they are unhappy with their pay or working conditions, for example refusing to work.

> *Prison officers will decide next week whether to take <u>industrial action</u> over staffing levels.*

● **grievance** (grievances) N-VAR
   grievance procedure (grievance procedures)
   N-COUNT

If you have a **grievance** about something that has happened or been done, you believe that it was unfair. A **grievance procedure** is a set of guidelines produced by a company or organization, which explains how to make a formal complaint against them.

> *The main <u>grievance</u> of the drivers is the imposition of higher fees for driving licences and certificates of proficiency.*
> *One of their biggest mistakes is failing to put a formal <u>grievance procedure</u> in place to deal with staff complaints.*

● **tribunal** (tribunals) N-COUNT

A **tribunal** is a special court or committee that is appointed to deal with particular problems.

> *His case comes before an industrial <u>tribunal</u> in March.*

● **working conditions** N-PLURAL

Working conditions are the conditions which exist in your job, such as the number of hours you are expected to work and the amount of holiday you get.

> *The strikers are demanding better <u>working conditions</u>.*

➲ **employee**: Topic 13.4; **personnel**: Topic 13.4; **staff**: Topic 13.4; **workforce**: Topic 13.4; **notice**: Topic 14.1

PRACTISE YOUR VOCABULARY

1 Use the terms in the box to complete the paragraph.

industrial action   arbitration   staff representatives   strike   works council   tribunal
trade union   grievance   industrial relations   co-worker

Management and trade unions are jointly responsible for _____. Management and _____ often come together on a firm's _____ to attempt to resolve problems before they become too serious. If, however, the issue cannot be solved, they may use outside _____ to assist them. If all attempts to find a solution fail, the _____ may call a _____, or take other forms of _____. If an individual employee has a complaint, a company usually has a _____ procedure to deal with it. Employees may also contact their trade union or an industrial _____ if they have a complaint about their treatment at work or about a colleague or a _____.

2 Which jobs are held by blue-collar workers and which are held by white-collar workers? Complete the table.

a computer programmer	**e** receptionist	**i** teacher
b plumber	**f** clerk	**j** architect
c washing machine repairman	**g** builder	**k** delivery van driver
d recruitment consultant	**h** electrician	**l** lawyer

BLUE-COLLAR	WHITE-COLLAR

3 Read the text and answer the questions.

> A recent EU directive requires every employer with more than 150 staff to establish a works council. Businesses will have statutory requirements for ongoing consultation on any proposed changes in working conditions, and to provide information about recent and probable developments and activities and about the establishment's economic situation.

a What will companies with more than 150 employees have to do?
b What will businesses be obliged to consult their workers about?
c What two types of information will businesses be obliged to give their workers?

4 When an employee begins a job they will sign a written contract of employment with the company, stating the conditions of work that have been agreed. Look at the list of conditions and put them under the correct heading.

NUMBER OF HOURS	TYPE OF EMPLOYMENT	PAY	BENEFITS	DISCIPLINARY PROCEDURES	NOTICE	GRIEVANCE PROCEDURES	EMPLOYEE RIGHTS

a 4 weeks paid holiday per year	**e** consequences of breaking company rules	**i** trade union membership
b paid sick leave	**f** who to contact to make a complaint	**j** permanent/temporary job
c 48 hours per week	**g** £20,000 per year	**k** full time/part time
d one month's notice	**h** $9 per hour	

● **equal opportunities** N-PLURAL

Equal opportunities refers to the policy of giving everyone the same opportunities for employment, pay and promotion, without discriminating against particular groups.

> The profession's leaders must take action now to tackle racist behaviour and to promote _equal opportunities_ for all.
> It recently appointed an _Equal Opportunities_ Monitoring Officer who examines all job applications.

Common Collocations

an equal opportunities _policy_
an equal opportunities _employer_
equal opportunities _legislation_

● **discriminate** (discriminates, discriminating, discriminated) VERB
discrimination N-UNCOUNT

To **discriminate** against a group of people or in favour of a group of people means to unfairly treat them worse or better than other groups. **Discrimination** is the practice of treating one person or group of people less fairly or less well than other people or groups.

> They believe the law _discriminates_ against women.
> ...legislation which would _discriminate_ in favour of racial minorities.
> The Commission for Racial Equality teaches organisations not to _discriminate_.
> She is exempt from sex _discrimination_ laws.
> India swiftly denounced the proposal as deplorable and patent _discrimination_ against minorities.

● **age discrimination** N-UNCOUNT
sexual discrimination N-UNCOUNT
racial discrimination N-UNCOUNT

Age discrimination is the practice of treating older people less fairly or less well than other people. **Sexual discrimination** is the practice of treating the members of one sex, usually women, less fairly or less well than those of the other sex. **Racial discrimination** is the practice of treating people of some races less fairly or less well than those of another race.

> The government finally published its code of conduct to combat _age discrimination_.
> Women's groups denounced _sexual discrimination_.
> ...the elimination of _racial discrimination_ and the promotion of equal opportunity.

● **positive action** N-UNCOUNT
positive discrimination N-UNCOUNT

Positive action or **positive discrimination** means making sure that people such as women, members of smaller racial groups, and disabled people get a fair share of the opportunities available. [BRIT]

> Labour has promised to change the law to allow political parties to use _positive action_ to boost the number of women candidates.

> ...a referendum on whether _positive discrimination_ in favour of women and blacks should be abolished.

● **disability** (disabilities) N-COUNT

A **disability** is a permanent injury, illness, or physical or mental condition that tends to restrict the way that someone can live their life.

> Facilities for people with _disabilities_ are still insufficient.
> ...athletes who have overcome a physical _disability_ to reach the top of their sport.

● **recruitment policy** (recruitment policies) N-COUNT

A company's **recruitment policy** is the set of attitudes and actions it uses for the selection of new staff.

> Editors of newspapers will never admit to a racist _recruitment policy_.

● **under-represented** ADJ

If a group of people is **under-represented** in a particular activity, there are fewer of them involved in the activity than you think there should be.

> Women are still _under-represented_ in top-level civil service jobs.
> ..._under-represented_ groups such as women and ethnic minorities.

● **interview** (interviews, interviewing, interviewed)

1 VERB

If you **are interviewed** for a particular job, someone asks you questions to find out if you are suitable for it.

> When Wardell _was interviewed_, he was impressive, and on that basis, he was hired.

2 N-COUNT

If you go for an **interview**, someone asks you questions to find out whether you are suitable for a job.

> ...an _interview_ for a job as a TV researcher.

PRACTISE YOUR VOCABULARY

1 Use the terms in the box to complete the paragraph.

> discriminated against   under-represented   disability   equal opportunities
> positive action   equal opportunities monitoring

When a company interviews a candidate for a job they are not allowed to discriminate against him or her on the grounds of race, sex, age or _____. In other words every candidate should have _____, or the same chance to get the job. EU laws help to promote this, as do other laws in other parts of the world. Figures suggest that candidates often are discriminated against on the grounds of race. Many people believe that _____ by employers is an important part of a good equal opportunities policy. This should help to increase the number of workers belonging to a particular racial group, if they are _____ in the firm. Firms need to be aware of the make-up of their labour force, and many companies carry out _____ during the selection procedure. As well as discrimination in the selection process, employees can also be discriminated against in the area of pay. In manufacturing, for example, women earn 72% of men's pay. Additionally, occupations that employ mainly women, such as hairdressing for example, tend to involve low pay. If an employee thinks that they have been _____ they can take their case to an industrial tribunal.

2 Look at the two tables showing employment trends in one country and answer the questions.

A. Percentage of the workforce by gender and occupation

	Men		Women	
Area of employment	Year 1	Year 5	Year 1	Year 5
Managers	16	19	8	12
Professional	11	13	8	9
Clerical	8	8	31	25
Manufacturing	25	17	4	3

B. Unemployment by ethnic groups

Ethnic Group	% Unemployment
White	5
Black	21
Asian	9
Others	14
Country average	7

a According to the information in the tables:
  i Has discrimination against women in management increased or decreased?
  ii Do men and women have equal opportunities to gain employment in the manufacturing sector?
  iii Is there any sexual discrimination in the clerical sector?
  iv Which ethnic group suffers the worst racial discrimination in employment?
  v Which ethnic group has the highest level of employment?

b If far-reaching programmes of compulsory positive discrimination were introduced, what trends might be seen in the tables above:
  i in the manufacturing sector?   **ii** among black workers?   **iii** among managers?

3 Read the text and answer the questions.

> A company that produces chocolate is keen on offering equal opportunities and thrives on the diverse cultural background of its staff that reflects the global reach of its many brands.

a What is the company's position on equal opportunities?
b Why is cultural diversity important to this company?

● **productivity** N-COUNT

Productivity is the rate at which goods are produced or work is completed.

The third-quarter results reflect continued improvements in <u>productivity</u>.

His method of obtaining a high level of <u>productivity</u> is demanding.

● **morale** N-UNCOUNT

Morale is the amount of confidence and cheerfulness that a group of people have.

Personnel officers and managers must work together to enhance employee <u>morale</u> and improve organizational performance.

One of your first priorities should be to work with managers to improve staff <u>morale</u>.

Many pilots are suffering from low <u>morale</u>.

Common Collocations

<u>low</u> morale   to <u>boost</u> morale
<u>staff</u> morale

● **sick leave** N-UNCOUNT

Sick leave is the time that a person spends away from work because of illness or injury.

I have been on <u>sick leave</u> for seven months with depression.

I have no paid holiday, no paid pension or paid <u>sick leave</u>.

● **unproductive** ADJ

Something or someone that is **unproductive** does not produce any good results.

Research workers are well aware that much of their time and effort is <u>unproductive</u>.

...vast, <u>unproductive</u> state farms.

For businesses to survive the tough times, and prosper in the good, they have to stand ready to cut costs and let <u>unproductive</u> staff go.

● **asset** (assets) N-COUNT

Something or someone that is an **asset** is considered useful or helps a person or organization to be successful.

We have here a very loyal, skilled and semi-skilled engineering workforce who would be an <u>asset</u> to any employer.

Anne has a wealth of experience in presenting and reporting and her obvious talent will be a great <u>asset</u>.

● **motivate** (motivates, motivating, motivated) VERB
motivated ADJ
motivation N-UNCOUNT

If you **are motivated** by something, especially an emotion, it causes you to behave in a particular way. Someone who is **motivated** has a strong wish to do something. **Motivation** is a strong wish to do something.

They <u>are motivated</u> by a need to achieve.

I don't want to be missing out. And that <u>motivates</u> me to get up and do something every day.

...highly <u>motivated</u> employees.

Some boredom and lack of <u>motivation</u> may be the result of heavy schedules and several years in the business.

Common Collocations

<u>highly</u> motivated   <u>self</u>-motivation
<u>lack of</u> motivation
the motivation <u>behind</u> something

● **job satisfaction** N-UNCOUNT

Job satisfaction is the pleasure that you get from doing your job.

I doubt I'll ever get rich, but I get <u>job satisfaction</u>.

Employees can benefit from reduced commuting time, more flexible work hours and increased <u>job satisfaction</u>.

They don't like their working conditions, they feel they are poorly supervised and have a lower level of <u>job satisfaction</u> than in any other European country.

● **absenteeism** N-UNCOUNT

Absenteeism is the fact or habit of frequently being away from work, usually without a good reason.

...the high rate of <u>absenteeism</u>.

<u>Absenteeism</u> among a group of female workers was more tolerated than the same level among males.

● **workplace** (workplaces) N-COUNT

Your **workplace** is the place where you work.

...the difficulties facing women in the <u>workplace</u>.

Their houses were <u>workplaces</u> as well as dwellings.

<u>Workplace</u> canteens are offering healthier foods than ever before.

⊃ **corporate culture**: Topic 13.3; **dress code**: Topic 13.3

PRACTISE YOUR VOCABULARY

1 Read the statement and put the three statements below into the right order.

> A strong corporate culture often motivates workers in their jobs. This may lead to increased productivity.

a workers are keen to belong to the company　　b output increases　　c the company develops a strong identity

2 Use the words in the box to complete the paragraph.

> *workplace　job satisfaction　unproductive　motivated　absenteeism　asset　productivity*

It is often said that the staff are a company's most important _____. A well-_____ worker
is more likely to work hard, which helps a company keep its costs low and improve profits. A lack of motivation often l
eads to an increase in _____ time, increased _____ and consequently a fall in the levels
of _____. A business can make the _____ attractive to workers, and increase their
motivation in various ways. If workers enjoy a high level of _____, and enjoy their work, then productivity
will benefit.

3 Look at the figures and answer the questions.

Sick leave taken in four comparable manufacturing companies – average from 4-year period.

Company	Days sick per worker per year
Oyez Engineering	6
Breakers Inc.	9
Iron & Steel to order	5
Daniel's Motor Co.	3
National average	5

a Which firms have higher than average absenteeism?
b Which firm probably has the highest levels of employee morale?
c Which firm probably has the lowest levels of employee motivation?
d Which firm probably has the lowest levels of job satisfaction?
e Which firm probably values its employees the most?

4 Read the statement and answer the questions that follow it.

> In a large British grocery chain, stores where staff were more satisfied (because they were better managed and looked after) generated a £200,000 increase in sales per month.

Are the sentences true or false according to the text?

	True	False
a Some stores in the same chain did better than others.	☐	☐
b In the stores that performed best the staff worked harder because they were paid more.	☐	☐
c In the stores that performed best the sales were better because the staff were happier.	☐	☐
d The staff were happier because of the attitude of the management of that particular store.	☐	☐

5 Read the paragraph and use a word or phrase from the text to complete the sentences.

> Friday used to be the most common day for employees to call in sick. Nowadays, though, sick leave is at its highest on Monday, with 55% of all time off through ill health occurring then. Fridays are now more attractive, with casual dress codes and early finishes, and employees are more motivated to work at the end of the week.

a The most common day for people to _____ is the first day of the week.
b Previously, _____ peaked on the last day of the week.
c Because companies have introduced _____ and allow employees to finish work early, they like working on a Friday.
d Productivity is now at its lowest on _____s.

MATERIALS BANK

1 IT AND WAYS OF WORKING

WHAT MAKES A BUSINESS MORE AGILE?

The introduction of text messaging, always-on internet connectivity and the possibilities of mobile working are prompting companies to fundamentally review their internal processes and the way they operate in order that they can keep up and survive in a more dynamic and demanding society.

As the world becomes increasingly interconnected through *a plethora* of fast and pervasive communications platforms and as customers demand service every day of the week, companies are having to introduce flexible working arrangements. The traditional *nine-to-five* model is no longer adequate in a *24/7* environment and employers also know if they want to retain skilled staff, especially those with children and other family obligations, they are going to have to be open to part-time working and job-sharing arrangements. Otherwise they could severely restrict the resources they can recruit from.

"Organisations can become more agile by deploying infrastructures that support them becoming agile. Your IT structure and networks have to permit flexible job patterns, instant messaging and videoconferencing," explains Danny McLaughlin, managing director of BT Major Business, a division of BT Retail. He argues that businesses need to take full account of the fact that electronic communications are fundamentally changing the nature of work. "Work is what you do and not where you go. We use web-based meetings so we can bring together the right specialists who may be based in different parts of the country. But there has to be the right infrastructure in place before you can have an *e-enabled* workforce."

Finding smart ways to apply technology is not easy. Technology can facilitate home working, for example, and create significant savings as space is not required in traditional office premises. Such practices are open to abuse and require a significant amount of trust. It is by no means clear to companies how you manage home workers effectively and keep them motivated. Nor is home working suited to everyone. Many prefer the social interaction of working with other people.

While there are clearly many new possibilities, there is still some way to go before the concept of business agility is successfully mastered by UK directors. "I don't think the process has been *cracked* yet," says Heath. "We're just at the stage where we are beginning to learn how to deal with this huge wave of technology innovation."

© *Justin Hunt, The Guardian (09/05/02)*

Glossary

- *a plethora* – a large amount
- *nine-to-five* – from nine a.m. to five p.m.
- *24/7* – 24 hours a day, 7 days a week
- *e-enabled* – able to make use of Internet communication
- *cracked* – mastered

(a) **Key word review**

Which paragraphs mention ideas which could be summarized by the following 'keyword' concepts?

1 teleworking   **2** flexible working patterns   **3** telecoms revolution

(b) **Vocabulary extension**

Find words in the text which have the same meaning as the following:

1 to keep (*para. 2*)
2 using or putting in place (*para. 3*)
3 people with particular skills (*para. 3*)
4 framework (*para. 3*)
5 place of work, building (*para. 4*)

ⓒ Questions on the text

1 Which word best describes business 'agility'?

i adaptability   **ii** speed   **iii** reliability

2 Give examples from the text of:

i technological innovation at work   **ii** flexible working arrangements

Add any of your own ideas to those mentioned in the text.

3 Explain in more detail why the writer says: 'Work is what you do and not where you go.'

ⓓ Discussion/Writing

1 What are the advantages and disadvantages of working from home? Add to the ideas in the text.

2 Think about the following jobs. In what ways could they be made more 'agile'? Use ideas from the text to help you.

    i a design engineer for a car company   **iii** a university lecturer

    ii a sales person for a computer company   **iv** an advertising executive

3 What are the advantages and disadvantages (for customers and employees) of:

i a 9–5 world   **ii** a 24/7 world

Which do you prefer and why?

② THE INTERNET

ⓐ Questions on the texts

1 Many people still like to see and pick up what they buy or shake the hands of those they're making deals with.

2 Reality consisted of *goofed-up* online orders, long delays in shipping and *cutthroat* competition.

3 Web advertising has become a serious *impediment* to Web usability. Pop-up ads now pop up at virtually every site, and many money-losing dot-coms are going even further, some to the point of covering up content with ads.

4 Each day, an estimated sixty-four million Americans go 'online', tapping into the worldwide Internet at work and at home.

5 Fast-growing dot-coms, if they don't get it right, can end up with too many customers and not enough product.

6 "We had a very adaptable business model by definition. We are constantly redesigning our website, bringing in new suppliers and improving the customer experience."

Glossary

• *goofed-up* – mistaken, wrongly taken

• *cutthroat* – very aggressive

• *impediment* – obstacle

1 Texts 1–6 above look at various advantages and disadvantages of doing business on the Internet. Match each text to one of the summaries i–vi below.

    i Many Internet businesses provide a poor service to their customers.

    ii The Internet is very popular.

iii Internet businesses can adapt and introduce better services quickly.

iv Successful Internet businesses often have problems keeping enough stock to meet demand.

v Many customers feel uncomfortable doing business with someone they can't see.

vi Many Internet businesses rely too heavily on advertising, making their sites difficult to use.

2 Which of the texts describe an advantage and which describe a disadvantage?

ADVANTAGES	DISADVANTAGES

3 Can you think of any more advantages or disadvantages to add to these two lists?

ⓑ Discussion

1 Do you ever buy products or services online? What kinds of products and services would you consider buying over the Internet? Are there any products and services you would not buy online?

2 What are the most popular Internet companies in your country?

ⓒ Questions on the texts

a Now that venture capitalists are no longer paying as much attention to Internet and computing startups, they're looking for new areas of interest.

b A lot of people building dot-coms were *looking for the fast buck*. They were looking to build their business and sell and get out.

c With the Web so easily catering to a huge number of competing properties, few websites attracted the size of user base that made television, until *the advent of* cable, such big business.

d It's a shift from just a few years ago, when college students were dropping out to pursue fortunes with dot-coms. Consider: Employment among college graduates has increased by more than 1.1 million jobs in the last year, even as less-educated *peers* saw 2 million jobs lost.

e A year ago, you couldn't get people with Java and HTML skills, but now there are more qualified staff than jobs available.

Glossary

• *looking for the fast buck* – looking for ways to make lots of money quickly

• *the advent of* – the arrival of

• *peers* – colleagues

1 Texts a–e above look at some of the causes and effects of the end of the dot-com boom. Which of the texts describe causes and which describe results?

CAUSES:

RESULTS:

2 Can you think of any other causes or results to add to the lists?

3 Which Internet companies have been successful in the last few years? Why do you think these companies have managed to be successful when so many dot-coms have failed?

ⓓ **Discussion/Writing**

1 Prepare a short talk/write a short report on a successful dot-com, describing the nature of its business and giving the reasons for its success.

2 Mobile phone technology is changing very fast. How many different things can you do with your mobile phone? List as many as you can.

ⓔ **Discussion**

1 It has been said that there are 4 main types of e-commerce:

  i business to business   **iii** business to consumer
  ii consumer to business   **iv** consumer to consumer

Think of examples of the types of business that can be done for each one. For the 3 involving consumers, think of actual companies that are involved in each type of e-commerce.

2 Some people involved in e-commerce believe that *any* kind of product can be sold on the Web. Look at the examples of products below. Which ones are already popular for buying online and which might be soon? Are there any that you think will never be popular online?

books   clothes   supermarket groceries   financial services   shoes   holidays   beauty products
fruit and vegetables   fast food   white goods (fridges, cookers etc.)   cars   garden plants   furniture

❸ WORD SEARCH

Put the following words and phrases in the correct column in the table below, and then find them in the word search grid on the next page. Words can go up, down or diagonally, backwards or forwards. The first one is shown as an example.

| *globalization* | *deregulation* | *just-in-time* | *outsourcing* | *freelance* |
| *teleworking* | *broadband* | *state-of-the-art* | *multinational* | |

production	IT	global issues	ways of working

```
F  J  U  S  T  I  N  T  I  M  E  W  H  F  O
D  S  T  A  T  E  O  F  T  H  E  A  R  T  U
B  E  K  S  K  D  I  B  S  R  O  K  L  M  T
L  R  R  G  L  E  T  H  I  M  D  A  F  G  S
D  Y  O  E  W  X  A  M  D  S  N  F  R  N  O
E  J  J  A  G  M  Z  A  W  O  Q  K  E  I  U
C  L  T  V  D  U  I  W  I  M  B  X  E  K  R
U  G  J  P  I  B  L  T  I  J  B  U  L  R  C
N  I  V  V  T  B  A  A  T  X  H  E  A  O  I
K  G  L  J  X  N  B  N  T  T  F  I  N  W  N
N  N  G  O  I  B  O  G  D  I  F  R  C  E  G
E  D  G  T  R  X  L  Y  V  W  O  T  E  L  M
Q  S  L  P  V  Y  G  B  J  O  Z  N  M  E  L
N  U  M  S  I  E  E  T  N  E  S  B  A  T  Z
M  F  P  I  V  V  G  Y  Q  S  S  I  D  I  Y
```

❶ CORPORATE STRUCTURE AND LEGAL STATUS

ⓐ **The following sections of text refer to the types of business and business structure listed in the box below. Decide what each section refers to and insert the correct forms of the terms shown in the box:**

sole trader	*franchise*	*Limited Liability Company*	*partnership*

STRUCTURING YOUR BUSINESS

1 A _____ gives the *fledgling* business person the advantage of the goodwill associated with the _____ name, and, perhaps more importantly, the use of a proven method of business.

The _____ is also likely to provide some level of support in the way of training and marketing, making it less *daunting* than going it alone, though this will vary from firm to firm.

As well as the initial license fee and its renewal, there are likely to be ongoing fees taking a percentage of your turnover or put onto the price of the goods or services you sell.

Despite the high success rate, when some set out to be their own boss, that's exactly what they mean, and the loss of control a _____ involves can be too high a price to pay.

2 By far the most popular choice is to set up as a _____. It's relatively easy; you just need to register as self-employed with the *Inland Revenue* and display your name, trading name and address on all business premises and stationery. Profits are treated as personal income and you can even use your personal bank account to run the business, though business transactions need to be clearly identifiable.

While the burden of paperwork may be pretty light for the self-employed, the financial liabilities are unlimited. The law makes no distinction between the business and its owner, so if it fails, your personal assets are at risk, which in itself is enough to put many people off.

3 This goes doubly for _____, which are for when two or more people want to go into business together. _____ are considered self-employed and, in the absence of any other agreement, will share the profits equally.

_____ are also personally liable for the debts of the business – jointly and severally liable, so if one _____ can't pay his share of the debt, the others will have to. It's also worth remembering that it is a _____, not a democracy, and each _____ can make binding business decisions and contracts without the others' consent.

4 The _____, and more recently the _____ Partnership, were designed for those people who wanted to go into business for themselves but did not want to *put* their house *on the line* doing so. The *mainstay* of both is that they are separate legal *entities* to their owners, so creditors can only claim against the business's assets, not the personal assets of the owners.

Against this are the increased costs of setting these structures up – to set up and register a _____ at Companies House often costs about £500 through a solicitor – and a far greater administrative burden, including the requirement to register audited company accounts.

©*Peter Davy, The Guardian (25/04/02)*

Glossary

- *fledgling* – inexperienced
- *daunting* – frightening
- *Inland Revenue* – government authority which collects taxes
- *put something on the line* – risk something
- *mainstay* – most basic part
- *entities* – things which have a separate identity

(b) **Vocabulary extension**

Find words in the text that have the following meaning:

1 the money a company makes (*section 2*)

2 the place or building of the business (*section 2*)

3 deals, items of business (*section 2*)

4 responsibilities, burden (*section 2*)

5 everything you own (*section 2*)

6 money you owe (*section 3*)

(c) **Questions on the text**

Based on your understanding of the text, which of the types of business could the following summaries of some of the advantages and disadvantages refer to?

1 risky but potentially very rewarding

2 has strict regulations and costly to start but little personal risk

3 less risk for a newcomer but you also have less control

4 a chance to share the risk and rewards with others

(d) **Discussion**

1 Which types of business or business structures are popular in your country?

2 How easy is it to start up a business in your country? Where do people get finance from? From banks, venture capitalists or other sources?

3 Do you know anyone who has set up a business? What type is it? What success have they had?

2 THE FUTURE OF THE COMPANY

Discussion

1 For each of the following organizations, discuss which characteristics are likely to be most important to managers:

　a a state-owned railway network

　b a high-tech computer software firm

　c a private nursing home

　d a hotel situated in a skiing resort

2 In the future, how do you think firms are likely to change in the following areas:

　i　　size of companies

　ii　 efficiency and leanness

　iii　brand values

　iv　importance of customer relations

　v　　advertising

　vi　 innovation

　vii　employees

3 Make a list of as many stakeholders as you can. Which of the aspects in question 2 are likely to be important and less important to these different stakeholders?

3 BUSINESS STRATEGY

1 A joint venture is often a particularly effective way of exploiting complementary resources and skills, with one firm, for example, contributing new technology and products and the other providing marketing expertise and distribution channels.

2 The main advantages of such a merger is that the new company has a larger market share and has reduced the number of competitors in the market. Greater economies of scale should occur if they are both producing similar products. However consumers may be faced with less choice.

3 Mr Cha said local knowledge was extremely important. Knowing the subtle differences between what goes on in one place compared to another could be the difference between making or breaking a project. 'That's why I want a local partner.'

4 From the firm's point of view a takeover can be advantageous because it may enable the firm to reduce production and distribution costs, acquire brand names, expand its existing activities or move into new areas, or remove troublesome competition and increase its market power.

(a) Vocabulary extension

Find words or phrases in the texts which have the same meaning as the following:

1 getting a benefit from (*para. 1*)
2 knowledge (*para. 1*)
3 methods (*para. 1*)
4 savings which are the result of being able to produce things in large numbers (*para. 2*)
5 beneficial, a good thing (*para. 4*)

(b) Keyword review/questions on the text

1 Match the texts with the statements below.

i This company wants to work with a company in another country in order to help them do business there more effectively.

ii This company wants to buy more shares in another country in order to take control of it.

iii This company wants to combine with another company and become one new company.

iv This company wants to work with another company in a business or project.

2 What are the benefits of the following types of business strategy, according to the texts?

i Joint ventures
ii Mergers
iii Local partners
iv Takeovers

3 Can you think of any other advantages to add to these lists?

4 INDUSTRIES AND SECTORS

Discussion/Writing

Either prepare a short talk OR write a short essay about the following:

1 Describe the economy of your country in terms of sectors, comparing 50 years ago and today.

2 How important are the primary/industrial/service sectors? Which does the government encourage most?

3 Within those sectors, describe the main types of business e.g. agriculture, banking, tourism etc.

5 CROSSWORD

Across
2 another word for business in general (8)
3 another word for a company (10)
5 a person or organization who provides finance for the start-up of a company (6)
8 the buying or taking over of another company (11)
9 another general word for a business; a business _____ (7)
10 the joining together of two companies (6)

Down
1 make enough money to cover costs (5,4)
4 organizations owned or funded by the government (6,6)
6 a business that is owned by or is part of another business (10)
7 an association of companies formed for a particular purpose (10)

1 INTERNATIONAL TRADE

Bush defends lifeline for US steel industry; Trade war

After weeks of agonising, President Bush yesterday imposed tariffs of up to 30 per cent on steel imports to the United States and *took the plunge* with a decision that cuts across global trade, domestic politics and potentially the future of the War on Terror. Describing the problem as like trying to solve a Rubik's cube, White House officials said that Mr Bush had tried to compromise.

Mr Bush, who *campaigned* for office *on a* free-trade *ticket*, argued that in order to remain a free-trading nation America had been forced to impose the tariffs "to provide a temporary *lifeline* so the industry can restructure itself". "This relief will help steelworkers, communities that depend upon steel and the steel industry adjust without harming our economy," Mr Bush said in a statement. "I take this action to give our domestic steel industry an opportunity to adjust to surges in foreign imports, recognising the harm from 50 years of foreign government intervention in the global steel market."

The tariffs range from 8 per cent to 30 per cent on 16 types of steel, much less than the 40 per cent demanded by the industry and by Democrats at home and far more than America's trading partners, especially in Europe, said that they could tolerate. Steel types attracting a 30 per cent tariff reflect Mr Bush's domestic priorities. They include tin mill steel, which is produced in West Virginia, a swing state in the 2000 presidential elections.

Officials said that Canada and Mexico, two of America's biggest trading partners and part of the North American Free Trade Agreement, would be exempt, as would developing countries such as Argentina and Thailand. But attempts to explain its reasoning *fell on deaf ears* in Europe, where there is suspicion that Mr Bush has his eye on the votes of the Ohio-Pennsylvania-West Virginia *steel belt*, which was critical to winning him the presidency and could be similarly important in November's mid-term elections.

The EU sends approximately £2.4 billion worth of steel to the United States each year, a fifth of America's total steel imports. In 2000 Britain sent £315 million worth, according to the Department of Trade and Industry. The WTO typically takes two years to reach a judgment in such cases, but the EU believes that in the meantime it would be entitled to erect barriers to prevent its own producers being swamped by a sudden glut of steel diverted from the US market. That could lead to further protectionist measures around the world. The EU could also retaliate by pressing for maximum damages from the United States after the WTO's January ruling that certain US export subsidies are illegal. The WTO is to decide on the amount on April 29, and the EU believes it is entitled to more than $4 billion. EU officials expressed concern that the steel dispute would undermine the new round of world trade liberalisation talks launched in Doha last November.

Roland Watson, Martin Fletcher and Philip Webster, ©Times (06/03/02)

Glossary

- *took the plunge* – made a difficult decision
- *campaigned on a … ticket* – used … as a key aspect of an election campaign
- *fell on deaf ears* – were ignored
- *Rubik's cube* – type of puzzle
- *lifeline* – help
- *steel belt* – area of the USA in which steel is manufactured

(a) **Key word review**

Fill in the gaps in the sentences with a suitable word or phrase from the article.

1 The American government plans to help the US steel industry by introducing _____, which make it expensive for companies to import steel into the USA.

2 The trade policies of the US government seems to be against the principles of _____, in which companies should be able to trade without restrictions.

3 The Americans' _____ principles are likely to annoy European governments, who want to protect their own steel industries from cheap _____.

ⓑ Vocabulary extension

Find words or phrases in the article which have the same meaning as the following:

1 sudden increases (*para. 2*)
2 countries with which another country trades goods (*para. 3*)
3 not included in a general rule (*para. 4*)
4 large amount of a product which arrives suddenly (*para. 5*)
5 fight back (*para. 5*)
6 amounts of money given to a company by the government to enable the company to export their goods more cheaply (*para. 5*)

2 WORLD ECONOMY AND INTERNATIONAL TRADE

ⓐ Key word review

Match the words to the sentences below:

*flight of capital   infrastructure   deregulation   dumping   subsidies   inward investment
income distribution   exchange rates   monopoly   domestic market*

1 European farmers receive large amounts of money from the EU to make their industry viable.
2 The pound (£) has fallen against the dollar ($) recently.
3 Roads, communication networks and power supplies were all damaged as a result of the war.
4 The country has received huge amounts of money from foreign companies wishing to establish a presence there.
5 When the Asian economic crisis hit, foreign countries were worried and started to take their money out of those economies.
6 Controls were removed from the UK stock market in the 1990s which contributed to its success.
7 There is a big gap, in terms of money earned, between the richest and the poorest people in the UK.
8 That Japanese car only has that brand name when it is sold in Japan itself (when it is exported, the name is different.)
9 There is only one company that has responsibility for maintaining the railway track in the UK.
10 Some Eastern European countries were accused of selling very cheap steel in the US to gain entry to their market.

ⓑ Discussion/Writing

1 Complete the following sentences about your own country's economy and trade:

i My country's main **imports** are _____ from _____, the main **exports** are _____ from _____.

ii My country's main industries are _____ and it has a **competitive advantage** in _____ because _____.

iii My country trades mostly with/within _____ and has problems with _____ (**protectionism, tariffs, quotas** etc) from _____.

iv In my country the _____ industry receives **subsidies** from _____ because _____.

v My country's **infrastructure** is _____ condition.

2 Now prepare a short *talk* or do a short piece of *writing* about the above – this time add some more details to each point.

ⓒ **Discussion**

  1 What are the arguments for and against free trade?

  2 Which countries have been in the news recently accused of protectionism? Are they justified in trying to protect their industries?

❸ BRANDING AND PRODUCT CYCLE

ⓐ **Key word review**

  Complete the following extracts with words or phrases from the box below.

development stage   *product lifecycle*   *product launch*   product portfolio   *tag line*   *brand image*

  1 The new phones, which also included a small and expensive cameraphone and a low-cost entry level model, further extended Nokia's _____, already the broadest in the industry. "We're convinced we're going to gain market share," Vanjoki said.

  2 A call centre is often the customer's first point of contact with the product – there is an onus on call-centre staff to communicate a positive _____ through excellent service.

  3 The company's _____ was delayed from last fall to April because of manufacturing problems. Earlier this year, it was pushed back to late May. Now, consumers will have to wait until at least late June to try out the technology.

  4 Scottish & Newcastle is to launch a £15 million advertising campaign for its Kronenbourg 1664 beer with the _____ Vive la vie Francaise.

  5 New products are critical to drive growth; more than 50 per cent of our revenues comes from products released in the previous two years … The _____ may be 10 years but as products age the price also goes down.

  6 At each stage, decisions have to be made about whether the product is likely to be successful; most products do not survive the _____.

ⓑ **Vocabulary extension**

  Find words or phrases in the extracts above which have the same meaning as the following:

  1 product designed for a first-time buyer (*para. 1*)

  2 get a higher percentage of the sales (*para. 1*)

  3 place where a company's business is conducted by telephone (*para. 2*)

  4 encounter (*para. 2*)

  5 pressure on (*para. 2*)

  6 postponed until (*para. 3*)

  7 vital (*para. 5*)

  8 encourage, push forward (*para. 5*)

  9 income (*para. 5*)

© Discussion/Writing

1 Think of a successful company you know. What makes it successful? Complete the following table with reference to the company and its marketing mix.

PRODUCT
PRICE
PROMOTION
PLACE

2 What are the company's core values, in your opinion?

3 What is the target market for the company's products?

4 Prepare a short presentation, or write a short report, describing the company and giving reasons for its success.

4 THE INTERNATIONAL MARKETING MIX

ⓐ Discussion questions

What are the following examples of?

1 A Cola company offers exactly the same product all around the world.

2 An international burger company sells a range of Indian style products in its restaurants in India.

3 Pizza companies often advertise by sending leaflets to individual homes.

ⓑ Discussion

How might a burger company adapt its marketing mix (product, price, promotion, place) in the following countries?

1 France

2 India

3 South Africa

5 CROSSWORD

Across

 2   a country experiences this when its imports exceed its exports (5, 7)

 5   a company's product which is bought by more consumers than any other product of its type (6, 6)

 7   people to whom a company is trying to sell something (6, 6)

10   **see 1 down**

12   **and 11 down** – plans which detail how a product will start to be sold in the market (6, 10)

Down

1 and 10 across – the difference between what a country pays to other countries and the money that it gets from those countries (7, 2, 8)

3   see 4 down

4 and 3 down – the situation where money is taken out of a country in large amounts e.g. because people feel the economy is in crisis (6, 2, 7)

6   when different currencies are valued against each other e.g. the £ against the $ (8, 5)

8   another word for competitors (6)

9   the situation where there is only one company providing a product or service; the situation where one company has total control over the market (8)

11 see 12 across

1 FAIR TRADE

GOOD BUSY-NESS

Some time ago alternative traders recognized that markets can be unfair, mostly because people bring unequal *bargaining power* with them to the market. Being fair – or at least fairer – implies that something has to be put right, a new balance *struck*. Achieving this, however, is less about abstract laws of economics or science than moral and political judgement.

Conventional companies cannot easily reconcile fair trade with the main objective of capitalist business – maximizing shareholder value. Most consumer concerns are, in the language of a typical executive-training institute, 'non-traditional considerations'. Though companies may react with 'cause-related marketing' and 'reputation management', they're a long way from admitting that trade done differently can overcome specific social and environmental problems caused in part by their 'traditional' practices. If their efforts are purely *cosmetic*, they make things worse not better – by *turning down the heat*. The interests of, say, small farmers or the informal economy get neglected, and the spotlight is deflected away from companies that show no interest whatever in fair trade. If superstores are made to look better or sound safer, specialist or independent companies and stores are dealt another heavy blow.

Everybody … seems to be talking about the 'ethical dimensions' of trade. What we have learned over more than a decade, however, is that it was campaigning, development education and mobilization that built the fair-trade *constituency*.

When the coffee market collapsed in 1989, creating a crisis for millions of small-scale farmers in the South, it was clear enough to those who knew about it that something grossly 'unfair' was going on. Britain's largest supermarket chain, Tesco, told Cafédirect that second only to complaints about the length of check-out queues (a *burning* issue at the time) were letters from customers demanding that they stock Cafédirect. Even as recently as 1997, half the women who had recently been made aware of Cafédirect said in interviews that they had heard about it through networks and word of mouth – churches, groups and friends. Only nine per cent remembered seeing the advertising.

There are, then, some pretty fundamental differences between alternative and conventional trade. Not least is the size of their communications budgets and the kind of customer they want to encourage. Alternative traders know that unless buyers think about what they are being sold, and approve of it, what they purchase won't make much difference. We prefer our customers *troublesome* – not simply buying our products.

©*Pauline Tiffen, New Internationalist, www.newint.org (April 2000)*

Glossary

- *bargaining power* – ability to make a deal
- *struck* – achieved
- *cosmetic* – on the surface
- *turning down the heat* – reducing the pressure
- *constituency* – group of consumers
- *burning* – important, controversial
- *troublesome* – challenging, difficult

(a) **Questions on the text**

1 Do the following phrases refer to FREE TRADE or FAIR TRADE?

conventional trade	specialist or independent companies	superstores
alternative traders	maximizing shareholder value	unequal bargaining power

2 Based on your understanding of the text, complete the sentences below in a suitable way:

    i Traditional companies' main focus is not on ....

    ii If traditional companies or supermarkets only pretend to take an interest in fair trade, ...

    iii Consumers who buy fair trade products are not just concerned with ...

    iv For alternative traders, marketing and advertising ....

ⓑ Discussion/Writing

Think about the following statement: 'Market forces will always be stronger than social responsibility. Price considerations will always outweigh any concern for producers in developing countries.' How far do you agree with this? Is there a future for fair trade?

2 ETHICAL CONSUMERISM AND CORPORATE RESPONSIBILITY

ⓐ Discussion/Writing

    1 How would you define business ethics?

    2 What are the advantages and disadvantages to a company of 'being ethical'?

    3 Can you give an example of a situation in which an employee could do something which is legal, but unethical?

    4 Can being ethical increase a company's profits?

    5 Can you give an example of an ethical dilemma that a manager might have to resolve?

    6 What people see as ethical or unethical is influenced by their national culture, religion, politics and so on. Think of something that you consider unethical but which someone from another culture might find acceptable.

ⓑ Look at the following examples of arguably unethical behaviour. Choose the five you find most unethical and put them in order from 1-5 (1 = worst). See if other people in your group agree. Give reasons for your point of view.

>   **i** *using child labour in developing countries to produce consumer products for developed countries*
>
>   **ii** *a company dealing in arms and selling them to any country who wants them*
>
>   **iii** *a company finding clever ways to avoid paying the full amount of tax*
>
>   **iv** *a company not providing adequate safety equipment for its workers*
>
>   **v** *a company ignoring laws on disposal of harmful waste products, e.g. leaving it on local land or in rivers*
>
>   **vi** *producing a product such as tobacco which is known to kill people*
>
>   **vii** *a company who pays their employees less than the minimum wage*
>
>   **viii** *food companies not labelling food properly so that consumers do not know what is in the product*

3 SUSTAINABLE DEVELOPMENT

Discussion/Writing

Prepare a short talk or write a short essay about the following:

How significant are the following issues in your country? Are people interested in them? Does the government promote them?

    green issues   *ethical tourism*   *business ethics*   *fair trade*

4 WORD SEARCH

Put the following words and phrases in the correct column in the table below, and then find them in the word search grid. Words can go up, down or diagonally, backwards or forwards. The first one is shown as an example.

sweatshop	cooperatives	eco-tourism	cash crop	social audit
infrastructure	raw materials	capital inflow	mass tourism	

free trade or traditional business	fair trade or non-traditional business	sustainable development

S	C	E	V	N	E	S	L	H	C	B	T	L	I	S
W	E	G	C	E	S	Z	J	A	Y	I	M	N	X	L
E	K	V	R	O	X	Z	S	H	D	U	F	P	B	A
A	Z	I	I	E	T	H	T	U	U	R	Q	O	W	I
T	O	A	N	T	C	O	A	V	A	M	A	I	G	R
S	Y	P	W	R	A	L	U	S	A	Q	U	X	L	E
H	X	L	O	P	A	R	T	R	T	O	L	D	Q	T
O	M	P	Y	I	Z	R	E	M	I	C	X	Y	I	A
P	N	Z	C	U	U	L	H	P	S	S	B	Z	F	M
O	V	O	Y	C	Q	T	I	K	O	P	M	A	F	W
Y	S	S	T	Q	K	I	Z	W	C	O	N	V	I	A
A	M	U	I	M	E	R	P	W	O	B	C	B	L	R
D	R	W	O	L	F	N	I	L	A	T	I	P	A	C
E	M	A	S	S	T	O	U	R	I	S	M	L	T	Z
W	P	Q	P	P	Y	G	C	F	Z	U	M	C	N	X

Topic 5 Production

■ MANUFACTURING AND PRODUCTION

FORD TAKES A LEAP IN MAKING CARS TO FIT;
CASE STUDY: STANDARDISING THE PARTS THAT GO INTO CARS
From 100 versions of petrol caps, the carmaker will use two.

Devotees of classic cars say that modern vehicles on the roads all look the same. However fair this view is, increasingly they do contain the same parts. But how do you reduce the number of components while ensuring that standards are maintained?

The problem: Traditionally motor cars have been designed by dedicated teams working on individual models. The result has been a proliferation of almost identical components, often produced by the same suppliers, being fitted into the different models. The designers are continually *reinventing the wheel*, coming up with near-identical solutions to the same engineering problems. But customers are unlikely to care if the individual working parts, which they rarely see, are identical across different models. There are huge cost-savings to be made if parts could be standardised. Ford took a decision, starting with its European plants, to introduce a programme of commonality across the group, while ensuring that the *intrinsic* differences between its various models were maintained.

The players: While he was head of Ford Europe, Nick Scheele, now overall chief operating officer, had appointed a "commonality *czar*" to ensure production lines used the same parts where they could. He was Jim McDonald, who took the job title of director, commonality and product development, factory improvement. He says: "One of the strategic applications we felt we weren't making enough of was the idea of sharing and re-using between our products." Mr Scheele recalls his astonishment, for example, on discovering that Ford Europe had been using about 100 different caps on its petrol tanks. By the end of this year there will be just two, a locking and a non-locking version. In January 2000 Ford hired AT Kearney, the management consultant, to work on a pilot project that would demonstrate that the principle would work for a limited range of parts.

The solution: Steve Young, vice-president in charge of Kearney's global automotive practice, says the team concentrated at first on the various components that went into the seats. This was to be the "proof of principle" that would show that commonality was practicable. Mr Young says: "We identified that 50 per cent of the value of a seat was made up of commonised parts. There was a further 30 per cent where this was a possibility." Ford brought in the maker of its seat parts, a Michigan manufacturer called Johnson Controls, to see how the range it produced could be rationalised, especially for the Fiesta and Focus models. "The reason you get such a lack of commonality and high level of complexity in the product is that the different teams are working in isolation,"

Mr Young says. "But does it matter to the customer if the electric motor that adjusts the seat is the same in a Ford, VW or Citroen? It is essential, Mr Young says, to ensure that quality is not compromised and the core values of the brand are maintained. "If the customer ever thought that in buying a Volvo or a Jaguar, they were buying a s*ouped-up* Ford, *you would be dead*." By May 2000, Kearney was set to hand over to Ford's own commonality team, which would extend the principle.

The result: The cost benefits will take time to work through, and will not be fully realised until all Ford's range has been remodelled. Mr McDonald says one advantage is that the economies of scale would allow the use of higher-quality parts. New models, meanwhile, will get to the marketplace faster since not every part has to be re-engineered, enabling savings in production and from stocking fewer accessories. An initial costing suggests that the rationalisation exercise could eventually save $1 billion (£710 million) over a six-year lifespan of an average model. Ford expects to launch about 45 new models, variations of its existing ranges, over the next five years, which is twice the average level in the past. The principle of commonality, meantime, is being extended across the company.

Martin Waller, ©Times, (05/03/02)

Glossary

• *devotees* – fans
• *reinventing the wheel* – inventing something which is not needed because a suitable alternative already exists
• *intrinsic* – important, recognized
• *czar* – person in overall charge of a particular area of business
• *souped-up* – superficially improved
• *you would be dead* – the company would suffer

ⓐ **Vocabulary extension**

Find words or phrases in the article which have the same meaning as the following:

1 individual parts which make up a product (*para. 1*)
2 great increase in the number of (*para. 2*)
3 changed so that they have the same features (*para. 2*)
4 ensuring that certain features are the same (*para. 2*)
5 initial test, designed to see if a system will work on a bigger scale (*para. 3*)
6 reduced in variety (usually in order to save money)(*para. 4*)
7 basic ideas about a brand (*para. 4*)
8 become apparent (*para. 5*)
9 life cycle (*para. 5*)

ⓑ **Questions on the text**

Based on your understanding of the text, are the following statements TRUE or FALSE?

	True	False
1 Until now, car manufacturers have used the same parts on various different models of cars.	☐	☐
2 It is more expensive to produce different parts for each make of car.	☐	☐
3 Ford has decided to use the same parts on all the models it manufactures.	☐	☐
4 Ford is testing the idea of commonality in a small range of parts.	☐	☐
5 Customers will not mind if Volvos are the same as Fords.	☐	☐
6 By standardizing components, the quality of the parts used can be improved.	☐	☐
7 Car owners replace their cars every six years on average.	☐	☐

ⓒ **Discussion/Writing**

1 Summarize in your own words the main differences between the traditional way of manufacturing cars and the principle of commonality.

2 The article describes the advantages of commonality. List these advantages in the table opposite. Do you think this system has any disadvantages?

ADVANTAGES OF COMMONALITY	DISADVANTAGES OF COMMONALITY

3 Can you think of any other products where the principle of standardization would be beneficial? Look at the list below, and in each case decide whether commonality/standardization could or could not be applied the the manufacturing process.

biscuits
mobile phones
a hotel chain
washing machines
birthday cards
bicycles

4 There has been a trend towards moving manufacturing to low-cost areas in developing countries. With the current trend towards 'mass customization' and the importance of service to the consumer, to what extent do you think this trend will be reversed?

② INNOVATION AND PRODUCTION METHODS

ⓐ Questions on the text/key word review

1 The group will select and define problems, brainstorm ideas, gather information and search for answers before presenting them to management.

2 Robots – computer-driven machines – can now be programmed to do most phases of automobile manufacture, performing tedious and often dangerous work that once required the labor of hundreds of human workers.

3 You are an engineer, confronted with an artifact you have found and don't understand. You make the working assumption that it was designed for some purpose. You dissect and analyze the object with a view to working out what problem it would be good at solving.

4 To produce the right quantity at the right time with the right quality. Putting this into practice means improving the flow of goods and cutting down on stocks.

5 It is a method which has the potential to help organisations understand more about their business practices and levels of performance. In particular, it can show how organisations compare with other companies engaged in similar activities.

1 The texts above are examples of different features of the production process. Match each text to the features in the list below:

JIT manufacturing
reverse engineering
quality circles
benchmarking
automation

2 Try to think of one advantage and one disadvantage of each aspect of production.

	ADVANTAGE	DISADVANTAGE
JIT manufacturing		
reverse engineering		
quality circles		
benchmarking		
automation		

[b] **Discussion**

1 The PC (personal computer) is often described as a 'disruptive' innovation. What do you understand by this term? Think of other examples in history of disruptive innovations.

2 Name some companies or countries which are known for their innovation. What makes them successful in this area?

3 How much importance is attached to invention and innovation in your country?

3 CROSSWORD

Across

3 manufacturing method producing goods only when required (1, 1, 1)

5 the amount an organization can produce in a given time period (8)

7 very advanced, ahead in its field (technology) (7, 4)

8 systems technology that helps designers and manufacturers in their work (3, 3)

9 the use of computers to improve every aspect of the production process (1, 1, 1)

10 the term for inexpensive products that people buy regularly e.g. toiletries, supermarket products (1, 1, 1, 1)

Down

1 started in Japan, a discussion group made up of a variety of workers who meet to identify and solve problems (7, 6)

2 _____ engineering: taking a product or system apart to see how it works and to try and improve on it (7)

4 the right to be the only person or organization to produce or sell a product (6)

6 the process of measuring your company's performance against a standard e.g. the best in the industry (12)

1 RETAILING AND DISTRIBUTION

WORKING AS A TEAM IS A PIECE OF CAKE

That *sinking feeling* experienced by airline passengers when they realise they will be among the last to be served food on a flight could soon be a thing of the past. The familiar message that the salmon is finished and the Indian vegetarian meal is the only food available might be heard no more, following the successful introduction of a new supply chain system by British Airways, Tony Dawe writes.

Called Aerocater, the Web-based system enables catering managers at BA stations around the world to know precisely the number and nationality of passengers on board each flight and to plan food supplies accordingly. In the past, they had to rely on phone calls and faxes, which sometimes failed to reach them or were out of date so that either too much, too little or the wrong food was loaded. "With about 10 million items being loaded each day across our 160 locations, the logistics are incredibly complex – and inventory management is critical to our cash flow," says Martin Blinkhorn, BA's senior manager, catering business support. "Aerocater will make a significant contribution to our programme to reduce the levels of inventory in the system and reduce the amount of written-off stock. Its provision of *real-time data* has helped our forecasting team to further improve operating efficiencies and has greatly simplified the task of managing the loading of aircraft worldwide."

The system has been developed by Sita, set up 50 years ago by the airline industry to provide telecoms and then IT systems. The company estimates that nearly £200 million is wasted on redundant *in-flight* catering every year and now plans to offer the technology to airlines around the world. Sita provides Aerocater through an Application Service Provider model via the Internet and through its own secure, global Internet Protocol network. The service is hosted at Sita's information hub in London.

Tony Dawe, ©Times, (19/02/02)

Glossary

- *sinking feeling* – feeling that something bad is going to happen
- *real-time data* – up-to-date information
- *in-flight* – during the flight

ⓐ **Vocabulary extension**

Find words or phrases in the text which have the same meaning as the following:

1 process of manufacturing and distributing goods (*para. 1*)

2 organization of stock levels (*para. 2*)

3 goods which have been paid for, but which cannot be used (*para. 2*)

4 time and/or money saved through improved working practices (*para. 2*)

ⓑ **Questions on the text**

1 **Based on your understanding of the article, put the statements below into the correct column in the table.**

i Passengers are often disappointed to find that the food they require is unavailable.

ii Managers can identify the exact number and nationality of passengers on a particular flight.

iii The wrong food is often loaded onto a flight.

iv The information received by managers is often out of date by the time the food is ordered for the flight.

v A lot of food is wasted because it is not used.

vi The system depends on faxes and telephone calls.

vii The system simplifies a very complex supply chain system.

TRADITIONAL SYSTEM	AEROCATER SYSTEM

2 Which of the following sentences best summmarizes the benefit of Aerocater?

   i It uses the Internet to run its business.

   ii It has been set up by a well-established company.

   iii It allows airlines to save money by reducing the amount of food wasted on their flights.

   iv It allows airlines to produce food for any nationality or number of passengers.

☐ SALES METHODS

Discussion/Writing

1 Make a list of 'direct marketing' methods.

2 What are the advantages and disadvantages of direct marketing compared to other marketing techniques such as the use of mass media, personal selling, sales promotion etc?

3 Why is direct marketing so popular today?

4 As new generations of customers become more familiar with computers, do you think the use of catalogues and other traditional direct marketing methods will decrease? Explain your answer.

☐ WORD SEARCH

ⓐ **Put the following words and phrases in the correct column in the table below, and then find them in the word search grid on the next page. Words can go up, down or diagonally, backwards or forwards. The first one is shown as an example.**

intermediary	*work-in-progress*	*warehouse*	*loyalty card*	*logistics*	*cold call*	*end user*

distribution	orders and stock control	sales methods	retailing

b There are also three words in the grid connected with money and sales. Complete the following, and then find the words in the grid.

    i The number of products a company expects to sell during a particular period. Sales _____.

    ii The value of goods and services a company has sold during a particular period. _____.

    iii The money a company receives from people. _____

L	I	N	T	E	R	M	E	D	I	A	R	Y	S	W
N	O	X	I	D	R	W	W	L	D	P	A	S	C	A
O	S	Y	K	A	V	E	O	M	N	A	E	F	L	R
I	I	A	A	L	Q	G	V	O	J	R	Q	L	K	E
T	K	S	C	L	I	T	T	E	G	M	A	L	N	H
A	B	Y	X	S	T	M	S	O	N	C	G	J	T	O
T	B	P	T	K	Y	Y	R	A	D	U	Z	M	Z	U
O	P	I	V	U	X	P	C	L	C	R	E	M	H	S
R	C	D	C	C	N	H	O	A	A	E	A	V	R	E
S	F	E	S	I	H	C	N	A	R	F	R	N	J	N
D	D	J	K	G	K	Q	B	U	G	D	X	O	E	D
Z	F	R	M	A	V	Y	W	J	T	P	X	O	F	U
N	O	N	W	W	D	E	N	B	D	M	O	F	F	S
W	E	F	S	U	K	A	V	C	Y	G	Y	O	E	E
A	S	F	T	U	R	N	O	V	E	R	O	C	Y	R

1 BOOM AND BUST

THE NEXT BUBBLE IS JUST ROUND THE CORNER

Ever since speculators in the 1630s were briefly persuaded of the investment merits of Dutch tulips, financial markets have been characterised by manic booms and spectacular crashes. The 1990s dot com bubble was just the latest in a long line of speculative investment *frenzies*, and it certainly will not be the last.

It is, of course, easy to spot a bubble after the event. It may seem obvious now that prices in the Japanese property market of the late 1980s, or in the dot com boom of the late 1990s, had easily outstripped anything that could reasonably be called fair value. But, at the time of the frenzy, there were *a host of* arguments advanced to justify the over-stretched valuations.

Where ought the investor to start if he is to minimise risk, and maximise return, in these volatile financial times? Most important of all to remember is that there will, without a doubt, be another bubble. For savers, then, the key is *to tread with the utmost caution*.

What are the bubble warning signs? First, and most obviously, is a sharp rise in prices that is sustained over a period of months. Another danger signal is when prices rise so far that they are *out of kilter with* historic valuation measures. If savers take notice of little else, they should at least think twice when virtually everyone appears to have *jumped on the same financial bandwagon*. Simple economics tells you that tens of millions of investors cannot earn extraordinary rates of return from a single savings vehicle for too long.

The asset class that springs most easily to mind in any discussion of bubbles is the property market. House prices are currently at more than five times earnings, a level not seen since the late 1980s. This has led many to argue that, just as 15 years ago, a potentially ruinous bubble is developing in UK property. There are good reasons why some of the recent rise in UK house prices may be sustainable. Over the 1990s and the early part of this decade low inflation means interest rates have been tumbling. Borrowing costs are expected to remain relatively low even when the rate of economic expansion begins to pick up. This means that homeowners can afford to take out larger mortgages than before, a factor that has helped to send house prices higher. But unfortunately this has not been the only cause of the property boom. New research by HSBC concludes that at least some of the recent rise in values cannot be explained by pure economic factors. The implication is that we could easily be on the verge of a new property bubble.

The Asian tigers were, of course, the place to invest in the mid-1990s. But like virtually all investment 'miracles', South-East Asia failed to live up to its *advance billing*. Although there was plenty that was good about the region's economies, investors failed to recognise that there was also a whole range of problems – with disastrous consequences. Asia's economies have made solid progress on reform since the panic and the capital flight of the late 1990s. The recent rise in stock prices in the region shows that investors are beginning to appreciate the change. It is probably too soon to worry about a second bubble in emerging markets: investors are still relatively cautious and appear to be correctly distinguishing the promising Asian economies from the struggling ones, and have yet to push up prices too far. But emerging markets are certainly not a place for *the risk-averse*, and investors ought to proceed with care.

The government bond market – so long seen as *a safe haven* in times of financial turmoil – is another area where the danger signals are flashing. The dismal performance of equities since the dot-com bust of 2000 has led many funds to increase their exposure to bonds. As with emerging markets, the recent surge in the popularity of bonds has not gone nearly far enough to push the sector into bubble territory. But there are reasons to be suspicious about long-term prospects. First, most traditional valuation measures now suggest government bonds are expensive. Worrying, too, is the suggestion that the investor rush to bonds may be far from over. *Anecdotal* evidence from money managers indicates that many pension fund trustees are just beginning to consider a change in mandate that would increase exposure to bonds at the expense of equities. It could take many months for these changes to feed through into the market. This means that the demand for bonds is likely to be sustained for some time to come – despite the fact that prices are already looking stretched.

Bubbles are a natural characteristic of financial markets, and macroeconomic shifts mean there are likely to be at least as many periods of investment mania in the future as there have been in the past. For the saver, *the golden rule* is to be wary of asset classes that promise extraordinarily high rates of return. If it sounds too good to be true, it probably is.

Lea Paterson, © Times, (06/08/02)

Glossary

- *frenzies* – periods of madness, unwise behaviour
- *to tread with the utmost caution* – to act as carefully as possible
- *jumped on the same finincial bandwagon* – bought the same financial products
- *the risk-averse* – people who do not like taking risks
- *anecdotal* – unofficial

- *a host of* – many
- *out of kilter with* – significantly different from
- *advance billing* – what was promised beforehand
- *a safe haven* – a safe place
- *the golden rule* – the most important thing to remember

(a) **Vocabulary extension**

Find words or phrases in the text which have the same meaning as the following:
1 outperformed (*para. 2*)
2 put forward, suggested (*para. 2*)
3 difficult (*para. 5*)
4 able to continue without problems (*para. 5*)
5 falling rapidly (*para. 5*)
6 very poor (*para. 7*)
7 rapid rise (*para. 7*)
8 appear in, become evident in (*para. 7*)
9 too high (*para. 7*)
10 be careful of (*para. 8*)

(b) **Questions on the text**

1 **The writer identifies three areas at risk of financial bubbles: property, emerging markets and government bonds. The list below summarizes the reasons why each area is at risk. Put each risk in the appropriate box in the table below.**

   i Prices have increased because of low inflation and low interest rates.

   ii This is traditionally seen as a safe investment by buyers, but prices are too high now.

   iii More people are buying because the market for stocks and shares is not performing well at the moment.

   iv This market is risky because of problems in the economies.

   v People are borrowing larger sums of money, so prices rise.

2 The writer also gives some reasons why these areas may not suffer from bubbles in the future. Add these to the appropriate boxes in the third column.

   i People are better at identifying which economies are safe and which are more risky.

  ii The cost of borrowing money is likely to remain low, so buyers can afford to pay more.

 iii Buyers are more careful in this market than they were in the past.

 iv Although this area has become more popular, it is not yet popular enough for a bubble to appear.

	RISK FACTORS	REASONS WHY A BUBBLE MAY NOT APPEAR
property		
emerging markets		
government bonds		

ⓒ **Discussion/Writing**

  1 What other bubbles do you know about in history? Have there been any in your country's history?

  2 Prepare a short talk or write a short article on a bubble in your country's history, or another bubble you know of.

2 STOCKS AND SHARES

Discussion/Writing

  1 Which countries' stock exchanges do the following indexes belong to?:

   i Hang Seng   **iii** FTSE 100   **v** Xetra DAX

  ii Nikkei 225   **iiv** Dow Jones Industrial Average   **vi** Nasdaq 100

  2 Are the American/British stock markets experiencing a 'bull market' or a 'bear market' at present? What seem to be the reasons for this? Are all stock markets around the world in a similar position or are there differences between them?

  3 Search the stock market data online or in the newspaper. Which companies currently have the highest market capitalization?

3 COMPANIES LOSING THEIR WAY

ⓐ **Reading/Discussion**

The following extracts present a number of arguments for and against strict bankruptcy laws. Divide them into arguments in favour of strict laws and arguments against strict laws.

 i Japan is a difficult country in which to suffer failure – not because of a lack of appropriate legislation, but because of social attitudes to debt and bankruptcy. 'This is a country in which bankruptcy is regarded by many people as a crime'.

 ii At issue in this case is whether one spouse can by declaring bankruptcy avoid paying another the fair share of the marital property in a divorce settlement.

iii For too long in this country bankruptcy laws have worked against entrepreneurs. I want them to work for them. The prospect of failure puts off many potential entrepreneurs from having a go.

iv America's relatively debtor-friendly bankruptcy laws explain why it has a more entrepreneurial culture than countries where the law provides greater protection to creditors.

v It is one thing for bankruptcy laws to make entrepreneurs less fearful of taking sensible business risks; it is quite another for them to encourage people to borrow, and spend, recklessly in the knowledge that they can bail out later.

vi Some borrowers use the law to escape debts they could afford to repay, with none of the shame that it once entailed.

vii Bankruptcy laws that provide no second chance therefore cut into the rate of innovation by discouraging risk. Only in America is it safe to joke that any businessman who has not gone bankrupt at least once by the age of 30 is a failure.

FOR	AGAINST

ⓑ Questions on the texts

From your understanding of the short texts above, which of the following statements are true of the United States?

   i Bankruptcy is regarded as morally wrong.

   ii The laws tend to favour the person who has become bankrupt rather than the people who are owed money.

   iii The laws tend to favour the people who are owed money, rather than the person who has beome bankrupt.

   iv The laws discourage people from taking risks in business.

   v It is quite easy for someone who has become bankrupt to start another business.

ⓒ Discussion

Find words or phrases in the text that have the same meaning as the following:

   1 Which of the arguments above do you agree/disagree with and why?

   2 How do people view bankruptcy in your country? Are these people prepared to take risks? Is there a fear of failure?

   3 How easy is it for companies to 'turn things around' if they are in trouble?

4 CROSSWORD

Across

5 to cover your costs (5, 4)

6 a form of borrowing money (4)

7 very good results can be described in this way (9)

8 the difference between the production costs and the price (6)

Down

1 the % investors receive on shares (5)

2 to do much better than your competitors (5, 5)

3 the situation where the company is closed down and and its assets sold (11)

4 trying to solve problems in a company (15)

Topic 8   Finance

1 FINANCING EXPANSION

SPORTING GOODS MAKER THAT TOOK ITS EYE OFF THE BALL
The European market for buyouts is suffering because it is almost mature

The management buyout can be the route to riches for executives and providers of funds alike. But how do you manage your way out of *the MBO from hell*, where brands and products are outstanding but the company turns out to be financially unviable?

The problem: Dunlop Slazenger Group, the world-renowned maker of tennis rackets and tennis and golf balls, was bought from BTR in 1996. The price was £240 million, rising to £341 million once the various forms of debt the company had been loaded with were taken into account. That £240 million price represented ten times earnings before tax and interest. But Cinven, the venture capitalist that funded the deal, found that the profits this implied were unachievable.

There was worse. Management systems and financial reporting structures were more suited to an engineering company than a consumer goods business with a very complex product mix. For example, it was almost impossible to track the flow of products around the world. Each had been given a different code for each country.

The harder the new management team looked, the more bad news they found. Inefficiency was *rife*, to the extent that a 1998 study found a third of orders were either incomplete or not delivered on time. Dunlop had been allowed virtually to disappear, both among professional players and at the grass-roots level. Sponsorship had been cut, while contacts with local clubs that could ensure the brand was taken up by younger players had *withered*.

The players: Cinven moved to put in a new management team. First to arrive, in November 1997, was Alan Lovell as finance director. He was joined three months later by Phil Parnell, who, as managing director of United Distillers in Europe, had a background both in financial controls and consumer goods.

The solution: The challenges facing the new team were *fourfold*. Management controls had to be completely rebuilt. Manufacturing had to be rationalised. Money had to be spent on marketing, in particular, the Dunlop brand. Most *pressingly*, the company had to be put on a sound financial footing. All this had to be done at a time when Dunlop Slazenger's traditional markets were becoming even more competitive.

Tennis balls, at the time of the buyout, were being made in three countries, the UK, Germany and the Philippines. But costs were much lower in the Philippines. A dozen standard balls cost £2.90 to produce there, as opposed to £6.50 in Europe. The team decided to close most of the plants, and by the end of this year 95 per cent of production will be in the Philippines.

The revival of Dunlop as a brand was perhaps the hardest part. The clubs had been used by Arnold Palmer and Bernhard Langer, the rackets by virtually every senior player. But the last significant victor was John McEnroe in 1984. Parnell says: "It's a long *slog*, but it's well under way." He *points to* the Australian Open in January, where three semi-finalists and both finalists were using Dunlop. Sales have been helped by innovation, including expanding the range of stronger rackets. McEnroe has been signed up to endorse the balls, and a new form of waterproof tennis ball will be launched at Wimbledon.

On the financial side, Cinven agreed to write off the entire value of its investment and withdraw. Lenders, which included banks and Invensys, were asked to swap debt for equity. As a result, Invensys wrote off £130 million of debt but now has a warrant over 40 per cent of the equity. After the refinancing, banks and management had half the equity each, although this will shrink to 30 per cent *apiece* if Invensys takes up the warrants. The final decision was to withdraw from licensing and the distribution of Maxfli and Slazenger golf balls, handing this over to taylormade. Maxfli was losing $10 million a year. Under the new supply contract, the brand will make about £4 million a year. Furthermore, taylormade has an option to buy the brand outright over the next year for $75 million, which would shrink the existing debt burden of £130 million further.

The result: Lovell says: "We have got a budget for this year which is modest in its profitability but will deliver at least £3 million of profit." In addition, more rigorous housekeeping virtually halved inventories over the year to February, from £41 million to £22 million. There are likely to be further talks with banks, which could lead to a stronger balance sheet.

Martin Waller, © Times, (23/04/02)

Glossary

- *the MBO from hell* – the worst MBO you can imagine
- *withered* – been allowed to die, disappeared
- *pressingly* – urgently
- *points to* – uses as an example

- *rife* – widespread
- *fourfold* – four in number
- *slog* – difficult piece of work
- *apiece* – each

a Vocabulary extension

Find words or phrases in the text which have the same meaning as the following:

1 not able to perform as intended (*para. 1*)
2 burdened with (*para. 2*)
3 most basic, ordinary (*para. 4*)
4 streamlined (*para. 6*)
5 be put in a stronger financial position (*para. 6*)
6 renewal (*para. 8*)
7 recommend (*para. 8*)
8 guarantee, right to buy (*para. 9*)
9 uses its right to buy (*para. 9*)
10 completely (*para. 9*)
11 amount of money owed (*para. 9*)
12 day-to-day management (*para. 10*)

b Questions on the text

1 Look at paragraphs 2–5, which outline the problems faced by the company after the MBO. Match the problems i–iv below with their causes v–viii.

PROBLEMS

i The company couldn't make enough profit to repay its debts.
ii It was very difficult to track movement of the company's products.
iii A third of orders were delivered late, or were not correct when they arrived.
iv The Dunlop brand was not as widely recognised as it had been in the past.

CAUSES

v The organisation of the supply chain was too complicated.
vi There was widespread inefficiency in the company's management systems.
vii The company had reduced the sponsorship of famous players and did not have a strong relationship with smaller golf and tennis clubs.
viii The company had borrowed heavily during the MBO.

2 Paragraph 6 identifies four general areas that need to be addressed. For each area, summarize what was done in the table below.

PROBLEM	SOLUTION
Management controls/supply chain had to be strengthened	
Manufacturing had to be streamlined	
Marketing had to be improved	
Company finances had to be strengthened	

(c) **Discussion**

1 In the 1990s there was a boom in Internet companies, followed by a slump in recent years. What effect do you think a growing market and a falling market have on venture capitalists' behaviour?

2 What are the most popular ways for companies to finance expansion in your country? How popular are MBOs?

2 ACCOUNTING

(a) **Discussion**

1 Who are the 'Big 5' accounting firms? Are they present in your country?
2 What is the purpose of a set of accounts? Who are they for? What should they show?
3 What are the advantages and disadvantages of an international accounting system?
4 Do you know which accounting system your country follows?
5 Have there been any scandals relating to companies' accounting practices in your country?
6 What is the view of accountancy as a job in your country?

(b) **Discussion/Writing**

1 In the so-called 'new economy', tangible assets such as buildings and equipment are not seen as being as important as intangible assets such as brands. Look at the following examples of intangible assets and decide which of the four headings they come under in the table:

   i customer satisfaction
  ii a highly qualified workforce
 iii a high level of spending on looking for ways to improve the product
  iv well-trained employees
   v speed of product to market
  vi 'Marks & Spencer', 'Virgin', 'Coca Cola'

vii a good client list

viii creating completely new products

intellectual capital	research and development	brands	other

2 What problems do you think might exist when trying to measure the value (not the cost or expenses) of intellectual capital, R&D and brands to a company?

3 WORD SEARCH

ⓐ **Put the following words and phrases in the correct column in the table below, and then find them in the word search grid on the next page. Words can go up, down or diagonally, backwards or forwards. The first one is shown as an example.**

insolvency   all-cash deal   expenditure   cash flow   rights issue
invoice   working capital   profit margin   bill

having no money	costs	paying money	financing expansion

ⓑ You will also find the opposite of the following words in the grid:

i fixed [cost] _____ [cost]   **iii** borrower _____

ii creditor _____   **iv** assets _____

ⓒ If you fail to pay a debt when it is due, you _____ _____ the debt.
This term is also in the grid.

R Z I W E M Z Q U B C C D L L

K O F S W P F P X T H E E Z I

D P F S Q L J A O K X T F P A

W O R K I N G C A P I T A L B

F O U O Y H R J E O V E U E I

B S L A F O B N G A Q C L U L

I N N F T I D M R R W I T S I

N N S B H I T I O G E O O S T

L S E E T S A M P P B V N I I

S D F U J B A H A B Y N H S E

E Z R R L Y Y C N R I I R T S

K E L E N D E R L S G L G H J

L A E D H S A C L L A I L G W

I N S O L V E N C Y A Y N I R

U T P M H F F O E T I R W R S

1 BRANDING

ⓐ **Key word review**

Fill in the spaces in the text. Choose from the following words and phrases:

brand extender	brand loyalty	brand	diversified
brand extension	stretching your brand		mother brand

You used to know where you were with a brand name but now a successful tag can fit anything. Claire Cozens charts the crossover hits and misses.

BRAND NEW WORLD

Once brands knew their place. Cosmopolitan was a magazine, Coca-Cola was a drink and Lynx was that *naff* after-shave that came in gift-packs at Christmas time.

Now, all that's changed. Cosmo girl can already enjoy her monthly magazine *fix* while lying on her Cosmopolitan sheets (Britain's second-biggest linen _____) and soon she'll be able to enjoy her favourite *glossy* while sipping a *skinny latte* in a Cosmopolitan café.

Meanwhile Coca-Cola has lent its name to a range of clothes, while French Connection – originally a clothes brand – has _____ into drinks with the launch of a new *alcopop* called FCUK Spirit.

The industry could be forgiven for thinking that when it comes to _____, anything goes. After all, if you can find a profitable new line of business and get a bit of extra exposure for your brand into the bargain, surely you can't lose. Or can you?

While Cosmopolitan is now one of the most successful examples of _____ generating profits in new areas, the magazine *notched up* at least one costly error before its recent successes. Cosmo yoghurt had to be quietly taken off the supermarket shelves a year ago after 18 months in business. Jane Wentworth, a senior consultant with the brand consultancy Wolff Olins, believes the most common mistake is to introduce a brand extension that isn't credible.

"I'm not surprised Cosmo yoghurts failed. But I can see the cafés working; you can imagine it being very *Sex and the City*, somewhere to have fun and gossip with your friends. Any brand extension has to be credible for the _____. Companies use brand extensions to reach new audiences and to make the most of their promotional spend – but the important thing is not to tarnish the original brand."

If the goal is to transfer your good reputation in one area into another, Virgin was the prime example of a successful _____. But its ill-fated *foray* into the cola market and unpopular trains have highlighted the dangers of _____ too far. And the bigger your brand, the more you have to lose.

Claire Cozens, ©The Guardian (11/03/02)

Glossary

- *naff* – unfashionable
- *fix* – dose
- *glossy* – magazine
- *skinny latte* – milky coffee
- *alcopop* – a mix of alcohol and fruit juice marketed at young people
- *notched up* – made
- *Sex and the City* – a popular TV series set in New York
- *foray* – venture

ⓑ **Vocabulary extension**

Find a word or phrase in the text that has the same meaning as the following:

1 introduction of a new product (*para. 3*)

2 money used for advertising the product (*para. 6*)

3 result to aim at (*para. 7*)

ⓒ **Questions on the text**

Are the following TRUE or FALSE?

1 Brands are no longer exclusively associated with one product.

2 Virgin has been successful with all of its many brand extensions.

3 Cosmo yoghurt is an example of the dangers of stretching a brand too far.

ⓓ **Discussion**

Think of some well-known companies who have extended their brand.

1 What products have they diversified into?

2 Which products have been successful? Which have been unsuccessful and why?

3 Have the failures of some brand extensions damaged the company's brand image?

4 Does the brand seem to have lost some of its 'core values'?

2 GLOBAL ADVERTISING

ⓐ **Key word review**

Fill the spaces in the article using the terms in the box below:

> *campaign (5)*   *agency (1)*   *advertising (1)*   *agencies (3)*   *brand (2)*
> *ad (2)*   *global advertising campaign (1)*

GUINNESS ORDERS RETHINK ON ADVERTISING

Guinness drinkers may believe that good things come to those who wait, but it seems the company behind the world's best-loved beer is less convinced.

After a four-year _____ trying to persuade publicans and drinkers alike that Guinness was a superior drink and should not be poured like a common lager or ale, the company has decided to *change tack* again.

Owner Guinness UDV is *ditching* the long-running advertising _____ that sought to persuade drinkers their pint was worth the wait as it faces up to an increasingly crowded drinks market.

The company has briefed its two advertising _____, Abbott Mead Vickers BBDO and Saatchi & Saatchi, to come up with a new _____ for the brand that will be shown across the world.

AMV is the _____ behind the current _____, which includes the highly acclaimed Guinness "Surfer" film, voted best _____ of all time by Channel 4 viewers.

It will be the first time Guinness, which spends more than £200m a year on _____, has run a _____ – the company has traditionally used different _____ around the world to create country-specific campaigns.

But last year Guinness cut its roster of international advertising _____ down to just two and the planned _____ is a further signal that Guinness UDV is trying to develop a more consistent global image for the _____.

Although the _____ continues to enjoy healthy sales across the world, its growth in Europe has *stalled* as bar-goers *eschew* beer in favour of wines and pre-mixed drinks.

One idea being developed would see Guinness returning to its Irish roots with a _____ based on hurling, the popular Irish sport it sponsors.

© *The Guardian (18/01/02)*

Glossary

- *change tack* – change direction, try a different way
- *ditching* – stopping, abandoning
- *stalled* – stopped
- *eschew* – stop (drinking)

ⓑ Questions on the text

Based on your understanding of the article, complete the sentences in a suitable way:

1 Guinness is changing its advertising campaign because …
2 It has never used … before.
3 Europe is the place where …
4 Irish sport may …

ⓒ Discussion/Writing

1 What are the advantages and disadvantages of having a global advertising campaign? Use Guinness and/or other brands to explain your ideas.
2 Make a list of other marketing techniques apart from mass media advertising. What advantages/ disadvantages do they have? Again, use Guinness and/or other brands as examples.

3 CROSSWORD

Across
1 offering a lower price than usual (11)
5 the final stage of the product lifecycle (7)
6 something that makes a brand different from its competitors (1, 1, 1)
7 to adapt (e.g. advertisements) to your particular needs (6)
8 if demand changes significantly with a small change in price, the product is price-_____ (9)
10 a high price (7)
11 when consumers always buy the same product whatever the competition offers (5, 7)

Down
2 unbranded (product) (7)
3 a brand's _____ is the impression people have of it (5)
4 another word for a poster (9)
5 another phrase for secondary data (4, 8)
9 when a market is full and there is no opportunity for growth (10)

■ DESCRIBING TRADING PERFORMANCE AND SALES OBJECTIVES

IT'S A GAME OF MORE BUBBLE FOR YOUR BUCKS

Marketing chiefs at Coca-Cola's head office in Atlanta are said to be working on a vanilla-flavoured version of its core soft drink, described as the biggest innovation in the world's most valuable brand in almost 20 years.

The plans are the first fruits of an attempt to put some *fizz* back into Coke. The brand and the wider business have suffered a *lacklustre* couple of years, largely because of a *morale-sapping* internal re-organisation of the company.

The Coca-Cola group lost 0.4% of crucial US market share, falling to 43.7% last year; it also suffered a 0.2% fall in sales, according to trade magazine Beverage Digest. Pepsi-Co gained 0.2% of market share, giving it 31.6% of the US soft drinks market and sales up by 1.3%.

Things have begun to *look up* for Coke. The group was *buoyed up* by its sponsorship of the Winter Olympics, an event that gained surprisingly good ratings in the US. A lemon-flavoured version of Diet Coke, launched last year, also proved popular. Last week, the group raised its sales forecasts for the first quarter to between 4% and 5%, and it expects to have regained momentum in North America.

Coke's shares are at half the level they were in 1998 but have rallied since the beginning of the year. They have climbed from $44 to almost $53. The emphasis on new brand development and the fresh shake-up in Atlanta have impressed Wall Street, and both Credit Suisse First Boston and Lehman Brothers raised their ratings on the group last week.

In the US, at least, there is little or no growth to be had in the cola market without some innovation.

Sales of both the core Coke and Pepsi cola brands have been faltering in recent years. Coke volumes fell by 2% last year and Pepsi dropped by 2.8%. The diet versions of both colas improved sales, but not by enough to make up the deficit.

With consumers becoming more health conscious, sweet fizzy stuff is losing share to plain old bottled water. But even there, Pepsi has been more *nimble*. It was faster to spot the growth than its competitor and is ranked number two in the US bottled water market after Perrier. Coke lies third.

© *The Guardian (02/04/02)*

Glossary

- *fizz* – energy
- *lacklustre* – disappointing
- *morale-sapping* – discouraging
- *look up* – get better
- *buoyed up* – encouraged
- *nimble* – quick-moving

ⓐ **Vocabulary extension**

Find words or phrases in the text with the same meaning as the following:

1 a particular form of something (*para. 1*)
2 main (*para. 1*)
3 re-arranging the structure inside the company (*para. 2*)
4 recovered (*para. 5*)
5 re-organization, major change (*para. 5*)
6 loss, shortfall (*para. 7*)

ⓑ Key word review

According to the text, are the following TRUE or FALSE?

	True	False
1 Sales of the core Coca-Cola and Pepsi brands have risen steadily recently.	☐	☐
2 Coca-Cola is planning an expansion of its product range.	☐	☐
3 The two companies' main priority seems to be to increase their market share.	☐	☐
4 Demand for cola seems to have reached a peak.	☐	☐
5 The two companies are engaged in a price war.	☐	☐
6 Coke's share price has shown an improvement this year.	☐	☐
7 The Coca-Cola group's sales turnover has increased while Pepsi's has fallen.	☐	☐

ⓒ Discussion/Writing

Discuss the following issues in relation to the Coca-Cola article:

1 What are the possible dangers of a company constantly introducing new product lines?

2 Why is there little growth in the cola market? Add to the ideas in the text.

3 What measures do you think Coca-Cola could take to improve sales? Evaluate the following possibilities:

　　i give the product a more contemporary look, re-evaluate its image

　　ii expand its product range – if so, how?

　iii sell into new markets

　　iv undercut its competitors

　　v use more merchandising

　vi change its promotion strategy

② REPOSITIONING THE BRAND

Charities are now considered big brands but what happens when the name, logo or corporate identity need a makeover? Nicola Hill picked up some tips from a leading consultant.

HOW TO TRANSFORM YOUR CHARITY INTO A TOP BRAND

Branding must be led by the chief executive and senior management, says David Coe, chief executive of Kingston Smith consultancy. Mr Coe should know, he led the rebranding of the charities Orbis and Amnesty International before becoming a consultant.

After conducting an audit of existing materials, Mr Coe recommends consulting with stakeholders, including staff, partners, volunteers, *service users* and suppliers. He also suggests setting up a branding group comprised of a range of stakeholders to lead the exercise and act as both brand *champions* and critics.

To help with the process, charities should conduct a product analysis. This involves seeing the charity as a product, looking at its positioning, its personality and its brand character. The product could be operating a *flying ambulance*, running a *meals-on-wheels service* or protecting children. To assess positioning, the charity needs to ask itself how it compares with competitors, who supports it and why, and what benefits it offers.

The personality of the charity will include its values, whether it is open, honest, has a good relationship with stakeholders and the colours and type of logo used. To assess the character of a brand, Mr Coe suggests describing the charity as an animal or symbol. At Amnesty, the rebranding group described the charity as an elephant – slow and bureaucratic. It wanted to become a cheetah.

To make sure branding fits in with the charity's operations, Mr Coe advises charities to consider other issues, for example, how the rebranding fits in with strategic plans and how the *vision*, mission and values of a charity might be affected. "These may be an integral part of the rebranding exercise but not if a charity is three years through a five-year strategic plan."

According to Mr Coe, the rewards of rebranding include integrating the organisation, increasing the public's trust and confidence, reducing fundraising costs, increased staff loyalty and as a result of all this, greater income.

Nicola Hill, ©The Guardian (21/02/02)

Glossary

- *service users* – customers of a service such as a charity or health service
- *champions* – supporters
- *flying ambulance* – medical team who work from a plane or helicopter
- *meals-on-wheels service* – service which takes hot meals to people's homes if they are too old or sick to cook for themselves
- *vision* – hopes and ideas for the future

(a) **Vocabulary extension**

Find words or phrases in the article that have the same meaning as the following:

1 independent expert (*para. 1*)   4 unnecessarily complicated, with too many rules (*para. 4*)
2 examination of a product (*para. 3*)   5 proposals for the future of the business (*para. 5*)
3 symbol (*para. 4*)   6 finding money for a charity (*para. 6*)

(b) **Questions on the text**

1 How did Amnesty want to change their public image?
2 How does Mr Coe suggest re-evaluating a brand?

(c) **Discussion**

1 Which companies have tried re-branding? Why did they do it? Have they been successful?
2 Which companies in your country are in need of rebranding in order to rejuvenate their images? What changes would you suggest they make?

3 WORD SEARCH

Put the following words and phrases in the correct column in the table below, and then find them in the word search grid on the next page. Words can go up, down or diagonally, backwards or forwards. The first one is shown as an example.

| price fixing   mission statement   greenfield site   undercut   cartel   enterprise zone |
| collusion   maximization   loss leader   relocate   new market |

sales objectives	relocating the business	the war for sales

```
M  N  K  N  J  H  Q  X  W  Y  J  S  Y  E  U  M
O  I  O  D  E  W  H  R  K  K  B  M  X  N  N  O
W  Q  S  I  B  W  L  J  R  X  E  M  M  T  D  J
R  Q  E  S  T  V  M  E  P  G  Q  T  D  E  E  U
G  L  D  W  I  A  L  A  D  F  X  S  S  R  R  M
N  F  L  L  O  O  Z  N  R  J  S  K  W  P  C  A
I  B  S  D  C  Q  N  I  B  K  L  G  R  R  U  X
X  U  C  A  Z  T  K  S  M  B  E  E  Y  I  T  P
I  T  T  O  W  R  F  K  T  I  D  T  Y  S  S  Q
F  E  L  E  T  R  A  C  S  A  X  O  T  E  X  S
E  I  L  I  D  F  N  E  M  T  A  U  Z  C  M
C  Y  P  O  Z  G  H  L  N  B  F  E  M  O  I  B
I  C  O  L  L  U  S  I  O  N  V  C  M  N  H  R
R  S  E  T  I  S  D  L  E  I  F  N  E  E  R  G
P  P  P  K  O  O  W  M  A  L  R  D  D  F  N  A
E  E  Y  L  U  K  A  W  W  U  H  G  K  L  R  T
```

1 ATTRACTING AND KEEPING CUSTOMERS AND CUSTOMER CARE

THE INSIDE TRACK

Customer complaints

It is said that the English never complain, but if that was ever true, things have changed. Research by the Institute of Customer Service (ICS) shows that compared with the other three nations in the United Kingdom, the English are more likely to complain about poor service.

Two-thirds of those surveyed anticipated making more complaints this year than they did last. It might be argued that it is not the English but the quality of services that has changed. And few will be surprised to learn that the organisation most complained about is a railway company.

Paradoxically, complaints can be good for business. ICS research shows that nine out of 10 people who have a complaint dealt with satisfactorily are likely to recommend the services of the company concerned to a friend.

In theory, at least, many marketing departments now argue that a company's brand is not its product but its people. The most visible symbol of this is the television advertisements that feature real employees – there is an underlying philosophy at work here. And the purpose of the ICS research is not to produce a *league table* of competence but to demonstrate that there is a correlation between share price and customer satisfaction. And its latest report, written by Robert Johnston of Warwick University, achieves exactly that.

Naturally everybody is in favour of good customer service, but not everyone is delivering it. "The boards of many companies in the UK still believe that, although good customer service may be desirable, it is a cost that they are not prepared to fully commit to," says Paul Cooper, business development director at the ICS.

Of course it might be argued that customer service is a wasted effort if employees are *flogging a dead horse*. For example, if rail management won't invest in new trains, there is little to be said that will cheer up the passengers. But it is not always that straightforward. For companies that deliver as much customer dissatisfaction as the rail firms, the *unschooled*, and presumably unauthorised, customer service announcement "Sorry, but the driver hasn't turned up" will fast become *a collector's item*.

© Bill Saunders, The Guardian (07/01/02)

Glossary

- *paradoxically* – strangely
- *league table* – list which shows how successful a company is compared with other similar companies
- *flogging a dead horse* – trying to achieve something that cannot be done
- *unschooled* – not the result of training
- *a collector's item* – very rare

a) Vocabulary extension

Find words or phrases in the text with the same meaning as the following:

1 hidden theory (*para. 4*)   3 relationship, connection (*para. 4*)

2 ability (*para. 4*)   4 done without permission (*para. 6*)

b) Questions on the text

1 What trend can be identified among English consumers?

2 Who is more likely to complain, an English person or a Scots person?

3 Explain the paradox mentioned in paragraph 3.

c) Discussion/Writing

1 The text mentions the cost of customer service. What factors are involved in providing good customer service?

2 Do you think that people in your country are more or less likely to complain than British people?

3 Imagine that you work in the customer services department of the following companies. In each case, discuss how you would deal with the complaints mentioned.

  i You work for an international airline. A businesswoman has arrived at her destination, but her suitcase, containing the documents and clothes she needs for an important meeting, has been left behind.

  ii You work for a busy restaurant. The people who live in the neighbouring area have been complaining about the noise from music and from customers leaving the restaurant late at night.

  iii You work for a railway company. A number of customers have complained that their commuter service has been late or cancelled on 28 of the last 35 days. It is autumn, and some of the delays have been caused by poor weather.

  iv You work for a large hospital. An elderly patient fell and hurt her leg at home. When her son brought her to the hospital, she had to wait five hours to see a doctor. Her son has also complained that she was left overnight on a bed in the corridor because there were no beds available on the wards.

OR

Write a letter responding to one of the complaints above.

2 CUSTOMER CARE

The following short texts deal with various aspects of customer care.

1 Every complaint must be put in writing and we undertake to respond to that complaint within 24 hours.

2 Despite booking wheelchair assistance, I had to ask a fellow passenger to push me to the departure gate for my Ryanair flight from Stansted to Biarritz.

3 Then there was the travel agent who told me about her customer losing a 'held booking' through having to wait more than 30 minutes on the phone to confirm.

4 'Managers should put in a call after a sale to check if the client is happy with the goods or services,' says Fosbrook. 'This will help to avoid late payments for dissatisfaction'.

5 Tradesmen who worked for Steve Clark began to get the idea he was serious about customer care when he arrived on site and threw their transistor radio in the bin. Other things that are banned on Clark Contracts sites include earrings and brand name clothing.

6 Hotel staff in Scotland have such poor language skills that workers in 97% of hotels were unable to answer basic questions in French and German from prospective customers, a survey has revealed.

7 Results in the survey showed that callers who managed to get through to an advertised business number spent more than 40% of their time either on hold, in a queue or being continually transferred.

8 If there is a shipping delay, a customer-care staffer contacts the buyer in question immediately. 'We don't want customers to have to call us to find out what's going on with their order,' says Mauriello.

a) Questions on the text

1 Which of the situations above represent good customer care, and which represent poor customer care?

GOOD CUSTOMER CARE: _____

POOR CUSTOMER CARE: _____

2 For each of the situations in the texts above which represent poor customer care, what could the company do to improve the situation?

ⓑ Discussion

1 Do you agree or disagree with the following statements? Give reasons for your answers.

i The quality of a company's product has the biggest effect on how people view a company.

ii Good customer service does not mean that that everyone in an organization has to have the same values.

iii Poor customer service always makes me take my business elsewhere.

2 Below is a list of factors which contribute to good customer care. Rank them in order of importance, giving reasons for your choices.

i Well-trained staff

ii Politeness of staff when dealing with customers

iii Efficiency and speed of dealing with customer enquiries

iv Smart appearance of staff

v Flexibility of staff

vi Service with a smile

vii Good pay and conditions of work

viii Staff familiarity with products

ix Satisfactory response to complaints

x Rewards for customer loyalty (e.g. air miles, money-off vouchers etc.)

xi Corporate hospitality

❸ CUSTOMER CARE, STAFF TRAINING AND DEVELOPMENT, CORPORATE IMAGE AND CONSUMER PROTECTION

Discussion/Writing

1 E-commerce is growing. It has been said that it is the quality of the experience which makes particular online retailers popular. What does good customer service involve in online retailing? Use your own experiences to give you ideas or just imagine how it might be different from (or similar to!) traditional retailing where face-to-face contact is so important.

2 What kinds of training and development make employees more motivated and lead to better customer service? Can the right kind of training overcome a) a boring job b) the wrong people in the company?

3 Think of some companies who have very strong corporate images. How do they promote the company image? Do they have a good image or a bad image? What factors have contributed to their image – customer service, quality of product, innovation, environmental record etc?

4 How important is the issue of consumer protection in your country? Give examples of laws or other measures which protect consumers. Give examples of companies who have treated consumers particularly badly or well.

❹ CROSSWORD

Across

5 a statement issued by a company to the media about something of public interest (5, 7)

6 business customers (7)

7 promotional methods that a company has direct control over, such as special offers or free samples in shops (5, 3, 4)

8 a law in the UK which aims to protect people against the misuse of information about them stored on computer (4, 10)

9 see 2 down

10 what is seen as the company's most important product (8, 5)

Down

1. written rules which describe how people working in a particular company or profession should behave (4, 2, 8)
2. **and 9 across** – the entertainment at events that a company provides for its most valued customers (9, 11)
3. a situation at work where a more experienced person gives help and advice to a new recruit (9)
4. the initial training that a new recruit gets when they join a company (9)
5. the work a company does to improve its image and relationship with the public (6, 9)

1 FINANCIAL SERVICES

EASY DOES IT WHEN YOU LOG ON

Smile got the nod for being the best financial services website

Every financial services company *worth its salt* has a website. And with half the UK adult population able to access the net from home or work according to the latest figures, consumer demand for quality service online is increasingly high.

Websites that are simple, secure and easy to *navigate* are crucial to the estimated 6.5m online banking customers who rely on them to manage their day-to-day transactions swiftly and efficiently at any time.

This is where Smile, the internet bank launched by the Co-operative Bank in 1999 and winner of the award for the best financial services website, *comes into its own*.

With more than a million customers and attracting between 15,000 and 20,000 new account holders a month, the bank with an ethical policy and *high street-beating* interest rates has consistently won praise for its website design and underlying customer service.

It scores highly in the wide range of functions customers can carry out online, from setting up and amending *standing orders* and cancelling *direct debits* to bill paying and transferring money.

For a bank that views itself as "multi-channel" rather than strictly "internet-only", the back-up services are also important. Without yet offering the facility to deposit or download cash, Smile makes cash withdrawals and deposits easier than some rivals. Customers can cash cheques or pay in money at any of 18,000 post offices and can use any Link cash machine to make withdrawals.

There's a 24-hour call centre staffed by a team of 200 people if you encounter any problems. "Providing full details of how to contact them in person is of critical importance for an online bank," says Sarah Mahaffy. "Many visitors to the internet prefer the sound of a sympathetic human voice rather than an impersonal email response."

Ms Mahaffy adds: "Internet banks have been quicker to get away from the *stuffy* image of banking projected by their high street competitors. I think that Smile and Egg *run neck and neck* on providing sites which really don't look like a bank at all."

Jill Papworth, © The Guardian (29/06/02)

Glossary

- *worth its salt* – deserving respect
- *navigate* – move around
- *comes into its own* – starts to perform very well
- *high-street beating* – better than traditional banks
- *standing order* – arrangement with a bank to pay someone a set amount regularly
- *direct debit* – arrangement with a bank for a person or company to take money regularly from your account
- *stuffy* – old fashioned
- *run neck and neck* – are almost equal

a) Vocabulary extension

Find words or phrases in the text which have the same meaning as the following:

1 regular pieces of business (*para. 2*)
2 rules about matters such as politics, the environment etc. (*para. 4*)
3 support services (*para. 6*)
4 money taken from a bank account (*para. 6*)
5 meet (*para. 7*)

ⓑ Discussion

Are the following features of *Internet-only* banking or *traditional high-street* banking? Sort the features into advantages and disadvantages of the two types of banking and write your answers in the table below.

1 less competitive deals e.g. lower savings rates, higher rates on credit cards, higher mortgage rates
2 possible worries over security
3 face-to-face contact possible
4 greater convenience e.g. with opening hours
5 cheaper costs per customer allow better deals on financial products
6 start-up costs of the business are very large
7 some lack of personal customer service
8 possible technical problems
9 less convenient in terms of opening hours and waiting for service
10 possibly greater trust associated with established brand names

	Internet-only banking	traditional high-street banking
advantages		
disadvantages		

ⓒ Discussion/Writing

1 To what extent will online banking remain a "niche product"? Consider some of the advantages and disadvantages of the different types of banking and the future direction of banking and its customers.
2 It has been said that services such as banking will adopt a multi-channel retail strategy; that is, a mix of the Internet, telephone banking, the high-street, use of mobile phones. What would be the advantages and disadvantages for a bank of following such a strategy?

2 CALL CENTRES

TIME TO SPEAK UP IF YOU'RE A REAL OPERATOR

Call centres are frequently described as *sweat shops*, yet the sector has continued to expand – 22% on average every year – and now employs more than 500,000 people in the UK.

But the industry has suffered some bad news of late. BT announced that it was closing 53 of its smaller call centres but spending £100m on creating "next generation multi-function customer contact centres."

"The call centre is becoming a thing of the past," says Nigel Paget, director of customer services at RAC Motoring Services. A new *vernacular*, "contact centres" *heralds* the arrival of an exciting era of high quality customer service.

Higher skills will be necessary in the call centres of the future, predicts Maddie Reed, responsible for call centres and telecoms within e-skills UK.

"All of a sudden it's more about diagnosing problems. The nature of what people are doing will evolve. It's good for the sector and it's very good for older people and mothers returning to work. The more advanced companies are recognising that a *bums-on-seats mentality* doesn't necessarily work. The challenge is how to *skill up* people."

One way of making the job more interesting is by varying tasks. BT's plans to introduce multi-function centres will do just that. What this means for the customer, is that rather than being *driven from pillar to post*, the same BT person will be able to help you with a wide range of queries.

But George Callaghan, a social scientist who has spent a lot of time studying the issues facing call centres is unconvinced about the changes being made by employers.

"They've created a pretty awful job and now they're having to find ways of *alleviating* the boredom," he says. "They're looking at teams, but teamwork is not necessary for the business to take place."

"People say that working in a call centre suits them because they can work flexible hours," he says. "But hardly anyone says: 'I like the work'. "

The number of people working in call centres is forecasted to rise to one million by 2005. But it might take some time before call centres manage to shake off their old image. And as for whether we'll all start calling them customer contact centres, *the jury is out.*

© *The Guardian (13/04/02)*

Glossary

- *sweat shops* – places where people work very hard for very little money
- *vernacular* – language used by a particular group of people
- *heralds* – announces
- *bums-on-seats mentality* – idea that quantity is more important than quality
- *skill up* – improve the skills of
- *driven from pillar to post* – sent from one person to another
- *alleviating* – reducing
- *the jury is out* – it is undecided

Questions on the text

1 Match the sentence halves together so that they make possible arguments **FOR** and **AGAINST** call centres.

a They allow flexible

b The work is monotonous

c Employees are closely

d The work is considered especially suitable for

e Shift work is often involved requiring employees

f The work will become increasingly skilled and customers will benefit from

g Call centres are increasingly likely to move to countries where

h The work is badly

i Call centres are the 21st century equivalent

j Employees' performance is judged on

i monitored and allowed few breaks.

ii one person being able to deal with all their questions.

iii women as they are believed to have good communication skills.

iv of an early 20th century factory.

v working patterns.

vi paid and it is hard work; stressful and tiring.

vii to work unsociable hours.

viii and 'narrow'.

ix how many calls they make in a certain time.

x set-up costs are lower and labour is cheap.

2 Which of these points are mentioned in the text?

3 Sort the points into FOR and AGAINST and write them in the table below.

FOR	AGAINST

4 Which of the above points do you think are probably true?

❸ SERVICES

Discussion/Writing

1 It has been suggested that the rigid distinction between what is called **manufacturing** and what are called **services** is disappearing. Discuss why this might be true. Think about a range of manufacturing and service 'products' and also consider the following concepts:

    mass customization   *increasingly demanding customers*   *advanced technology*

2 Discuss the following in relation to your country:

  i the balance between services and other sectors of the economy

  ii the importance of the leisure industry in the economy and the nature of 'work-life balance' for people

  iii the significance of online services and call centres in the economy

  iv examples of companies who provide good and bad service in your country

❹ WORD FINDER

What are the phrases below? Some mixed-up clues are given underneath:

1 m _ _ _ _ _ f _ _ _ _ _

2 m _ _ _ _ _ s _ _ _ _ _ _ _ _ _ _ _

3 m _ _ _ _ _ s _ _ _ _

4 t _ _ _ _ _ _ _ i _ _ _ _ _ _ _

5 p _ _ _ _ _ s _ _ _ _ _ b _ _ _ _ _

6 c _ _ _ p _ _ _ _

7 s _ _ _ _ _ c _ _ _ _ _ _

a where you can get money anytime

b dividing up the market into different parts

c supply and demand

d the sector that does not produce goods

e one company's proportion of the sales of a product

f organizations run or funded by the government

g an EU law that deals with conditions at work

1 MANAGEMENT AND LEADERSHIP STYLES

PACKAGES; PREMIER EXECUTIVE

HOW well do you manage your team? Executives dismissing "pink and fluffy" skills such as listening, communicating and empathy now have reason to adjust their prejudice; employers are increasingly appraising them on such abilities – and linking this to pay. A new study by Ashridge Management College revealed the surprising finding that over a third of employers in the survey offer some kind of performance bonus based on the way in which managers treat their staff.

The logic is that the teamwork, motivation and skills in an organisation play a *pivotal* role in the success of the business. Managers who are good at fostering this ought to be rewarded. The Ashridge report notes: "If people management skills are as crucial as data suggest, then surely every effort should be made to measure and reward them?"

The problem is, how to measure something as complex and intangible as leadership style? Pam Jones, head of the Performance Through People programme at Ashridge, says, however, that the measurement is not impossible. She adds that the traditionally 'hard' *yardsticks* such as profits and sales, are just as difficult to measure in modern organisations, because it can be difficult to attribute financial performance to individuals with any clarity. "So-called 'hard' matters are difficult to measure, because of the matrix structures in organisations. It is difficult to pay Joe as the guy who has brought in the money when there are so many influences affecting targets," says Ms Jones.

To measure people management skills, employers can use results of appraisals of a manager's performance by his or her staff. They can also assess the competencies of individual managers; and they can measure the climate of a team – staff answering questionnaires on how motivated, rewarded and autonomous they feel. These are *fraught with* difficulties, however, particularly when using appraisals. If the staff know that their view has an influence on their manager's pay, and they also consider managers' pay to be too high, the chances of an honest appraisal diminish.

Similarly, managers may be reluctant to discipline poor performers, knowing that they have an indirect say in the level of their bonus. Employers need measures that are subtle, fair, as objective as is possible and immune to *perverse* incentives. No one has yet answered all the requirements but that is true of all performance-related pay schemes.

Philip Whiteley, © Times, 04/07/02

Glossary

- *pivotal* – key, important
- *yardsticks* – ways of measuring
- *fraught with* – full of
- *perverse* – abnormal

(a) **Vocabulary extension**

Find words or phrases in the text which have the same meaning as the following:

1 understanding how other people feel (*para. 1*)
2 judging, assessing (*para. 1*)
3 developing, nurturing (*para. 2*)
4 very important (*para. 2*)
5 indefinable (*para. 3*)
6 demonstrate who is responsible for (*para. 3*)
7 abilities (*para. 4*)
8 independent (*para. 4*)
9 reduce (*para. 4*)

According to the text, are the following statements TRUE or FALSE?

	True	False
1 Managers should be rewarded for being good at communicating with their staff.	☐	☐
2 A team which works well together is likely to make a business more successful.	☐	☐
3 It is more difficult to measure good management skills than traditional indicators of performance such as sales and profits.	☐	☐
4 Staff sometimes have some influence on how much their managers are paid.	☐	☐
5 There is a danger that staff appraisal of managers may prevent weak employees from being disciplined effectively.	☐	☐
6 Staff feel more motivated if they are allowed to appraise their managers.	☐	☐

ⓒ Discussion

1 What are the benefits to a company of the 'pink and fluffy' skills mentioned in the text?

2 Do you agree with the writer that these skills are just as important as the more traditional measures of performance? Why/why not?

3 Which kinds of management skills are regarded as important by businesses in your country?

4 Is it possible to learn these skills? How can people be taught to be better at:

listening and communicating   **teamwork**   **motivating staff**

5 Some people argue that the growing importance of communication skills in business is the result of having more women in management positions. Do you agree?

6 Look at the list of management skills below. Try to rank them in order of importance. Would you add any other features to the list?

  i good communication skills
  ii leading by example
 iii openness
  iv customer focus
  v collaboration skills
  vi delegation skills
 vii ability to motivate staff
viii knowledge of market
  ix problem-solving skills
  x ability to maintain staff discipline

2 ENTREPRENEURS

ⓐ Discussion

1 Which of the following examples and pieces of evidence support the idea that you are BORN with leadership qualities, and which support the idea that leaders can be MADE? Put them under the relevant heading in the table below:

  i Innate personality traits such as charisma are essential for leadership.

 ii Leaders vary their leadership style depending on the situation; for example, the type of organizational culture, the nature of the task involved, the experience of subordinates.

iii Leaders need extensive experience before they can become good leaders.

iv There is some evidence that tall people make good leaders.

v Leadership is a collective enterprise whereby a group of people working together have a vision and implement a strategy; it does not depend on one individual.

vi People need to learn about the process of leadership (including how to motivate and communicate with people) by doing courses and receiving training from mentors.

BORN	MADE

2 Are leaders born or made? What do you think about the above ideas?

3 ORGANIZATIONAL CULTURE, HUMAN RESOURCE MANAGEMENT AND ENTREPRENEURS

Discussion/Writing

1 What are the visible (tangible) and not so visible (intangible) aspects of a company which distinguish it from another company? For example, how might a computer company in Silicon Valley differ from a bank in terms of its culture?

2 Which do you agree with most and why: Theory X or Theory Y?
What are the consequences of managers treating their employees according to these ideas?

3 Think of some examples of well-known, successful entrepreneurs. In your opinion, what factors have led to their success?

4 WORD SEARCH

Match the terms in the box with the following descriptions. Then find each term in the word search grid below. Words can go up, down or diagonally, backwards or forwards. The first one is shown as an example.

facilitating   hotdesk   delegate   laissez-faire   CEO   the board   empowerment *tycoon   autocratic   democratic   subordinates   guru   performance*

1 two phrases about 'people at the top' (one is an abbreviation)
2 three words which describe different leadership styles
3 two other words about leadership which are linked in that 'leaders _____ to _____'
4 two words which describe different types of organizational culture
5 two other words about organizational culture – both involve employees
6 two words which are used about people who have some kind of power or influence

E	E	F	J	Q	D	P	K	O	A	C	C	S	Y	E
X	R	R	T	G	L	S	Z	U	P	I	P	E	Z	T
P	Z	I	Y	D	E	R	T	G	T	P	O	T	E	A
B	E	G	A	D	R	O	O	A	U	E	G	A	M	G
X	F	R	T	F	C	A	R	O	C	R	C	N	P	E
J	S	O	F	R	Z	C	O	N	E	C	U	I	O	L
Z	H	K	A	O	U	E	A	B	O	E	J	D	W	E
V	L	T	X	A	R	G	S	X	E	G	U	R	E	D
Y	I	D	E	U	P	M	O	S	N	H	I	O	R	H
C	V	R	D	M	Y	Y	A	Q	I	P	T	B	M	C
Z	U	G	W	F	C	S	E	N	L	A	K	U	E	C
B	T	Y	C	O	O	N	L	Q	C	V	L	S	N	V
C	I	T	A	R	C	O	M	E	D	E	J	S	T	K
F	A	C	I	L	I	T	A	T	I	N	G	F	D	Y
Q	B	K	Z	F	M	V	S	B	D	P	O	K	O	C

1 INCREASING PRODUCTIVITY

POWER TO THE PEOPLE

Empowerment is an interesting concept for a business manager. In principle, most managers would agree that a workforce that feels part of the company is going to be motivated, but it's easy to overlook the downsides. Some people may feel intimidated by the idea, and the more cynical *contingent* might suspect it's a *thinly veiled* means of building more responsibility into employees' jobs without extra pay to compensate.

This is why it is essential to bear in mind the managerial and cultural changes that empowering employees will involve. People who had power bases built on islands of information within an organisation will need to give them up if other employees are to be empowered in any meaningful way; others may need persuading to *buy into* the IT systems that *underpin* the sharing of knowledge a business needs to put in place.

This sharing of knowledge and flexibility of approach to working is possible largely through the technology currently available. The basic tool is a corporate intranet: a network based on internet technology and comprising loads of web pages that can be viewed on just about any computer with the right security access to look at them. Staff can then use these for e-learning, for information on their job while they're working and for extending their workplace into their home or on the road. It puts them very much in charge of their area of work.

The flexibility to work where and how you want is another key benefit of empowerment. Again, employers can expect to see an increasingly motivated workforce as a result.

The Telecottage Association represents home workers and notes a number of reasons why people prefer to work this way. "Cutting out the *commute* and being able to spend the time saved with your family are probably the benefits that appeal most to people," says TCA executive director Alan Denbigh.

Richard Thwaite, joint managing director of technology systems company Conchango, encourages staff to work remotely and use the company's knowledge systems from wherever they are. "The important thing is to create a culture that makes it easy for people to ask for the information and support they need, without feeling inadequate or stupid," he says. "This 'lack of blame' culture is fundamental to effective flexible working, as it means that everyone is focused on a common goal."

So, there's a lot to come in terms of flexibility in approach to employing someone. For the moment there's a lot that can be done in terms of improving a company's flexibility. And this is becoming less of a choice and more of a necessity. Recent research from printer manufacturer Epson says that 46% of smaller businesses are having to change their products according to their customers' requirements, 48% say their customers require a more tailored approach, and 62% were building flexibility into their business plans.

And the technology to start making this happen, at least on the employee side, is there already.

Guy Clapperton, ©The Guardian (09/05/01)

Glossary

- *contingent* – group
- *thinly veiled* – poorly disguised
- *buy into* – become involved in
- *underpin* – form the basis of
- *commute* – travelling to and from work

ⓐ **Questions on the text**

1 According to the text, what is the *main* way that 'empowerment' can be achieved?

　i giving employees more authority over other people i.e. giving them more opportunities to supervise others and to delegate to others

　ii allowing employees to have access to all necessary information at any time, giving them the autonomy to work anywhere

　iii providing regular training and development sessions so that employees can update their skills

2 Write definitions for the following concepts mentioned in the text – use your own words:

　i power bases　　　　**iv** work remotely
　ii corporate intranet　　**v** 'lack of blame' culture
　iii e-learning　　　　　**vi** tailored approach

3 Summarize the advantages and disadvantages for *managers* and for *employees* of empowerment – use information from the text and add any ideas of your own.

ⓑ **Discussion/Writing**

What factors do you think motivate employees? Remuneration such as bonuses, perks, share options, performance related pay? Or empowerment through, for example, increased responsibility, the freedom to work flexibly, the chance to update and widen skills? Or are there other factors which motivate?

❷ EQUAL OPPORTUNITIES

AGE-OLD PROBLEM FOR BABY-BOOMERS

The issue of age in the workplace is rapidly moving up the political and business agenda. First, there's the changing demographics of the population. The *baby boomers* of the 60s are approaching retirement age at the same time as fewer younger workers are coming into the workplace.

Medical advances also mean people are healthier and living for longer, raising expectations of what they can achieve in their 60s and 70s. Then there's the pensions crisis, sparked by the mis-selling scandals of the 80s and 90s.

Either way, workers of all ages, but particularly those in their 30s and 40s, are suddenly *waking up to the fact* they may have to work well beyond the traditional 65 if they want a comfortable retirement.

Yet, despite the best efforts of enlightened employers – retailers such as B&Q and Asda are probably the best known for hiring older workers – getting and staying in work once you've passed 50 remains an *uphill struggle* for many.

"Some employers are less likely to *dispose of* older people," concedes Eric Reid, chairman of the Association of Retired and Persons over 50. "But the ability of older people to obtain work once they are over 50 is still pretty much *nil*."

There are a variety of reasons for such prejudice, he argues. Bosses often fear an older worker will cost more in salary, pension and occupational health insurance than a younger employee.

Then they worry about integrating older workers if they have a predominantly younger workforce, believe they will not be *up to speed* with new technology, will be less *mouldable*, inflexible in their thinking and less able to move around the country. Beyond that, there's often simply a sense that, if you're over 50, you're somehow "past it".

Unlike the majority of European Union members, which either already have or are near to having age discrimination legislation in place, all Britain has is a voluntary code of conduct.

This will change in four years' time when the EU Employment Directive, which covers age discrimination, becomes law. One point yet to be resolved is whether the government intends to abolish a mandatory retirement age.

Yet older workers, say supporters, are generally more loyal, committed, punctual, *worldly wise* and empathetic than their younger counterparts, particularly where they deal with members of the public. Often, too, with children grown up or moved away, they will have fewer family commitments than, say, a 30-year-old.

"The benefit of getting someone in their 50s is that you are likely to retain them for longer than someone in their 20s. There is a greater awareness around that they are *a good deal*," explains Sally Russell, principal consultant at HR consultancy RightCoutts.

©*Nic Paton, The Guardian (06/07/02)*

Glossary

- *baby boomers* – people born after the second world war: a period with a high birth rate
- *waking up to the fact* – realizing
- *uphill struggle* – difficult task
- *dispose of* – get rid of
- *nil* – zero
- *up to speed* – up-to-date
- *mouldable* – easy to change or influence
- *worldly wise* – experienced
- *a good deal* – good value for money

ⓐ **Vocabulary extension**

Find words in the text with the same meaning as the following:

1 the particular characteristics of a population e.g. age (*para. 1*)
2 having modern, forward-looking attitudes (*para. 4*)
3 unreasonable attitudes and behaviour towards a particular group of people (*para. 6*)
4 involving somebody fully in a group so that they feel part of it (*para. 7*)
5 essential because laws or rules say that you must do it (*para. 9*)
6 prepared to work hard (*para. 10*)
7 on time; being somewhere at the agreed time (*para. 10*)
8 being able to understand how other people feel because you can imagine yourself in their position (*para. 10*)

ⓑ **Questions on the text**

1 According to the text, are the following TRUE or FALSE?

	True	False
i In the UK, there is an increasing shortage of young people in the workforce.	☐	☐
ii People over 50 do not find it too difficult to find a new job at present.	☐	☐
iii Education is the sector which is most willing to employ older workers.	☐	☐
iv Companies are afraid that older people will find it more difficult to fit into the organizational culture.	☐	☐
v At the moment, Britain is subject to stricter rules and laws than the rest of Europe.	☐	☐
vi Most workers in Britain have to retire at a certain age because the law says so.	☐	☐
vii Younger workers tend to be better at dealing with the public because they are more 'in touch' with their ideas and interests.	☐	☐
viii Companies find it easier to keep younger employees because they are keen to make a good impression and to establish their careers.	☐	☐

2 Summarize the arguments *for* and *against* employing older workers – use the information from the text and add your own ideas.

3 HIRING AND FIRING, INDUSTRIAL RELATIONS AND EQUAL OPPORTUNITIES

Discussion/Writing

1 Describe the most common methods that companies use to recruit people in your country. How do companies 'fire' people? Is it easy for companies to do so or do employees have rights in that situation?

2 How powerful are trade unions in your country? Are strikes common?

3 What types of discrimination exist in your country? On the grounds of sex, ethnic group, age, disability? Are there laws against discrimination? How effective are they?

4 CROSSWORD

Across

1 to tell someone they no longer have a job (*informal*) (4)

3 **and 14 across** – the smallest amount of money – which is set by law – that can be paid to an employee by an employer (7, 4)

4 **see 6 down**

7 not being at work when you should be (11)

9 **see 8 down**

11 how employees feel about their situation at work at a particular time (6)

12 **and 10 down** – used to describe those who do office work rather than manual work (5-6)

13 when you lose your job because you are no longer needed, or when the company cannot afford to keep you (10)

14 **see 3 across**

Down

2 money an employee receives because something bad has happened to them e.g. they have lost their job (12)

5 money given to an employee when they leave a company; _____ handshake (6)

6 **and 4 across** – the process of trying to persuade employees to leave their current job and move to a new job (4, 7)

8 **and 9 across** – employees protest in some way e.g. a strike, to show that they disagree with their employer's policies (10, 6)

10 **see 12 across**

ANSWER KEY

Topic 1.1

Exercise 1
a business model **b** vertical integration **c** outsourcing
d IT **e** virtual integration

Exercise 2
i b **ii** a **iii** d **iv** e **v** f **vi** g **vii** c

Exercise 3
a true **b** true **c** true **d** true **e** true

Topic 1.2

Exercise 1
a IT has become more accessible **b** interconnect with
the World-Wide Web **c** the falling cost of telephone calls
d the increasing willingness of consumers to try products
from abroad **e** different brands of mobile phones

Exercise 2
a computer **b** the Internet **c** satellite communications
d mobile phone **e** cable TV

Exercise 3
a pay-as-you-go **b** telecoms revolution **c** mobile phone
operators **d** social changes **e** tariffs

Topic 1.3

Exercise 1
a Internet Service Provider **b** World-Wide Web
c personal computer

Exercise 2
a going online **b** surf the net **c** websites **d** ISP
e broadband **f** Internet

Exercise 3
a false **b** false **c** true **d** true **e** true **f** true

Exercise 4
a personal computer **b** Internet Service Provider
c World-Wide Web **d** website

Topic 1.4

Exercise 1
a
an enterprise = a business
a global market = a worldwide market
a multinational = a global enterprise
the market = the marketplace
b
i global products **ii** global economy **iii** global enterprises
iv global market

Exercise 2
a globalization **b** global economy **c** liberalized
d multinational **e** deregulation

Exercise 3
a no **b** yes **c** no **d** no

Topic 1.5

Exercise 1
a flexitime **b** shifts **c** teleworking **d** freelance
e short-term contract **f** job sharing

Exercise 2
a true **b** true **c** false **d** false **e** false **f** true **g** true

Exercise 3
company: smaller premises, lower overheads, wider choice
of potential employees
employee: flexible working hours, no commuting, no
restrictions on where you live

Topic 2.1

Exercise 1
a firm **b** commerce **c** big business **d** corporations
e small businesses

Exercise 2
List A: a, b, c, d, f   List B: e

Exercise 3
a business/commerce **b** businesses/companies/firms/
business concerns **c** business **d** businesses/companies/
firms/enterprises/business concerns/business ventures

Exercise 4
a corporation **b** large **c** small businesses

Topic 2.2

Exercise 1
Primary Sector: b, f, g, l, q
Industrial Sector: e, i, j, k, p, r
Service Sector: a, c, d, h, m, n, o

Exercise 2
a Country B **b** Country C **c** Country A

Exercise 3
a industries **b** private **c** public, public sector enterprises
d goods, productive **e** financial, service

Topic 2.3

Exercise 1
Backers: a, b, d, g, h

Stakeholders: all of them

Exercise 2

a backers **b** business plan **c** break-even **d** cash flow
e overheads **f** budget

Exercise 3

a book d **b** book b **c** book c **d** book f **e** book a
f book e

Topic 2.4

Exercise 1

Organizations that control another company: a, c
Organizations whose shares are held by another company:
b, d

Exercise 2

a group **b** holding company **c** sister companies
d associated companies

Exercise 3

a franchising **b** franchise **c** franchiser **d** franchisees
e franchise agreement

Exercise 4

a a sole trader/sole proprietor **b** a plc **c** a limited
company **d** a partnership

Topic 2.5

Exercise 1

a consortium, joint venture **b** expansion, grow the
business **c** acquisition, takeover **d** join forces, merge

Exercise 2

a true **b** false **c** false **d** true **e** true **f** false **g** false

Exercise 3

a business strategy **b** local partner **c** expansion strategy
d global reach

Exercise 4

a local partner **b** takeover **c** joint venture

Topic 3.1

Exercise 1

a protectionism **b** tariffs/customs duties **c** tariffs/customs
duties **d** free trade **e** quotas **f** imports **g** exports
h exchange rates

Exercise 2

Encourage the movement of goods across borders:
favourable exchange rates; WTO; free trade agreements

Exercise 3

a ii **b** iii **c** v **d** iv **e** vi **f** vii **g** i

Exercise 4

visible imports: bananas, oil, cars, processed food, rice
invisible imports: tourism, insurance

Exercise 5

a true **b** false **c** true **d** true **e** false

Topic 3.2

Exercise 1

a iv **b** viii **c** iii **d** vii **e** ii **f** i **g** vi **h** v

Exercise 2

plus points: b, c, e, h minus points: a, d, f, g

Exercise 3

a true **b** false **c** true **d** true **e** false **f** false **g** true
h true

Topic 3.3

Exercise 1

a competitors **b** compete **c** competitive
edge/competitive advantage **d** competitive
advantage/competitive edge **e** key players
f monopolies

Exercise 2

i b ii a iii d iv c

Exercise 3

a Moto **b** Moto Swift C **c** Airlie Rapide, Auto Vitesse
d no **e** Moto **f** Thomson

Exercise 4

a true **b** false **c** false **d** true **e** true

Topic 3.4

Exercise 1

a product mix **b** product portfolio **c** product range
d global brands **e** brand **f** product differentiation
g brands **h** aligned

Exercise 2

a product mix **b** product lines **c** product differentiation
d product portfolio, product range

Exercise 3

a v **b** vi **c** i **d** ii **e** iv **f** iii

Topic 3.5

Exercise 1

a one product with a different price for each market
b products customized to each market **c** customized
marketing campaign **d** country-specific advertisements

Exercise 2

standarized products

Exercise 3

a, c, e, f

Exercise 4

a ii **b** iii **c** i

Exercise 5

a product **b** price **c** place **d** promotion

Exercise 6

a product **b** promotion **c** price **d** place

final column: use your own examples

Topic 4.1

Exercise 1

a and d

b and c

Exercise 2

i developed countries: b, c, d, h, developing countries: a, e, f, g **ii** b, c, d, h **iii** a, e, f, g **iv** a, e, f, g

Exercise 3

a, d, e, g, h

Exercise 4

Keith and Steve

Exercise 5

a false **b** false **c** true **d** false **e** true **f** false

Exercise 6

co-operative retail society: a, b, c, d

ordinary retail company: e

Topic 4.2

Exercise 1

increase corporate responsibility: d, e

barriers to corporate responsibility: a, b, c

Exercise 2

a corporate responsibility **b** social costs/social benefits
c social costs/social benefits **d** trading relationship
e social audit **f** ethical policy

Exercise 3

a point 2 **b** point 3 **c** point 1

Exercise 4

a yes **b** yes **c** no **d** yes

Topic 4.3

Exercise 1

a i raw materials **ii** infrastructure
b i taxation **ii** political stability **iii** inflation
iv income distribution **v** green issues
c i labour **ii** labour costs

Exercise 2

a i the economy **ii** positively **b i** raw materials
ii negatively **c i** labour **ii** negatively **d i** labour
ii negatively **e i** the economy **ii** negatively

Exercise 3

a availability of labour; availability of raw materials; state of

the political environment **b** political stability **c** investment
in infrastructure **d** labour costs; government taxes **e** low

Topic 4.4

Exercise 1

a fair trade **b** developing **c** fairly-traded products
d producers and growers **e** cash crops **f** world market
prices **g** commodities **h** Fairtrade mark **i** fair trade

Exercise 2

free trade system: a, c, e fair trade system: b, d, f

Exercise 3

Paolo is producing a cash crop.

Topic 4.5

Exercise 1

a yes **b** capital inflow **c** critical **d** economy: making
little contribution to economies in developing countries;
workforce: not employing enough local people;
accommodation: offering low contract rates **e** added
value (by dealing with negative environmental and social
impacts of tourism)

Exercise 2

advantages: b, c, e, f, h, j disadvantages: a, d, g, i

Exercise 3

a Tourists **b** Tour operators **c** Global tourism **d** tourism
sector **e** Mass tourism

Exercise 4

Signs a, d, f and g would appeal to eco-tourists.

Topic 5.1

Exercise 1

a lean production **b** production process **c** factory
d just-in-time **e** production

Exercise 2

a factory **b** manufacturer **c** output **d** output **e** works

Exercise 3

a true **b** true **c** false **d** true **e** true **f** true

Exercise 4

a It will be low **b** It will be low **c** There will not be much
bulk-buying **d** low, because of levels of stock

Exercise 5

a

i industrial/secondary **ii** primary **iii** service/tertiary
b The different stages a product passes through before
reaching the consumer. In this case, from cocoa beans,
through manufacturing to the finished chocolate product in
a restaurant.

Topic 5.2

Exercise 1

a product **b** goods **c** product-led **d** new products
e existing products **f** R & D **g** research laboratories
h reverse engineering

Exercise 2

a ii **b** iv **c** i **d** v **e** iii

Exercise 3

a ii **b** v **c** i **d** iii **e** iv

a research and development **b** research laboratories
c reverse engineering **d** staff suggestion schemes **e** focus
groups

Topic 5.3

Exercise 1

a total quality management **b** quality control/quality
assurance; routine checks **c** quality assurance/quality
control **d** subcontract **e** benchmarking

Exercise 2

a iii **b** i **c** ii **d** iv

Exercise 3

a, c, d, g

Exercise 4

QC: b, d, g TQM: a, c, e, f

Topic 5.4

Exercise 1

a invention **b** innovation **c** researchers **d** NIH
syndrome **e** patenting **f** under licence **g** intellectual
property rights

Exercise 2

a vi **b** iv **c** i **d** v **e** ii **f** iii

Exercise 3

a technologists **b** researchers **c** inventor

Exercise 4

a yes **b** no **c** no

Topic 5.5

Exercise 1

a assembly line/production line **b** assembly line/
production line **c** robots **d** automation **e** robotics
f computer-aided design/computer-aided manufacturing

Exercise 2

a

a ii **b** iii **c** i

b

i job production **ii** flow production **iii** batch production

Exercise 3

d, e, f

Exercise 4

a continuous-flow production **b** they are highly
standardized, so all products are likely to be identical
c automated and staffed by less skilled workers

Topic 6.1

Exercise 1

a sales force **b** sales executives **c** sales executives
d salespeople **e** salesmen/saleswomen **f** salesmen/
saleswomen

Exercise 2

a sales figures **b** unit sales **c** sales revenue/sales turnover
d sales revenue/sales turnover **e** sales target

Exercise 3

a sales figures **b** the sales force **c** unit sales **d** sales
e sales territory

Exercise 4

a

people involved in selling: salesmen, salespeople, sales
team, sales executive, sales force, saleswomen
amount of sales: sales figures, sales revenue, sales target,
sales turnover, sales forecast

b

i sales target **ii** sales figures **iii** salespeople/salesmen/
saleswomen **iv** sales force/sales team **v** sales executive
vi sales revenue/sales turnover

Topic 6.2

Exercise 1

a distribution **b** end users **c** distributor **d** distribution
network **e** wholesalers **f** warehouse **g** agent **h** factory
shops

Exercise 2

a manufacturers **b** wholesaler/agent **c** wholesaler/agent
d factory shop **e** warehouse **f** end users

Exercise 3

a true **b** false **c** true

Exercise 4

a freight forwarder, forwarding agent, forwarder **b** goods
c factories, depots **d** sea ports, airports etc.

Topic 6.3

Exercise 1

a components **b** stocks **c** lead times **d** orders **e** work-
in-progress

Exercise 2

a logistics **b** the purchasing department **c** raw material: metal; component: electric motor **d** hotels, launderettes

Exercise 3

Supplier B

Exercise 4

a true **b** false **c** false **d** true

Topic 6.4

Exercise 1

a sales which are made without the use of intermediaries **b** because customers can choose how and when to shop **c** because they do not have to pay intermediaries **d** direct mail (sending advertising material to people by post); personal selling (direct contact between a company sales representative and a potential customer); cold calls (sales representatives phoning or visiting people in their homes to tell them about the company's products); catalogues (sending people books containing illustrations of products for sale by mail order)

Exercise 2

a cold calls **b** online retailing **c** free samples **d** loyalty cards **e** direct sales channel **f** direct mail **g** personal selling

Exercise 3

a iii **b** iii **c** i **d** ii

Exercise 4

a point of sale **b** Merchandising **c** in-store demonstrations

Exercise 5

a, c, d, e

Topic 6.5

Exercise 1

retail outlets: supermarket, shopping centre, retail park, department store

retailing methods: mail order, online retailing, franchising, home shopping

Exercise 2

a 2 **b** 0 **c** 1

Exercise 3

a checkout **b** bar code **c** computerized checkout system

Exercise 4

a false **b** true **c** false

Topic 7.1

Exercise 1

prices rising: boom, bull

prices falling: bust, bear

Exercise 2

a boom **b** slump **c** boom-bust **d** booming **e** stock-market collapse

Exercise 3

a no **b** sold **c** increase **d** decrease **e** yes

Exercise 4

a bond **b** bond **c** defaulting **d** defaulting on its bonds

Topic 7.2

Exercise 1

a publicly **b** a dividend **c** do not **d** preference

Exercise 2

a B **b** D **c** A **d** G **e** A **f** C

Exercise 3

b The price for Company A's shares was £2.05. This was an increase of 2.3%. Investors can expect to receive a yield of 9%.

c The price for Company B's shares was £13.39. This was an increase of 1.4%. Investors can expect to receive a yield of 2.9%.

d The price for Company C's shares was £1.81. This was a decrease of 0.9%. Investors cannot expect to receive any yield.

e The price for Company E's shares was £3.66. This was a decrease of 1.6%. Investors can expect to receive a yield of 2.6%.

f The price for Company F's shares was £3.75. This was a decrease of 1.4%. The yield figures are unavailable.

g The price for Company G's shares was £1.80. This was a decrease of 3.4%. Investors can expect to receive a yield of 4.4%.

Exercise 4

a stock exchange **b** investors **c** go public **d** invest **e** investment

Topic 7.3

Exercise 1

a, b, c, g, h, i

Exercise 2

a true **b** true **c** false **d** false

Exercise 3

c The telecommunications industry is experiencing a downturn.

d After a downturn in the oil industry, there was a sudden spike in oil prices.

Topic 7.4

Exercise 1

a fold/go out of business **b** fold/go out of business
c ailing **d** management consultant **e** turn...around
f troubleshooting **g** going bankrupt

Exercise 2

a iii **b** ii **c** iv **d** i **e** v

Exercise 3

1 a **2** c **3** d **4** b

Exercise 4

pleased: c, f worried: a, b, d, e

Topic 7.5

Exercise 1

a gross **b** profit margin **c** mark-up **d** profitability
e break-even

Exercise 2

a story 1 **b** story 2 **c** story 5 **d** story 3 **e** story 4

Exercise 3

a return on capital employed **b** profit and capital invested
c because it shows them how well the company is performing

Topic 8.1

Exercise 1

a sales revenue **b** trade credit **c** accounts receivable
d accounts payable **e** bills **f** invoicing **g** cash flow

Exercise 2

column 1: money owed to the company
column 2: money the company owes

Exercise 3

a, b

Exercise 4

a invoice **b** credit card **c** debit card **d** letter of credit

Topic 8.2

Exercise 1

a costs **b** cost structures **c** fixed costs **d** direct costs
e indirect costs **f** overheads

Exercise 2

cost of producing goods: a, d
non-production costs: b, c

Exercise 3

b, c, d

Exercise 4

a v **b** i **c** iv **d** ii **e** vi **f** iii

Exercise 5

a £112 000 (= insurance+equipment+rent)

b £925 000 (= heating+wages+raw materials+canteen)

Exercise 6

a true **b** true **c** false **d** true **e** true

Topic 8.3

Exercise 1

profit and loss
asset and liability

Exercise 2

a iv **b** iii **c** i **d** v **e** ii **f** vi

Exercise 3

b, c, a

Exercise 4

a results **b** profit and loss account/balance sheet **c** profit
and loss account/balance sheet **d** auditors **e** accounting
standards **f** assets **g** liabilities **h** interim

Exercise 5

fairly priced (current assets): e, f; undervalued (fixed
assets): a, d, g, j; seriously undervalued (intangible assets):
b, c, h, i

Topic 8.4

Exercise 1

creditor: lend
debtor: borrow, owe, repay

Exercise 2

a Eva Co. Ltd. **b** Delaware Inc. **c** Bright Brothers
d £250,000 and £600,000 **e** £50,000 **f** Chris Ltd.

Exercise 3

a false **b** true **c** false **d** false

Exercise 4

benefit from high interest rates: banks, loan companies,
people with savings, credit card companies; benefit from
low interest rates: manufacturing industry, consumers

Topic 8.5

Exercise 1

a 2 **b** 3 **c** 1 **d** 5 **e** 6 **f** 4

Exercise 2

a raise capital **b** participate in a rights issue **c** share
issue/flotation **d** by arranging a bank loan

Exercise 3

a takeover **b** working capital **c** liquidity **d** financing

Topic 9.1

Exercise 1

a market-led **b** market research **c** desk research **d** field
research **e** secondary data **f** primary data **g** surveys

h consumer panels **i** market test

Exercise 2

a primary data - field research; secondary data – desk research

b primary data: iv, v, vi secondary data: i, ii, iii

Exercise 3

a iii **b** i **c** ii **d** iv **e** vi **f** v

Topic 9.2

Exercise 1

a launched **b** growth **c** maturity **d** saturated **e** decline
f product life cycle

Exercise 2

a 2 **b** 6 **c** 1 **d** 3 **e** 5 **f** 4

Exercise 3

correct order is: d, a, f, c, e, b, g

Topic 9.3

Exercise 1

a ii **b** ii

Exercise 2

a print **b** advertising campaign **c** advertising agencies
d account executive **e** advertising budget **f** tailor
advertisements **g** advertisement **h** advertising standards

Exercise 3

a 2 **b** 4 **c** 3 **d** 1 **e** 5

Topic 9.4

Exercise 1

a brand name **b** brand awareness **c** own brand
d generic products **e** USP **f** brand image

Exercise 2

a brand recognition **b** own brand **c** brand loyalty
d brand name **e** brand image **f** brand awareness
g brand stretching

Exercise 3

a false **b** true **c** false **d** true

Topic 9.5

Exercise 1

a cost **b** list price **c** discounting **d** market price
e price-sensitive **f** price-sensitive **g** pricing strategies

Exercise 2

a ii **b** iv **c** iii **d** i

Exercise 3

a penetration pricing **b** market-orientated pricing
c competition-based pricing **d** cost-based pricing

Topic 10.1

Exercise 1

column 1: to rise, to increase, to improve, to reach a peak, to peak column 2: to level off, to stabilize, to remain constant column 3: to decrease, to fall, to drop

Exercise 2

a true **b** the noun forms are the same as the verb forms, except for 'improvement' and 'growth'

Exercise 3

1 levelled off **2** increased gradually/improved steadily
3 fell slightly **4** increased gradually/improved steadily
5 peaked dramatically **6** remained constant **7** rose sharply/grew rapidly **8** rose sharply/grew rapidly

Exercise 4

a increased **b** temporary fall **c** steadily

Topic 10.2

Exercise 1

a maximize profit **b** new markets **c** growth in sales turnover **d** market share **e** mission statement

Exercise 2

a iii **b** v **c** ii **d** i **e** vi **f** iv

Exercise 3

a ii **b** iii **c** i

Exercise 4

a false **b** true **c** true **d** false **e** true

Topic 10.3

Exercise 1

a undercuts **b** price wars **c** predatory pricing **d** collude
e price fixing **f** restrictive practice **g** cartel

Exercise 2

predatory pricing: the consumer
price cutting/price wars: the consumer
price discrimination: the seller
cartels: the seller
restrictive practices: the seller
loss leaders: the consumer

Exercise 3

a loss leaders **b** predatory pricing **c** price discrimination
d price cutting/price wars **e** restrictive practices **f** cartels

Exercise 4

a ii **b** ii **c** i

Topic 10.4

Exercise 1

a manufacturing base **b** relocate **c** enterprise zones

d low-wage centre

Exercise 2

b, c, f

Exercise 3

a ii **b** i **c** iii **d** iv **e** v

Exercise 4

a enterprise zone **b** brownfield site **c** greenfield site

Exercise 5

a true **b** false **c** true **d** true

Topic 10.5

Exercise 1

a worried **b** moving the brand downmarket **c** to rejuvenate the brand/ appeal to discount shoppers **d** it could damage the brand image with existing customers

Exercise 2

moving the brand upmarket:
advantage: **d** disadvantage: **a**
moving the brand downmarket:
advantage: **b** disadvantage: **c**

Exercise 3

a ii **b** i

Exercise 4

a false **b** true **c** false **d** true **e** true **f** false

Topic 11.1

Exercise 1

a yes **b** yes **c** no **d** yes

Exercise 2

box 1: **e** box 2: **a** box 3: **b** box 4: **d** box 5: **c**

Exercise 3

a iii **b** iv **c** i **d** ii
i code of practice **ii** corporate hospitality **iii** emotional capital **iv** repeat business

Exercise 4

customer care, customer loyalty, customer satisfaction, customer relations

Exercise 5

i customer relations **ii** customer loyalty **iii** customer satisfaction **iv** customer care

Exercise 6

a customer relations **b** serve customers **c** service with a smile **d** code of practice

Topic 11.2

Exercise 1

a consumers **b** clients **c** customers

Exercise 2

a customer base **b** warranties and guarantees **c** after-sales service **d** repeat customers

Exercise 3

after-sales service: a, c, e
other types of customer care: b, d, f, g

Exercise 4

a iii **b** i **c** ii

Exercise 5

a company c **b** company b **c** company a

Topic 11.3

Exercise 1

a iii **b** v **c** i **d** ii **e** iv

Exercise 2

a iii **b** i **c** ii **d** iii

Exercise 3

Alan **b** Bill **d** Colin **a** Doreen **e** Edwina **c**

Topic 11.4

Exercise 1

below-the-line promotion: b, e
public relations activities: a, c, d, f

Exercise 2

a false **b** false **c** true **d** true **e** true

Exercise 3

below-the-line promotion: advantage: **a** disadvantage: **d**
corporate advertising: advantage: **c** disadvantage: **b**

Exercise 4

below-the-line promotion: **a** corporate advertising: **b**

Exercise 5

a corporate advertising **b** corporate image **c** corporate values

Topic 11.5

Exercise 1

a caveat emptor **b** consumer laws **c** consumer protection **d** consumer rights

Exercise 2

a iv **b** iii **c** i **d** v **e** ii

Exercise 3

a ii **b** iii **c** iii

Exercise 4

a false **b** false **c** true **d** true **e** false

Topic 12.1

Exercise 1

a market **b** market economy **c** market forces

d marketplace **e** segment **f** market segmentation
g market share
Exercise 2
a market forces **b** market share **c** market segmentation
d market conditions **e** market economy **f** market entry
g market sector **h** marketplace
Exercise 3
b, c, e
Exercise 4
a Jordan **b** Pat

Topic 12.2

Exercise 1
a false **b** true **c** true **d** false
Exercise 2
a distribution **b** retail **c** engineering **d** men **e** 10%
f 34% **g** 1% **h** 35%
Exercise 3
a iii **b** i **c** iv **d** ii

Topic 12.3

Exercise 1
a services **b** service/customer service **c** service/customer
service **d** service providers **e** service criteria
Exercise 2
a service criteria **b** service sector **c** customer service
d service business **e** service provider
Exercise 3
a providing a service **b** the service sector **c** providing a
service **d** providing a service **e** the service sector
Exercise 4
a yes **b** safety

Topic 12.4

Exercise 1
a leisure revolution **b** core sectors **c** service quality
Exercise 2
Public sector bodies: c
Trade associations: a, b, e, f, h
Companies: d, g, i
Exercise 3
a ii **b** iii **c** i

Topic 12.5

Exercise 1
a personal banking **b** telephone banking/online banking
c telephone banking/online banking **d** cashpoints

e financial services **f** call centres **g** financial services
providers
Exercise 2
a financial **b** i financial adviser ii financial services
iii financial services providers
Exercise 3
a Benny **b** Derek **c** Alex **d** Edward **e** Carl **f** Paul

Topic 13.1

Exercise 1
a shareholders **b** board of directors **c** managers
Exercise 2
a senior executives **b** chief executive officer **c** managing
director **d** board of directors/board **e** chair **f** board of
directors/board **g** company secretary
Exercise 3
a, b, c, e
Exercise 4
a ii **b** iii **c** iv **d** i

Topic 13.2

Exercise 1
i c **ii** b **iii** a
Exercise 2
a ii **b** i **c** i **d** ii **e** iii
Exercise 3
a Ian **b** Geoff **c** Sally **d** Bob
Exercise 4
a ability to know which direction company is going; ability
to lead company through change; ability to plan how to
achieve goals; ability to persuade others that decisions are
right; ability to motivate staff
b give examples of management abilities from your own
experience

Topic 13.3

Exercise 1
beliefs and values: organizational culture
examples: bureaucratic culture, facilitating culture,
performance culture
Exercise 2
a i **b** ii **c** ii **d** ii
Exercise 3
a fragmented organization **b** mercenary organization
c communal organization **d** networked organization

Topic 13.4

Exercise 1
Individual in an organization: a, c

Collective term for people in an organization: b, d, e

Exercise 2

i b ii a iii c

Exercise 3

a, b, d, f, g

Exercise 4

Hierarchical structure

Exercise 5

Theory X: b, d

Theory Y: a, c

Topic 13.5

Exercise 1

a entrepreneur b run their own business c flair
d technical skills e self-employed

Exercise 2

c, a, d, b

Exercise 3

a true b true c true d true

Exercise 4

a from India to the USA b inventing software c very
successful

Topic 14.1

Exercise 1

finding and appointing new employees: a, b, f, k
termination of an employee's contract: c, d, e, g, h, i, j

Exercise 2

b

Exercise 3

1 a 2 c 3 b

Exercise 4

a recruitment consultant b headhunted c constructive
dismissal

Topic 14.2

Exercise 1

cash: a, b, f, g, i
other: c, d, e, h

Exercise 2

a, c, e, f, g

Exercise 3

b

Exercise 4

a Anna b Carlos c Julia d Gianfranco e Florence

Exercise 5

a false b true c false

Topic 14.3

Exercise 1

a industrial relations b staff representatives c works
council d arbitration e trade union f strike g industrial
action h grievance i tribunal j co-worker

Exercise 2

blue-collar: b, c, g, h, k
white-collar: a, d, e, f, i, j, l

Exercise 3

a establish a works council b proposed changes in
working conditions c recent and probable developments;
establishment's economic situation

Exercise 4

number of hours: c
type of employment: j, k
pay: g, h
benefits: a, b
disciplinary procedures: e
notice: d
grievance procedures: f
employee rights: i

Topic 14.4

Exercise 1

a disability b equal opportunities c positive action
d under-represented e equal opportunities monitoring
f discriminated against

Exercise 2

a i decreased ii no iii yes iv black v white
b i more women ii increased employment iii more women

Exercise 3

a it aims to offer equal opportunities to all b because its
products have a global reach

Topic 14.5

Exercise 1

c, a, b

Exercise 2

a asset b motivated c unproductive d absenteeism
e productivity f workplace g job satisfaction

Exercise 3

a Oyez Engineering, Breakers Inc. b Daniel's Motor Co.
c Breakers Inc. d Breakers Inc. e Daniel's Motor Co.

Exercise 4

a true b false c true d true

Exercise 5

a call in sick b sick leave c casual dress codes d Monday

MATERIALS BANK ANSWER KEY

Topic 1

1 (a) **1** para. 4 **2** para. 2 **3** para. 3

(b) **1** retain **2** deploying **3** specialists **4** infrastructure
5 premises

(c) **1** i

2 i text messaging/always-on internet
connectivity/instant messaging/videoconferencing/
web-based meetings

ii part-time working/job sharing/home working

3 'Work is what you do and not where you go':
technology means that teleworking etc allows
people to work away from an office, so place of
work is no longer so important.

2 (a) **1** i – 2 ii – 4 iii – 6 iv – 5 v – 1 vi – 3

2 Advantages: 4, 6 Disadvantages: 1, 2, 3, 5

(c) **1** Causes: b, c Results: a, d, e

3 production: outsourcing, just-in-time
IT: broadband, state-of-the-art
global issues: deregulation, globalization, multinational
ways of working: freelance, teleworking

F	J	U	S	T	I	N	T	I	M	E	W	H	F	O
D	S	T	A	T	E	O	F	T	H	E	A	R	T	U
B	E	K	S	K	D	I	B	S	R	O	K	L	M	T
L	R	R	G	L	E	T	H	I	M	D	A	F	G	S
D	Y	O	E	W	X	A	M	D	S	N	F	R	N	O
E	J	J	A	G	M	Z	A	W	O	Q	K	E	I	U
C	L	T	V	D	U	I	W	I	M	B	X	E	K	R
U	G	J	P	I	B	L	T	I	J	B	U	L	R	C
N	I	V	V	T	B	A	A	T	X	H	E	A	O	I
K	G	L	J	X	N	B	N	T	T	F	I	N	W	N
N	N	G	O	I	B	O	G	D	I	F	R	C	E	G
E	D	G	T	R	X	L	Y	V	W	O	T	E	L	M
Q	S	L	P	V	Y	G	B	J	O	Z	N	M	E	L
N	U	M	S	I	E	E	T	N	E	S	B	A	T	Z
M	F	P	I	V	V	G	Y	Q	S	S	I	D	I	Y

Topic 2

1 (a) section 1: franchise, franchiser's, franchiser, franchise

section 2: sole trader

section 3: partnerships, partners, partners, partner,
partnership, partner

section 4: Limited Liability Company, Limited Liability,
Limited (Liability) Company

(b) **1** profits **2** premises **3** transactions **4** liabilities **5** assets
6 debt

(c) **1** sole trader **2** Limited Liability Company **3** franchise
4 partnership

3 (a) **1** exploiting **2** expertise **3** channels **4** economies of
scale **5** beneficial

(b) **1** i – 3; ii – 4; iii – 2; iv – 1

2 i Joint ventures – allow companies to combine their
particular areas of expertise

ii Mergers – reduce the number of competitors;
reduce costs; increase market share

iii Local partners – provide information about a market
and how it's different from other markets

iv Takeovers – reduce costs of production and
distribution; allow acquisition of brand names; allow
movement into new areas; remove competitors;
increase market share

4 ACROSS: **2** commerce **3** enterprise **5** backer **8** acquisition
9 concern **10** merger

DOWN: **1** break even **4** public sector **6** subsidiary
7 consortium

Topic 3

1 (a) **1** tariffs **2** free trade **3** protectionist, imports

(b) **1** surges **2** trading partners **3** exempt **4** glut **5** retaliate
6 export subsidies

2 (a) **1** subsidies **2** exchange rates **3** infrastructure **4** inward
investment **5** flight of capital **6** deregulation **7** income
distribution **8** domestic market **9** monopoly
10 dumping

3 (a) **1** product portfolio **2** brand image **3** product launch
4 tag line **5** product lifecycle **6** development stage

(b) 1 entry level model 2 gain market share 3 call centre
4 point of contact 5 onus on 6 pushed back until
7 critical 8 drive 9 revenues

4 (a) 1 standardization 2 customization/country-specific
products 3 direct marketing

5 ACROSS: 2 trade deficit 5 market leader 7 target market
12 and 11 down launch strategies

DOWN: 1 and 10 across balance of payments
4 and 3 down flight of capital 6 exchange rates
8 rivals 9 monopoly

Topic 4

1 (a) 1 **free trade:** conventional trade, superstores,
maximizing shareholder value

fair trade: specialist or independent companies,
alternative traders, unequal bargaining
power

2 i Traditional companies' main focus is not on
producers/supporting fair trade.

ii If traditional companies or supermarkets only
pretend to take an interest in fair trade, it draws
attention away from the real alternative traders and
hides the fact that some countries have no interest in
fair trade/it increases the feeling that everything is all
right for the producers.

iii Consumers who buy fair trade products are not
just concerned with the lowest prices, but how the
product was produced and whether people were
treated fairly.

iv For alternative traders, marketing and advertising
are a small part of their budget and consumers find
out about their products in other ways.

4 free trade or traditional business: sweatshop, mass
tourism, cash crop

fair trade or non-traditional business: social audit, eco-
tourism, cooperatives

sustainable development: infrastructure, raw materials,
capital inflow

S	C	E	V	N	E	S	L	H	C	B	T	L	I	S
W	E	G	C	E	S	Z	J	A	Y	I	M	N	X	L
E	K	V	R	O	X	Z	S	H	D	U	F	P	B	A
A	Z	I	I	E	T	H	T	U	U	R	Q	O	W	I
T	O	A	N	T	C	O	A	V	A	M	A	I	G	R
S	Y	P	W	R	A	L	U	S	A	Q	U	X	L	E
H	X	L	O	P	A	R	T	R	T	O	L	D	Q	T
O	M	P	Y	I	Z	R	E	M	I	C	X	Y	I	A
P	N	Z	C	U	U	L	H	P	S	S	B	Z	F	M
O	V	O	Y	C	Q	T	I	K	O	P	M	A	F	W
Y	S	S	T	Q	K	I	Z	W	C	O	N	V	I	A
A	M	U	I	M	E	R	P	W	O	B	C	B	L	R
D	R	W	O	L	F	N	I	L	A	T	I	P	A	C
E	M	A	S	S	T	O	U	R	I	S	M	L	T	Z
W	P	Q	P	P	Y	G	C	F	Z	U	M	C	N	X

Topic 5

1 (a) 1 components 2 proliferation of 3 standardised 4
commonality 5 pilot project 6 rationalised 7 core
values 8 work through 9 lifespan

(b) 1 false 2 true 3 false 4 true 5 false 6 true 7 false

(c) 1 (example) In traditional manufacturing, each model
of car had parts specifically designed for that model,
whereas with commonality, certain parts are shared in
a number of different models.

2 Advantages of commonality: designers do not waste
time designing new versions of existing products;
costs can be reduced by standardising parts; the level
of complexity in production can be reduced;
economies of scale mean better quality products can
be used; new models can get to the market more
quickly; fewer accessories need to be stocked.

2 (a) 1 JIT manufacturing – 4; reverse engineering – 3;
quality circles – 1; benchmarking – 5; automation – 2

3 ACROSS: 3 JIT 5 capacity 7 leading-edge 8 CAD/CAM
9 CIM 10 FMCG

DOWN: 1 quality circle 2 reverse 4 patent 6 benchmarking

Topic 6

1 (a) 1 supply chain system 2 inventory management
3 written-off stock 4 operating efficiencies

(b) 1 Traditional system: i, iii, iv, v, vi

Aerocater system: ii, vii

2 iii

3 (a) distribution: warehouse, end user

orders and stock control: work-in-progress, logistics

sales methods: loyalty card, cold call

retailing: intermediary

(b) **i** forecast **ii** turnover **iii** revenue

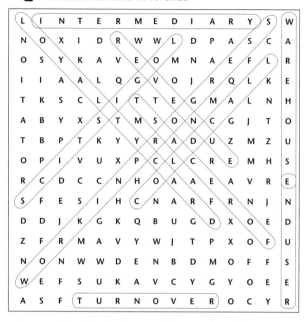

Topic 7

1 (a) 1 outstripped 2 advanced 3 volatile 4 sustainable
5 tumbling 6 dismal 7 surge 8 feed through into 9
stretched 10 be wary of

(b) 1 **i** property **ii** government bonds **iii** government
bonds **iv** emerging markets **v** property
2 i emerging markets **ii** property **iii** emerging markets
iv government bonds

2 (a) 1 Hong Kong 2 Japan 3 UK 4 USA 5 Germany 6 USA

3 (a) for: ii, v, vi

against: i, iii, iv, vii

(b) ii, v

4 ACROSS: **5** break even **6** bond **7** sparkling **8** margin
DOWN: **1** yield **2** steam ahead **3** liquidation
4 troubleshooting

Topic 8

1 (a) 1 unviable 2 loaded with 3 grass-roots 4 rationalised 5
to be put on a sound financial footing 6 revival

---

7 endorse **8** warrant **9** takes up its warrant **10** outright
11 debt burden **12** housekeeping

(b) 1 i & viii; ii & v; iii & vi; iv & vii

2 management controls/supply chain: more rigorous
housekeeping; reduced inventories
manufacturing had to be streamlined: tennis ball
manufacturing concentrated in Phillipines
marketing had to be improved: reange expanded;
McEnroe to endorse balls; introduction of
waterproof balls
company finances had to be strengthened: debt
converted to equity; licensing and distribution of
Maxfli/Slazenger handed to taylormade, with option
to buy

2 (b) 1 intellectual capital: ii, iv
research and development: iii, viii
brands: vi
other: i, v, vii

3 (a) having no money: insolvency
costs: profit margin, expenditure
paying money: cash flow, invoice, bill
financing expansion: all-cash deal, rights issue,
working capital

(b) **i** variable **ii** debtor **iii** lender **iv** liabilities

(c) default on

Topic 9

1 **a** 1 brand 2 diversified 3 brand extension 4 brand loyalty 5 brand extender 6 mother brand 7 stretching your brand

b 1 launch 2 promotional spend 3 goal

c 1 true 2 false 3 true

2 **a** 1 campaign 2 campaign 3 agencies 4 ad 5 agency campaign 7 ad 8 advertising 9 global advertising campaign 10 agencies 11 agencies 12 campaign 13 brand 14 brand 15 campaign

b 1 Guinness is changing its advertising campaign because there is so much competition in the market and the campaign was not effective enough.

2 It has never used a global advertising campaign before.

3 Europe is the place where sales of Guinness are not growing, as people increasingly prefer other drinks.

4 Irish sport may be used in the new campaign.

3 ACROSS: 1 discounting 5 decline 6 USP 7 tailor 8 sensitive 10 premium 11 brand loyalty

DOWN: 2 generic 3 image 4 billboard 5 desk research 9 saturation

Topic 10

1 **a** 1 version 2 core 3 internal re-organisation 4 rallied 5 shake-up 6 deficit

b 1 false 2 true 3 true 4 true 5 false 6 true 7 false

2 **a** 1 consultant 2 product analysis 3 logo 4 bureaucratic 5 strategic plans 6 fundraising

b 1 By creating a less slow and bureaucratic public image

2 By consulting stakeholders, setting up branding groups and conducting a product analysis

3 sales objectives: maximization, mission statement, new market

relocating the business: relocate, enterprise zone, greenfield site

the war for sales: loss leader, collusion, cartel, price fixing, undercut

Topic 11

1 **a** 1 underlying philosophy 2 competence 3 correlation 4 unauthorised

b 1 They are becoming more willing to complain about poor customer service. 2 An English person 3 People who complain are more likely to recommend a company than people who don't (if their complaint is dealt with effectively).

2 **a** good customer care: 1, 4, 5, 8
poor customer care: 2, 3, 6, 7

4 ACROSS: 5 press release 6 clients 7 below-the-line 8 data protection 10 flagship brand

DOWN: 1 code of practice 2 and 9 across corporate hospitality 3 mentoring 4 induction 5 public relations

Topic 12

1 **a** 1 day-to-day transactions 2 ethical policy 3 back-up services 4 withdrawals 5 encounter

b Internet-only banking advantages: 4, 5
Internet-only disadvantages: 2, 6, 7, 8
Traditional banking advantages: 3, 10
Traditional banking disadvantages: 1, 9

2 1 a v b viii c i d iii e vii f ii g x h vi i iv j ix
2 Points a, b, f, h
3 For: a, d, f
Against: b, c, e, g, h, i, j

4 **1** market forces (c) **2** market segmentation (b) **3** market share (e) **4** tertiary industry (d) **5** public sector bodies (f) **6** cashpoint (a) **7** social chapter (g)

Topic 13

1 ⓐ **1** empathy **2** appraising **3** fostering **4** crucial **5** intangible **6** attribute...to **7** competencies **8** autonomous **9** diminish

ⓑ **1** true **2** true **3** false **4** true **5** true **6** false

2 ⓐ born: i, iv
made: ii, iii, v, vi

4 **1** CEO, the board **2** laissez-faire, autocratic, democratic **3** delegate, subordinates **4** facilitating, performance **5** hotdesk, empowerment **6** tycoon, guru

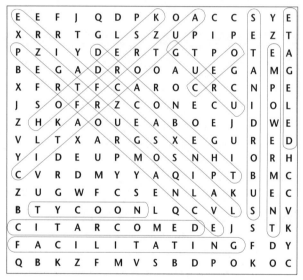

Topic 14

1 ⓐ **1** ii
2 (*examples*) **i** positions or centres of authority **ii** a computer network for the use of a particular organization only **iii** educational or training courses which are based on using the Internet to access information and receive guidance **iv** work at a distance from the office, using technology to keep in touch **v** an organization which has the values of encouraging employees not to be afraid to seek help when needed **vi** policy developed to suit individual preferences

2 ⓐ **1** demographics **2** enlightened **3** prejudice **4** integrating **5** mandatory **6** committed **7** punctual **8** empathetic

ⓑ **i** true **ii** false **iii** false **iv** true **v** false **vi** true **vii** false **viii** false

4 ACROSS: **1** sack **3 and 14 across** minimum wage **7** absenteeism **11** morale **12 and 10 down** white-collar **13** redundancy

DOWN: **2** compensation **5 and 14 down** golden **6 and 4 across** headhunting **8 and 9 across** industrial action

INDEX

The numbers refer to the topic numbers in the main text.